This is the first book-length study of the collaboration between Tennessee Williams and Elia Kazan. Their intense creative relationship, fueled by a deep personal affinity that endured until Williams's death, lasted from 1947 to 1960. The production of *A Streetcar Named Desire* established Williams as America's greatest playwright and Kazan as its most important director. Working with producers Irene Selznick and Cheryl Crawford, designers Jo Mielziner and Lemuel Ayers, and actors such as Marlon Brando, Jessica Tandy, Paul Newman, and Burl Ives, Williams and Kazan created some of the most important theatrical events of the post-war era.

In this book Brenda Murphy analyzes this artistic partnership and the plays and theatrical techniques the artists developed collaboratively in their productions of *A Streetcar Named Desire*, *Camino Real*, *Cat on a Hot Tin Roof*, and *Sweet Bird of Youth*. In addition, Murphy suggests new ways to examine the working relationship between playwright and director which can be applied to other practitioners in twentieth-century drama.

The book will be of interest to students and scholars of theatre history and American literature as well as to practitioners. It contains numerous illustrations from important productions.

Tennessee Williams and Elia Kazan

Tennessee Williams and Elia Kazan

A collaboration in the theatre

Brenda Murphy

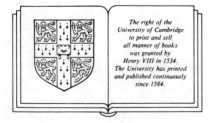

The right of the
University of Cambridge
to print and sell
all manner of books
was granted by
Henry VIII in 1534.
The University has printed
and published continuously
since 1584.

Cambridge University Press

Cambridge   New York   Port Chester
Melbourne   Sydney

Published by the Press Syndicate of the University of Cambridge
The Pitt Building, Trumpington Street, Cambridge CB2 1RP
40 West 20th Street, New York, NY 10011-4211, USA
10 Stamford Road, Oakleigh, Victoria 3166, Australia

© Cambridge University Press 1992

First published 1992

Printed in Great Britain at the University Press, Cambridge

A catalogue record for this book is available from the British Library

Library of Congress cataloguing in publication data

Murphy, Brenda.
Collaborative drama: Tennessee Williams and Elia Kazan / by
Brenda Murphy.
        p.   cm.
Includes bibliographical references and index.
ISBN 0 521 40095-3 (hardcover)
1. Williams, Tennessee, 1911–1983 – Stage history – United States.
2. Kazan, Elia.   I. Title.
PS3545.I5365Z78   1992
812'.54 – dc20   91-16237 CIP

ISBN 0521 40095 3 hardback

SE

To George

Contents

Illustrations

Preface

This book began as an attempt to translate one of the current truisms of critical theory – that a play is not simply a dramatic text but a text realized in performance – into practical criticism. While it has become a cliché to recognize this fact at the beginning of a critical piece, it has also become a cliché to note that we have yet to find a satisfactory method for analyzing performance and text simultaneously. Hence most studies of plays remain either studies of dramatic texts as literature or studies of performances as such. In this book, I wanted to look specifically at the process by which the initial performance of a play was inscribed in the text that was subsequently published, either as an "acting version" to be used as a blueprint for subsequent performances or as a "reading version" to be read and studied as a literary text.

I chose Tennessee Williams and Elia Kazan for this study because they had a long, well-known, and productive collaborative relationship. Kazan had directed the initial Broadway productions of four of Williams's best-known plays – *A Streetcar Named Desire* (1947), *Camino Real* (1953), *Cat on a Hot Tin Roof* (1955), and *Sweet Bird of Youth* (1959) – and the two had, in collaboration with designer Jo Mielziner, created "the American Style" in the 1950s, a recognizable and influential theatrical idiom that has been mentioned by many critics and scholars but given no really exhaustive analysis.

My original intention was to discover what specific elements in the published texts of the plays that convention ascribes to the playwright Tennessee Williams – elements such as set, props, movement, costumes, music, and vocal intonation as well as dialogue – actually originated with director Kazan or designer Mielziner. As I studied the evidence in memoirs, letters, notes, drawings, lighting charts, property lists, etc., related to the performances, and the changes that were made in the versions of the scripts as the writing proceeded before, during, and sometimes after the rehearsal process, however, I found that there was a more intriguing subject in the process of the collaboration itself.

My study of the development of the plays, particularly those after

Streetcar, showed that the models we currently employ for the collaboration of playwright and director are inadequate to describe the process
that actually occurred with Williams and Kazan. These models fall
generally into two categories which Richard Hornby has called the
"symphony model" – director as conductor, merely interpreting the
playwright's fixed text – and the "cinema model" – director as *auteur*,
bringing to life the playwright's mere scenario. These models describe a
clear hegemony within the creative process. Either the playwright's text
or the director's concept is sacrosanct. In the theatre of the fifties, before
directors like Richard Schechner took control of the creative process,
critics have assumed that the "symphony model" was at work. The
playwright handed a finished play to a director, who did his best to realize
the playwright's vision on the stage. During the fifties, Kazan himself
used this language to describe his work with playwrights.

The creative interaction between Williams and Kazan, however, was a
far more complex process. As soon as he had a recognizable script,
Williams would send it off to Kazan for his reaction. Kazan responded
with detailed suggestions about how the play might be changed and
reshaped. He suggested adding or deleting scenes, emphasizing various
themes, developing or changing aspects of characterization, and in
general helped to shape the play that finally emerged in the script that
went into rehearsal. In rehearsal, Kazan and Williams worked together,
with Williams cutting lines or writing new dialogue to go with the kinesic
and pictorial stage language that Kazan developed. The published text(s)
of the play recorded the script as it had evolved at one or another stage in
this process and described the set designed by Jo Mielziner or another
designer in collaboration with Kazan for this specific production.
Although Tennessee Williams wrote every word that appeared in a
published script, the play the script described was clearly a collaborative
venture. On the other hand, as the one who made the final decision on
every word of dialogue, Williams was hardly writing "scenarios" for
Kazan to develop.

The study of this collaboration demonstrates clearly that we can not
employ the critical convention of ascribing everything that appears in a
play's text to the playwright and everything that occurs in rehearsal to the
director. It also shows that the process of Broadway "playwrighting" in
the fifties, before the advocates of performance rose up in the sixties and
took control of the script's development, was not the clear-cut division of
labor it has been assumed to be. In the case of Williams and Kazan, at
least, the director was involved in the play's writing from very early on
and the playwright was involved in the production process throughout its
development. Within this process occurred a dynamic of struggle – for

ownership, for control, for hegemony over the creative process – that is masked by the rhetoric of cooperation with which the process of theatrical collaboration is usually described. From the earliest versions of the script to the Broadway opening, Kazan sought to shape the play within his vision of its meaning. While he keenly desired his director's collaboration to a point, Williams resisted it – sometimes explosively – when he felt that Kazan's suggestions were violating some inner vision of his own. In the end, exacerbated by critics such as Eric Bentley, the struggle for control, and the complex emotions that it generated, fatally undermined the creative dynamic that had sustained this collaborative relationship for thirteen years. Did this relationship run a natural course that might help to explain the explosive dynamics that characterize many creative collaborations in the theatre?

In the end, a study like this inevitably raises more questions than it solves. My investigation suggests broader questions that need to be answered before we can arrive at a more accurate model for the process of playwrighting in the fifties. There is evidence to suggest that Kazan worked in a similar way with playwrights such as Arthur Miller, Robert Anderson, and Archibald Macleish. Was there a similar struggle for control in the creative dynamic with them? Kazan was one of the most influential figures in the American theatre of the fifties, and Williams was its greatest playwright. Did their working relationship establish a model for others? If so, what is its relationship to the rise of the director in the sixties?

Even more broadly, we need to think more about what it means to call Tennessee Williams, or any playwright, the "author" of a play and how the conventional language of scholarship and criticism can be altered to reflect the collaborative art that went into creating "his" plays. Most importantly, we need to study the collaborative dynamic among theatre artists in order to discover more about the forces that lie beneath the rhetoric of cooperation that we have used to mask them. Is the struggle for creative hegemony inevitable? How are the forces with the collaborative dynamic related to creativity? How does collaborative art differ essentially from art created by an individual? Pursuing answers to these questions will bring us closer to understanding the complex aesthetic process by which drama is created in the twentieth century.

Acknowledgments

The first and primary debt I owe is to George Monteiro, who read several drafts of this book and gave me excellent advice, some of which I took. The second debt is to libraries and their staffs, without which this book could not have been written at all. In particular, I must acknowledge the invaluable help of Ken Craven, Kathy Henderson, Patrice Fox, and the rest of the staff at the Harry Ransom Humanities Research Center of the University of Texas at Austin; Dorothy L. Swerdlove and her staff at the Billy Rose Theatre Collection, Performing Arts Research Center, New York Public Library; and the staffs of the Olin Library and the Cinema Archive of Wesleyan University, the University of Connecticut Libraries, the Owen D. Young Library of St. Lawrence University, the University of Rhode Island Libraries, the Newport Public Library, the Brown University Libraries, and the San Diego State University Libraries.

Financial support and research time to pursue this project were provided to me by the National Endowment for the Humanities, St. Lawrence University, and the University of Connecticut.

The manuscript was altered for the better on the advice of Phillip Larson, my former colleague at St. Lawrence University, and Sarah Stanton, my editor at Cambridge.

Although his substantial archive at Wesleyan University remains sealed to scholars as I write this, Elia Kazan and his assistant Eileen Shanahan were generous in helping me to pursue my research in other collections.

All of the photographs are included here by consent of the Billy Rose Theatre Collection, New York Public Library, Astor, Lenox, and Tilden Foundations. The two photographs by Fred Fehl are reproduced with his permission. My efforts to contact Seymour Milbert have been unsuccessful, but I have used the materials he donated to the New York Public Library with gratitude.

The publishers have kindly granted permission to quote from the following: "To a Friend Whose Work Has Come to Nothing," in *The*

Variorum Edition of the Poems of W. B. Yeats, edited by Peter Alt and Russell K. Alspach (New York: Macmillan, 1957); "Do Not Go Gentle Into That Good Night," in Dylan Thomas: *Poems of Dylan Thomas*, copyright 1952 by Dylan Thomas; reprinted by permission of New Directions Publishing Corporation.

1 Tennessee Williams and Elia Kazan: the aesthetic matrix

The dynamics of collaboration

A director who works with a playwright on the first production of a play is a full collaborator in the work that is eventually described in the published script. This is now a critical commonplace. When Tennessee Williams began working with Elia Kazan on *A Streetcar Named Desire* in 1947, it was more like an accusation. The Broadway theatre of the forties was still functioning on a model for the production process that had originated at the turn of the century, just as the director had begun to assume a separate identity from the producer and actor-manager. In the days of the great regisseurs – men like Augustin Daly, David Belasco, and Steele MacKaye – director, playwright, and sometimes theatre owner and star actor, were often one person, the company manager. In the early part of the twentieth century, the playwright gained greater and greater respect as a literary artist while the functions of producer and director gradually were separated into those of the business manager who tended to the money side of the production and the artistic director who actually staged the play.

By the early thirties, the model for interaction among producer, playwright, and director had solidified into convention. In the conventional model that had arisen in the twenties, the playwright delivers a finished script to a producer, working out with him or her the changes that are deemed necessary for commercial success. The producer hires a director and casts the play, usually in cooperation with the director, although the producer's decision about casting overrides the director's, and the playwright must give at least tacit consent to all decisions. The director takes the finished script and interprets it for the stage, providing a unified physical realization of what he sees as the playwright's intended meaning in the play. This includes helping the actors to develop their characters, providing movement and gestures in the form of blocking and business, cutting and sometimes revising the script to meet the needs of the production, working with the designers to create scenery and costumes that will support the overall concept of the play's meaning, and in general serving as the coordinator of the performance.

According to this model, the playwright works in isolation, alone in the proverbial study, to produce the script, having complete ownership of the play up to the point of production. At the point of production the director takes over and becomes the author of the performance. When the play is published, whether it be in the "reading version" meant to take its place in the library of dramatic literature or the "acting version" meant to serve as a blueprint for subsequent performances, convention again ascribes all of its elements to the playwright. Since the playwright, as writer, owns the published script, she also owns the non-verbal elements described in the stage directions, despite the fact that the playwright may have had little or nothing to do with creating them.

Playwright Robert Ardrey wrote of his relationship with the typical Broadway producer in 1939:

Before the production starts, the two of you will have put in many hours, hundreds of hours, perhaps, going over the script, cutting, rewriting, arguing, clarifying. By the time rehearsals start, you've settled everything with him. The job is in his hands. You have only to sit back, watch, make suggestions, have an occasional emotional discussion with him in the back of the empty theatre.[1]

Ardrey said that the Group Theatre changed this conventional relationship during the thirties because it included the playwright in the production process, extending his collaboration to the director and actors, and opening the script up to revision by the author well into the rehearsal period. It also changed the position of the producer, however, transferring the artistic relationship of the playwright in effect from the producer to the director. When he had gained enough power through a string of successful productions, Elia Kazan was to force Broadway producers to accept the situation that had prevailed when he was a member of the Group, with the exception that as director he was definitely in control, with the actors firmly under his authority.

As is particularly true of Tennessee Williams's plays, the differences between the pre-production version and the published version(s) of a script are often great and, as Elia Kazan has written, the play described in the published script is seldom the work of the playwright alone:

A published play is often the record of a collaboration: The director's stage directions are incorporated, as are some of the contributions of others working on the show – actors' "business," designer's solutions, and so on. The theatre is not an exclusively literary form. Although the playscript is the essentially important element, after that is finished, actors, designers, directors, technicians "write" the play together.[2]

To refine on this, we should remember that plays have never been merely written but "wrought." The playwright may write every word of the published script, but the language of a play is not simply words. The language of the theatre is also form and color and movement and sound, a language that cannot be created by a playwright writing, or by one artist without the creative collaboration of others. The script merely records the stage language that results from this creative collaboration.

To criticize a playwright for engaging in collaboration with the theatre artists with whom he works to create the piece on stage seems now to evince a very narrow view of the creation of a play. In the forties, however, critics were working from the already out-dated model that treated the playwright as a "writer," working alone and outside the presumably corrupting influence of the theatre, and the director as a subordinate talent concerned only with realizing the writer's imagination as well as he could within the constricting limits of the stage production. The playwright's job was to write the play, from start to finish, presumably consulting only his creative imagination. The director's job was to know his place and keep it. The creative process by which Williams's plays were realized in performance under Kazan's direction clearly differed from the conventional model, so much so that Eric Bentley raised the issue of what he called Kazan's "co-authorship" of Williams's plays as early as his 1947 review of *Streetcar*. Quickly picked up by other critics and discussed with increasing intensity throughout the fifties, the issue was constructed as a question: whether Williams was a "weak" playwright who allowed his director to "tamper" with his plays, or whether Kazan was an overbearing director who violated the writer's artistic integrity, or both.

The process by which *Streetcar* was produced was actually much closer to the conventional model than what was to become the collaborative process of Williams and Kazan during the fifties. Williams had presented a finished script to producer Irene Selznick, who had, at Williams's request, hired Kazan to direct the play. The three had worked together in casting the major roles, leaving the minor ones up to Kazan alone. Williams had watched the rehearsal process, primarily as a passive observer, making minor revisions in the script at Kazan's request. The set had been designed and realized by Jo Mielziner under Kazan's direction. Both published versions of the script included descriptions of the set designed by Mielziner and the gesture, movement, and business devised by Kazan in conjunction with the actors, although the "reading version" that Williams prepared for publication by New Directions contained less of this specific information than the "acting version" prepared directly from the stage manager's script for Dramatists Play Service.

Kazan had a much more direct influence on the construction of the plays after *Streetcar*. Beginning with *The Rose Tattoo* in 1950, Williams's practice was to send Kazan an early draft of the script, to which Kazan would respond with a long letter suggesting ways of shaping the plot, developing the characters, and emphasizing the potential meaning he saw in the play. Williams responded in various ways to these letters, becoming increasingly resistant to Kazan's suggestions as the years went by, but he always made substantial changes in his plays as a result of Kazan's advice and criticism. Williams and Kazan together chose the producers for the plays after *Streetcar*, producers who were increasingly cut off from the rehearsal process. Kazan directed the whole production process for the later plays, with Williams's active participation. The scripts for these plays remained flexible for a good part of the rehearsal period. Williams added or deleted whole scenes as well as changing or adding lines to develop the play that was taking shape on stage. With the exception of *Cat on a Hot Tin Roof*, the scripts that Williams published – both "acting" and "reading" versions – described the play as it had developed in collaboration with Kazan and the other artists involved in the production without commenting on the extent of this collaboration.

After Williams published a note with the *Cat* script explaining that he had felt pressure from Kazan to make changes in the play he hadn't been sure of, most critics in the fifties tended to describe Kazan's involvement in the script's development as an intrusion of commercial values into the artist's domain and Williams's acceptance of it as caving in to the desire for success. In one of the most influential attacks, Henry Hewes wrote in *The Saturday Review* in 1956 that, "because he is a sensitive romantic, Williams has an insecurity which sometimes leads him into giving in to inferior suggestions from stronger people rather than to do nerve-shattering battle for his own judgement. His relationship with director Elia Kazan is a case in point."[3] Hewes went on to build a whole scenario of interference based on Kazan's alleged commercialism in opposition to Williams's supposedly higher artistic motives.

Academic critics, on the other hand, have tended to be concerned that Williams was somehow not doing the whole job of artistic creation if his final scripts reflected the contributions of the theatre artists he worked with. In the first serious critical book on Williams in 1961, Nancy Tischler implied that Williams's collaborative aesthetic made him less of a playwright than those who wrote independently of theatre artists: "Since Tennessee Williams has owed much of his success to the designers, directors, and actors who have caught the fire of his conception and conveyed it vividly and artistically to the audience," she wrote, "the belittling rumors are partially justified."[4]

For most of its duration between 1947 and 1960, the artistic collaboration between Williams and Kazan was carried on within a climate of critical disapproval and distrust which naturally made for tension between playwright and director. Partly because of this, with *Camino Real* in 1953, Williams began to resist some of Kazan's suggestions. The tension heightened with *Cat*, finally surfacing in Williams's public statement in 1955 that he felt Kazan had usurped his authority as writer with that play, and Kazan's understandable resentment. This did not deter Williams from rather desperately wanting Kazan to direct *Orpheus Descending* (1957), *Sweet Bird of Youth* (1959), and *Period of Adjustment* (1960). The personal and artistic relationship between Williams and Kazan intensified rather than diminished during the late fifties.

At work here was a fundamental dynamic in the relationship between these two men, a struggle for artistic control that is masked by the rhetoric of cooperation typically used to describe the collaborative relationship among theatre artists. In the old conventional model, the director is the willing servant of the playwright, subordinating his or her personal vision to the expression of the play's meaning as the director understands the playwright to intend it. In new models arising from the work of alternative theatres in the sixties and seventies, the playwright becomes the servant of director and actors, as all work to stage the group's performance under the director's guidance. Within the dynamics of Williams and Kazan's relationship, however, there was clearly a struggle between playwright and director to maintain artistic control, to own the play. Kazan has made no secret of his drive for hegemony over the productions he directed. He understood, as he remarked to Robert Anderson, that "a director takes the play away from the playwright, and then the actors take it away from both of them."[5] He tried to realize the writer's vision, but it was his version of that vision:

I think there should be collaboration, but under my thumb! I think people should collaborate with *me*. I think any art is, finally, the expression of one maniac. That's me. I get people who help me, but I'm the center of it . . . Art is the overwhelmingly strong impression that one obsessed visionary puts on his work. It's important that the people who collaborate with you are able to see things as you do, but also that they're willing to ask you what you want and try to give it to you. When I have people I like, it's enormously pleasurable. And I like being contradicted because it helps the work, so long as I can, at a point, say: "That's it."[6]

For his part, Williams usually acceded to Kazan's ideas and synthesized them with his own in reworking his plays because he had a great faith in what he called the "Kazan magic" – the director's ability to take even a shaky script and realize it powerfully on the stage. But there was a point at which Williams would dig in his heels and refuse to go Kazan's way – which happened in small ways with *Camino Real*, and a point at which his creative powers simply refused to function – which happened in small ways with *Cat* and in major ways with *Sweet Bird*. The struggle for ownership is clear in gestures such as Williams's publishing an early version of *Cat*'s Act 3 along with what he called the "Broadway Version," in order to distinguish his vision of the play from Kazan's. It was there almost from the beginning of this collaboration, and it could be debilitating, but it was also part of the creative dynamic.

The close artistic collaboration between these two men was also based on a deep personal affinity that both recognized but neither could explain. Williams wrote that "Kazan understood me quite amazingly for a man whose nature was so opposite to mine."[7] Kazan has written:

Tennessee and I took to each other like a shot and without any of the usual gab about mutual friends, tastes, experiences, and so on to bridge the gap. It was a mysterious harmony; by all visible signs we were as different as two humans could be. Our union, immediate on first encounter, was close but unarticulated; it endured for the rest of his life. How did it happen? Possibly because we were both freaks. Behavior is the mystery that explains character. (L 334–35)

The relationship between Williams and Kazan was based on a mutual affection, trust, and admiration that supported their freedom to experiment artistically. It also contained destructive elements that strained the relationship as time went on, and resulted in its eventual dissolution. Williams conceived of Kazan as an Apollonian consciousness who could bring order to the Dionysian chaos of his artistic genius. He relied on his director to advise him about the structure of his plays, and he trusted Kazan to uphold his artistic values throughout the pragmatic negotiations with producers, theatre owners, agents, and lawyers. Over the years, Williams also developed an emotional dependence on Kazan that made him increasingly reliant on his director for approval and support, while at the same time he resented his own dependence and what he came increasingly to view as Kazan's interference with his artistic vision.

For his part, Kazan was at first enthusiastic about his role as interpreter of and catalyst for Williams's creative vision. As time went on, however, he felt an increasing need to express his own ideas and imagination, fighting for greater and greater control over the process of artistic collaboration in all of his directing work, both plays and films. Combined with Williams's emotional dependence on him, this need to assert his own creativity led to the imposition of what he has acknowledged were his aesthetic values rather than Williams's on the productions of *Cat* and *Sweet Bird*. By 1960 the fragile dynamic of their collaborative relationship had become destructive rather than productive of the free play of creativity that had made it so successful in the beginning. Their collaboration perhaps ran a natural course that helps to explain the explosive dynamics that characterize many creative collaborations in the theatre, and that are masked by the rhetoric of cooperation we now employ to describe the production process.

Despite its eventually destructive dynamic, the Williams–Kazan relationship was central to some of the best work that either man did. Kazan understood that Williams's work was his life. He wrote:

Work is what held Tennessee Williams together; he did it every morning, and nothing was allowed to interfere. He would get up, silent and remote from whoever happened to be with him, dress in a bathrobe, mix himself a double dry martini, put a cigarette into his long white holder, sit before his typewriter, grind in a blank sheet of paper, and so become Tennessee Williams. Up until then he'd been nothing but an aging faggot (his phrase, to me), alone in a world he had always believed and still believed hostile. (L 261)

Williams, writing about the centrality of work to his existence, said, "I don't think anyone has ever known, with the exception of Elia Kazan, how desperately much it meant to me and accordingly treated it – or should I say its writer – with the necessary sympathy of feeling."[8]

The collaborative aesthetic

Within the dynamics of their collaboration, Williams and Kazan brought together a nexus of aesthetic values from their varied training and experience that they combined with the visual aesthetics of Jo Mielziner to create the unique theatrical idiom that came to be known throughout the world in the fifties as "the American Style." In 1944, Tennessee Williams was a young playwright with several moderately successful regional productions and a rather spectacular Theatre Guild flop to his credit. With a brashness born of having little to lose, he wrote what is now recognized as a theatrical manifesto that defined the most significant development in the twentieth-century American theatre. In his production notes to *The Glass Menagerie*, Williams took a defiant stand against the theatrical realism that was the dominant mode in American drama before World War II. Calling his new work a "memory play," he suggested that it could be presented "with unusual freedom of convention."[9] Directly confronting the assumed dichotomy between representational and presentational drama that had divided the American theatre of the twenties and thirties into two sharply defined camps, Williams declared that

expressionism and all other unconventional techniques in drama have only one valid aim, and that is a closer approach to truth. When a play employs unconventional techniques, it is not, or certainly shouldn't be, trying to escape its responsibility of dealing with reality, or interpreting experience, but is actually or should be attempting to find a closer approach, a more penetrating and vivid expression of things as they are. (7)

After suggesting that greater depth of thought was possible with the techniques associated with expressionism, he dismissed what he called "the straight realistic play with its genuine frigidaire and authentic ice-cubes, its characters that speak exactly as its audience speaks," noting that "everyone should know nowadays the unimportance of the photographic in art" (7). Instead, he wrote, "truth, life, or reality is an organic thing which the poetic imagination can represent or suggest, in essence, only through transformation, through changing into other forms than those which were merely present in appearance" (7). Lest any reader miss the point, the young playwright declared that "these remarks are not meant as a preface only to this particular play. They have to do with a conception of a new, plastic theatre which must take the place of the exhausted theatre of realistic conventions if the theatre is to resume vitality as a part of our culture" (7).

Williams was suggesting here a marriage of the two theatrical idioms most at odds during the thirties and early forties, the realism associated with the commercial, middle-class and middle-brow theatre of Broadway and the expressionism associated with the experimental and leftist theatre imported from Europe during the twenties and appropriated by such socially conscious groups as the Federal Theatre Project and the various workers' theatres of the thirties. During the thirties, Williams had been writing mildly leftist plays about miners and flop-houses for regional theatres that thought of themselves as avant-garde. Now he was trying to assimilate what he had learned aesthetically with a subject matter and social point of view that were appropriate to the Broadway theatre, and were also much more indicative of Williams's own interests and concerns than his early efforts. His "manifesto" was a way of domesticating the avant-garde in order to make it suitable to a Broadway audience. At the same time, it was meant to free the domestic drama of middle-class life from what Williams considered the severe limitations of realism as a theatrical mode.

The notion of a "plastic theatre" derives from precursors of Tennessee Williams as remote as Edward Gordon Craig and Richard Wagner. One critic has suggested that it derives directly from Wagner's concept of synthesis: "Wagner sought a fusion of music, poetry, and all areas of design. Similarly, Williams strives for a synthesis of poetry, music, dance, mime, and all theatrical elements of design, including such modern devices as the film screen."[10] Most critics, however, have followed Esther Jackson's lead in locating the elements of Williams's theatrical language in his American contemporaries and their immediate precursors. As she noted, something uniquely American had developed from the work of playwrights as disparate as Eugene O'Neill, Thornton Wilder, Clifford Odets, Elmer Rice, and William Saroyan: "a system of communication with its own themes, types of character, modes of speech, styles of acting, and patterns of staging."[11] Most importantly for Williams, "this poetic language had a parallel in an emerging art of the *mise-en-scène*."[12] Jackson maintains the importance of Williams's academic training in "the rudiments of this theatrical syntax,"[13] and a number of biographical and critical studies have emphasized particularly the influence of Hamilton Wright Mabie at Iowa and John Gassner and Erwin Piscator at The New School for Social Research in acquainting Williams with recent developments in both the American and European theatres.[14]

For Williams's particular theatrical idiom, the most important development in the American theatre of the twenties and thirties occurred in scene design, a development spearheaded by the great American designers Robert Edmond Jones, Lee Simonson, and Norman Bel Geddes, and continued by the generation of Donald Oenslager, Boris Aronson, and Jo Mielziner. In 1941, Jones published his seminal little book on scene design, *The Dramatic Imagination*, which might be seen as a summation of his generation's work and an outline for that of the next. With uncanny prescience he wrote:

Some new playwright will presently set a motion-picture screen on the stage above and behind his actors and will reveal simultaneously the two worlds of the Conscious and the Unconscious which together make up the world we live in – the outer world and the inner world, the objective world of actuality and the subjective world of motive. On stage we shall see the actual characters of the drama; on the screen we shall see their hidden secret selves. The drama will express the behavior of the characters set against a moving background, the expression of their subconscious mind – a continuous action and interaction.[15]

Williams used slides and "screen legends" instead of motion pictures in *The Glass Menagerie*, but he did sketch out a series of silent movies to develop Alma Winemiller's character in early versions of *Summer and Smoke*. In any case, he will be recognized as the kind of playwright Jones was describing. The episteme beneath Williams's new theatrical idiom was the "continuous action and interaction" of the objective and the subjective, social reality and memory, past and present. Williams's drama exploded conventional notions of truth by exposing the inadequacy of the language used to convey them, and did so precisely as Jones had imagined, by exposing the "hidden secret selves" of its characters at the same time as it maintained the illusion of objective reality regarding the events happening in the present of the stage action.

In *The Glass Menagerie*, the dramatic assumption on which the conventions that allow the audience to understand the play are built is the basic assumption of realism, the illusion of the fourth wall. The audience "believes" Tom when he makes his opening speech because the convention is that he is a "real person," not a character in a play. When it witnesses the action behind the transparent wall, the audience accepts not only the convention that the characters are Tom's family and friend, but that the action is really what happened to Tom in the past, as Tom remembers it. In other words the fundamental suspension of disbelief operating in realistic drama is operating here. The audience accepts the premise that the stage action is based on something that happened in a particular time and place, that it represents objective reality. The play's departure from realism comes of course in the assumption that Tom's memory has intervened in the audience's perception of that objective reality, and that the spectator is perceiving the past through the layers of memory represented by the consciously public discourse of Tom's speeches as narrator and the scrims through which the audience first views the action. The play's fundamental aesthetic is realism, but it is subverted by some elements of its theatrical language in order to suggest that the fundamental epistemological assumption behind realism – that the aesthetic object represents objective reality – must be tempered by an element of subjectivity. This play represents not "what is," but the way Tom understands and remembers "what was."

Some elements of the play's theatrical language are completely in keeping with the aesthetic of realism, in that they do not shatter the fourth-wall illusion by calling attention to their theatricality. The fact that the glass menagerie is a symbol or an objective correlative for Laura's state of mind, for example, does not interfere with its iconic function as a realistic prop; it is the collection of glass she keeps in the living room. Only elements of the production that call attention to themselves as theatrical, such as the scrims, the music, and some of the lighting, shatter the illusion of representational realism. These effects thrust the play into another mode, but because the fundamental assumption of the play is that of realism the spectator is unable to categorize it as expressionism or as fantasy. The particular mode of drama in *The Glass Menagerie*, a fundamentally realistic aesthetic subverted by suggestions of a mediating consciousness, is more accurately described as "subjective realism." This term is useful, I believe, for describing not only *Menagerie*, but the whole group of important mid-century plays that became recognizable to the theatrical world as being in "the American Style" during the fifties. Subjective realism was the aesthetic base for Williams's collaboration with Elia Kazan and designer Jo Mielziner.

When Williams began collaborating with Elia Kazan on *A Streetcar*

Named Desire in 1947, Kazan was on the brink of becoming the most successful director and perhaps the single most influential person in the American theatre. In 1953 Eric Bentley was to write that "the work of Elia Kazan means more to the American theatre than that of any current writer whatsoever."[16] Kazan had begun his career by establishing himself as a more than competent actor with the Group Theatre in the thirties, capable of great intensity within a limited range. He first attracted attention as the cab driver who runs up onto the stage at the end of *Waiting for Lefty* and calls passionately for a strike, with both the other actors and the audience joining in. As Eddie Fuseli in *Golden Boy*, he created the character of the hoodlum aristocrat that was to become a mainstay in films, played occasionally by Kazan himself.

Kazan had always wanted to be a director, however. The story is told that when he was asked by Lee Strasberg at his interview for a Group Theatre apprenticeship what he wanted to do, he replied, "What I want is your job" (L 57). No one, including Kazan, quite knew at the time the significance of this remark. Kazan was to become the Group Theatre's most famous director, and as co-founder with Cheryl Crawford of the Actors Studio, was eventually to give Strasberg the teaching job that would establish the legend of Lee Strasberg and the Method. While stage managing and eventually acting with the Group, Kazan gained directing experience with a workers' theatre group called the Theatre of Action and eventually was allowed to direct several Group productions, although none achieved great commercial success.

After the Group dissolved in 1940, Kazan directed a string of successful plays, including Thornton Wilder's *The Skin of Our Teeth*, a Helen Hayes vehicle about Harriet Beecher Stowe entitled *Harriet, One Touch of Venus* by S. J. Perelman and Ogden Nash, and S. N. Behrman's *Jacobowski and the Colonel*. By 1944 Kazan was a director in demand, one who was offered the best scripts and was in a position to choose what he wanted to direct. His choice of *Deep Are the Roots* in 1945, a self-described problem play about racism based on a white family's differing attitudes toward a black veteran, was indicative of both his socially conscious roots and his deepening interest in the psychology of family relationships. In a short-lived producing association with Harold Clurman, he directed Arthur Miller's *All My Sons*, the production that made Tennessee Williams decide Kazan was the person to direct *Streetcar*.

Asked about his aesthetic development in a 1974 interview, Kazan replied, "I was influenced by three things: the Stanislavsky method as taught by Clurman and Strasberg, my readings of Vakhtangov, and films. I was very struck by *Potemkin* and Dovzhenko."[17] One other influence, which he described in his autobiography, was his academic training at

Williams College and the Yale School of Drama. Although at pains to explain how little of what he learned in school was of use to him in the theatre, Kazan wrote that the invaluable technical training he had at Williams meant he never had to fear an electrician when he directed. Of Yale he wrote:

> I did learn a good deal that was useful from the professor of directing, Alexander Dean. He taught directing as an art of position, picture, and movement . . . The director's job was to contrive a kinetic pattern that told what was happening. The actor, as a vehicle of expression, was not to be relied upon. The stage picture, as it developed, told the event. Rhythm and pace, "builds" and "drops," would do the rest. (L 49)[18]

This emphasis on the pictorial and kinesic codes in the production complemented the Group Theatre's Method, but Kazan was always to acknowledge that the Group's influence was primary. "I owe Lee a great deal," he wrote, "and owe to the movement Harold and he started, the Group Theatre, everything" (L 143). From Strasberg he learned to be an actor, and consequently, "learned never to be afraid of actors, so I've never treated them . . . as counters in a game to be moved about as I pleased" (L 143). From Clurman he learned respect for the actor and the role, the ability to inspire actors to do more than they thought themselves capable of, a collaborative attitude toward the production, and the rejection of an authoritarian stance (L 121). It was these qualities that made actors consider Kazan the ideal actors' director.

The artistic center of the Group Theatre was of course the acting system developed by Constantin Stanislavsky for the Moscow Art Theatre, and adapted by Strasberg and Clurman into the Method. Its central principle was that all of the actors' performances were "actions," small units of what Stanislavsky called the "through-action" of the play, or what the Method director calls its "spine". As Kazan told an interviewer in 1967, the concept of action was the central element in his direction.[19] In 1972 he explained his own formulation of the Method:

> The idea with the Method was to consider the play like the trunk of a tree with the branches coming out and you had a branch that led you to another branch and slowly you came to the first climax of the play which contained the theme. The idea was that if you performed all the tasks on the way you would be able to perform the task at the end. We used to refer to it as the spine with all the vertebrae coming off it . . . We used to say in the theatre: "What are you on stage *for*? What do you walk on stage to get? What do you want?" I always asked that of actors; what they're in the scene to obtain, to achieve. The asset of that is that all my actors come on strong, they're all alive, they're all dynamic – no matter how quiet . . . Another thing in the Stanislavsky system that I always stress a lot when I direct actors is what happened just before the scene. I not only talk about it, I sometimes improvise it . . . Another thing I've tried to stress is a basic simplicity; that

is, listening to the person who's talking to you, and talking to him, not declaiming.[20]

The most controversial element of the Method as taught by Lee Strasberg and others was emotional memory, or the re-creation of an emotional state within the actor by recalling the circumstances that produced that emotion in her own life. Kazan described this as an "essential and rather simple technique, which has . . . been complicated by teachers of acting who seek to make the Method more recondite for their commercial advantage" (L 63).

Kazan's personal deviation from the Method began very early, long before his career as a director. In his autobiography he describes a conversation with Molly Day Thacher, his future wife, in which he set forth his views on directing:

Nor is direction what the Group directors seemed to think it is, a matter of coaching actors. It is turning psychological events into behavior, inner events into visible, external patterns of life on stage. I could and I would . . . apply what I'd learned about direction from Alexander Dean at Yale – the shaping of scenes and the manipulation of the positions and movements of actors so that the stage pictures revealed, at every moment, what was happening – to the Group's Method, which had found the way to create spontaneous, surprising, and true inner experiences . . . My work would be to turn the inner events of the psyche into a choreography of external life. (L 90)

This was precisely what he was to do. Kazan's direction was in fact a combination of the fundamental elements of the Method in working with actors and an expressive use of the visual elements of a play – space, movement, gesture, props, set, costumes – to externalize the psychic life of the characters, to objectify the subjective. During the late forties and the fifties, he was to be the perfect collaborator for playwrights who were writing plays that attempted to do just that, playwrights like Tennessee Williams, Arthur Miller, Robert Anderson, and William Inge.

The visual side of Kazan's aesthetic can be seen in his intense interest in Vsevolod Meyerhold and Evgeny Vakhtangov. He said that during the Group years, "we adored their theatre: Meyerhold, Vakhtangov, Stanislavsky. We did imitations of their methods. I typed up Vakhtangov's notes and made a few carbons and gave them out to other members."[21] From Meyerhold he learned the liberating force of theatricality, which could come from the simple rejection of the objective realism that confined Stanislavsky and most directors associated with the Method to the fourth-wall illusion. As Vakhtangov said,

For Meyerhold "theatricality" means a spectacle during which the audience doesn't forget that it is at the theatre, nor do they cease for a moment to perceive the actor as a master playing a role. Stanislavsky demanded the opposite, i.e. that the audience forget they are at the theatre, that they feel they are part of the atmosphere and milieu in which the play's characters live.[22]

From Vakhtangov Kazan learned about plasticity in the expressive quality of the actor's body. Kazan recognized that movement was an important part of his own training as an actor as well as his directing. In the thirties the experience of dancing with Helen Tamiris and Jerome Robbins led him to be more free in his movements on stage. As a director, he said, "I choreographed scenes more than purely psychological directors do."[23]

The other significant element of Vakhtangov's aesthetic that was to appear in Kazan's work was the notion of "imaginative realism," which Kazan formulated for himself as "poetic realism" – a unique combination of elements from his many aesthetic influences forming a unifying principle that amounted to subjective realism. In his fullest statement of the concept, he explained the influence of film:

The scene I remember in Dovzhenko is the scene in the forest, in *Aerograd*, when the old men yell at each other. I think that changed my life, just one scene like that where I thought a film can be both true – realistic – and completely poetic. And that became the ideal of my aesthetic – to the extent that I was conscious of my aesthetic. Suddenly you look at it and it's as plain as a loaf of bread, and it's completely poetic at the same time. It has overtones, it has suggestions, it has poetry all around it, but then, it can also be just nothing, a loaf of bread. This is what I feel when I see paintings by Cézanne: he shows you an apple, it's just an apple on a table, but it's somehow poetic. I like that.[24]

Kazan recognizes the necessity of the artist's subjective view of the object in creating this kind of representation, and he is proudest of the films where he conveyed his own viewpoint successfully.

In different ways, the aesthetics of both Williams and Kazan embodied deep conflicts. Williams fluctuated between realism and expressionism in trying to represent both objective and subjective versions of reality on the stage at once. Like his admired Vakhtangov, Kazan was torn between the naturalistic, representational theatre of Stanislavsky and the abstract, presentational theatricality of Meyerhold. In collaboration, their visions were enough alike that they understood each other, but their artistic views had different sources and different goals. In forging their new theatrical idiom along with Jo Mielziner, these artists capitalized on their contradictory impulses. Mielziner developed a design language that he called "abstract realism," in which objective reality is suggested but attentuated and subjectivity is indicated without being precisely delimited. Kazan juxtaposed Stanislavsky with Meyerhold, creating a naturalistic environment in which his actors addressed the audience in increasingly presentational ways. Williams created an illusion of objective reality into which subjective perception intruded insistently. The interaction of these aesthetic impulses made for exciting and dynamic theatre, perhaps because the art they produced was always an unstable compound – not the vision of "one maniac" as Kazan thought, but the juxtaposition of many visions within one work of art.

2 Subject and object: *A Streetcar Named Desire*

Assembling the team

In 1947 Irene Selznick, newly separated from her celebrated movie-producer husband David, was attempting to begin a career as a theatrical producer. Williams's agent Audrey Wood, who had heard about Selznick's plans from various friends and colleagues in Los Angeles, carefully watched the work she was doing on *Heartsong* and decided that Selznick was the right producer for Williams's new play, *A Streetcar Named Desire*. Wood recalled in her autobiography that she had received a wire from Williams after suggesting Selznick during a phone call to him in New Orleans. It read, "THIS WOMAN HAD BETTER BE GOOD."[1] According to Williams, his first meeting with Selznick "was arranged by Audrey with the atmosphere of high-level espionage."[2] In the spring of 1947, Williams was wired to come to the best hotel in Charleston, South Carolina. The decision for Selznick to produce *Streetcar* was made then and there and confirmed with a wire sent to her New York office in code: "BLANCHE IS COMING TO STAY WITH US" (M 112).[3] Williams found the intrigue very exciting, but was soon back in New Orleans for Mardi Gras. The producing arrangement was actually made between Wood and Selznick, with Williams paying little attention to its details.

Williams was much more concerned about the choice of a director. He wrote that when he saw *All My Sons*, he "was so impressed by [Elia Kazan's] staging of that message drama, by the vitality which he managed to put into it, that [Williams] implored Audrey Wood and Irene Selznick to do everything possible to procure [Kazan] as director for *Streetcar*" (M 130).[4] This was not easily done. Kazan was not attracted by the play at first. Both Williams and Wood remembered that it was his wife, Molly Day Thacher Kazan, who had convinced Kazan to direct *Streetcar*. Kazan wrote in his autobiography that Selznick had all but promised the play to Joshua Logan when Williams, "following an instinct, something irrational," told her that he had to have Kazan.[5] Kazan remembers that at that point, he had still not read the play, "but my wife, overwhelmed by it,

kept after me. When I read it, I must confess, I had reservations"
(L 328).[6] He said that he and Williams met twice to resolve Kazan's
problems, and then shook hands and embraced. "As far as we were
concerned, the matter was settled. [Williams] 'removed himself' to Cape
Cod" (L 328).

At this point, however, negotiations began to get complicated. Kazan
suggests that Selznick and his lawyer were engaged in prolonged negotiations that he and Williams were not party to. Williams, apparently told by
Selznick that Kazan was demanding a great deal of revision, began
writing directly to him, suggesting that they meet and talk about the
script. "I'm sure a lot of good will come out of consultation between us,"
he wrote. "The cloudy dream type, which I admit to being, needs the
complementary eye of the more objective and dynamic worker. I believe
you are also a dreamer. There are dreamy touches in your direction which
are vastly provocative but you have the dynamism my work needs"
(L 328). Kazan said that after this letter, he "belonged" to Williams
(L 328). He wrote Williams a letter saying that he worked best "in single
collaboration with the author," and that he was not about to consult with a
producer on every point of production. He said he and his lawyer had
worked out a proposal that he hoped Mrs. Selznick would find acceptable,
adding, "it will depend somewhat on how much you want me" (L 329).
According to Selznick, this proposal included an unprecedented demand
to "co-produce and own a chunk of the show" as well as a "top percentage
of the gross."[7] In the negotiations that followed, Selznick agreed to give
Kazan 20 percent of the show, taking half from her own share and half
from the investors' share. The demand to co-produce was reduced to a
second credit – "IRENE SELZNICK PRESENTS ELIA KAZAN'S
PRODUCTION of" – still a significant statement of the power the
director was demanding.

Kazan was fully aware of what he was doing in these negotiations.
Assured by now of an author who wanted him and no one else to direct the
play and a producer who, because she was just beginning, would be
willing to give up a good deal for the professional status that a success of
the magnitude she expected from *Streetcar* could provide, Kazan was
making his move to establish the position of "artistic tyrant" he had
always thought the director should occupy on the production staff. He has
written that, "on *Streetcar* [he] established a concept in support of which
all other craftsmen working on the show had to shape their contributions.
The producer was reduced to the status of an owner who observed the
production process but had little part in it" (L 338).

Williams had no interest in the contract negotiations, and little understanding of what was going on. After two unhappy experiences with

producers – the Theatre Guild on *Battle of Angels* and a rather unstable partnership on *The Glass Menagerie* – he was not in a very good position to judge Selznick's effectiveness or Kazan's demands. In May of 1947 he wrote to Margo Jones that Selznick had signed Kazan virtually on her own terms, stating that Kazan had wanted to be co-producer but Selznick had faced him down.[8] It is likely that Selznick and Woods were putting the best face on a bad deal from their point of view, and their ingenuous playwright was all too eager to believe them. In fact, from an artistic standpoint, which Williams proved over and over again was the only one he really cared about in the production of his plays, the deal was a good one. Williams made less money from the production than he might have, but its artistic development was completely up to him and the director whose collaboration he knew would help his play (see plate 1).

The designers had already been engaged when Kazan finally signed his contract, but he said that in Jo Mielziner, Selznick had "engaged the scene designer [he] would have chosen – 'buying the best,' as David [Selznick] would have done" (L 338). After serving a valuable apprenticeship with Robert Edmond Jones, Mielziner had begun designing for Broadway on his own in 1924. By 1947, he was the most sought-after designer in New York, with such credits as *Street Scene* (1929), *Winterset* (1935), *Hamlet* (1936), *Carousel* (1945), and *Annie Get Your Gun* (1946) under his belt. As the one who had created the crucial scenic design for *The Glass Menagerie*, he was Williams's first choice. Wood wrote to Williams in April of 1947 that Mielziner had demanded tremendously high terms, but that Selznick had hired him because Mielziner said this was going to be the best job he'd ever done.[9]

Kazan and Mielziner met many times without the producer, planning the set together. Working from Kazan's ground plan, the two discussed every aspect of Mielziner's design, "the colors, the materials, the transparency, the effects, and the lighting – which [Mielziner], wisely, was to do for himself" (L 338). When the two had arrived together at the scheme they wanted, Mielziner made a number of sketches, which they presented jointly to Williams and Selznick. Kazan worked in the same way with costume designer Lucinda Ballard, but not quite so amicably. Ballard's volatile temperament caused problems, particularly with Selznick, and Kazan and Williams were to turn to others to design costumes for the rest of their productions. According to Kazan, it was he who selected Alex North to score the music, which turned out to be quite a bit different from what was indicated in Williams's pre-production script. Throughout the production process, Kazan had a clear idea of the role he had defined for himself as director:

I had to gather all the artistic contributions – Tennessee's, Jo's, Lucinda's, Alex North's, and that of each member of the cast – into one intention. Since they were all talented people of decided opinions, this was not always an easy task. Williams's play was to undergo the great change, become a production, no longer what Thornton Wilder called a "text" – a word I loathe in the theatre. It now had to be transformed into a living thing, and I had the responsibility of supervising the metamorphosis. (L 339)

The play's casting was a collaborative effort, with the most aggressive participation coming from Kazan. Selznick favored movie star Margaret Sullavan for the part of Blanche, but Williams complained that "she didn't seem right to me, I kept picturing her with a tennis racket in one hand and I doubted that Blanche had ever played tennis" (M 132). The other strong possibility was Jessica Tandy, who was appearing in Williams's *Portrait of a Madonna* in Los Angeles. Williams, Selznick, and Wood travelled from New York to join Kazan, who was in Hollywood finishing the work on his latest film, and see the production. Williams has written that "it was instantly apparent to [him] that Jessica was Blanche" (M 132). The others agreed, and Blanche was cast.

The Brando story is now legendary. Kazan gave Marlon Brando, a young actor he knew from Actors Studio and his production of *Truckline Cafe*, twenty dollars for bus fare and sent him to Provincetown to read for Williams. Brando arrived three days later, having hitched to Provincetown to save the money for food. There, according to Williams, Brando fixed the broken plumbing and the electricity, and then sat down to read. After ten minutes Margo Jones, who was staying with Williams, "jumped up and let out a 'Texas Tornado' shout. 'Get Kazan on the phone right away! This is the greatest reading I've ever heard – in or outside of Texas!'" (M 131). Kazan reports that he received "an ecstatic call from our author, in a voice near hysteria. Brando had overwhelmed him" (L 341–42).[10] Stanley was cast.

As he thought about the casting of Brando, Williams adopted Kazan's point of view on the relative ages of Blanche and Stanley, realizing how well the casting would serve the play's theme. In August he wrote to Audrey Wood that it had not occurred to him before what casting a very young actor in the role would do for the play: "It humanizes the character of Stanley in that it becomes the brutality or callousness of youth rather than a vicious older man. I don't want to focus guilt or blame on any one character but to have it a tragedy of misunderstandings and insensitivity to others."[11] After Blanche and Stanley were cast, Williams told Kazan that he should cast the rest of the parts as he wished, and this is pretty much what happened. Karl Malden, who played Mitch, had acted in both

Truckline Cafe and *All My Sons*. It was Selznick who suggested Kim Hunter for Stella, but the rest of the cast, as was to become typical for Kazan, came out of his newly established Actors Studio, which he was to treat as a kind of permanent company, drawing on it for both plays and films throughout the forties and fifties.

The evolution of the script

Tennessee Williams had begun to work on the play that was to become *A Streetcar Named Desire* during rehearsals for *The Glass Menagerie* in 1944. He says in *Memoirs* that the play began as *Blanche's Chair in the Moon*, of which he had written only a single scene during the winter of 1944–5. In that scene, he wrote, "Blanche was in some steaming hot Southern town, sitting alone in a chair with the moonlight coming through a window on her, waiting for a beau who didn't show up." Williams stopped work on the play because he "became mysteriously depressed and debilitated" while writing it (M 86). In a 1981 interview he said that the play had originated with an image of his sister, who was in love with a young man: "Whenever the phone would ring, she'd nearly faint. She'd think it was he calling for a date, you know? They saw each other every other night, and then one time he just didn't call anymore. That was when Rose first began to go into a mental decline. From that vision *Streetcar* evolved."[12]

Williams actually had done more work on the play that winter than he remembered. He sent Audrey Wood a scenario on March 23, 1945, writing that he intended it for Katherine Cornell and suggesting as possible titles "The Moth," "The Poker Night," "The Primary Colors," or "Blanche's Chair in the Moon."[13] In the scenario, Williams suggested three possible endings:

One, Blanche simply leaves – with no destination.
Two, goes mad.
Three, throws herself in front of a train in the freight-yards, the roar of which has been an ominous under-tone throughout the play.[14]

The title *A Streetcar Named Desire* first appeared in a letter to Audrey Wood on January 15, 1946, but Williams favored *The Poker Night* right up until the last revisions. On February 16, 1947, Williams sent the manuscript to Wood for typing, and he sent a set of revisions on March 18. Williams began talking to Kazan about the play in April, 1947. In May he went to Provincetown to work on further revisions. It was there, he said, later, that he thought of Blanche's exit line, "I have always depended on the kindness of strangers" (M 130–31). Williams continued to revise the script throughout the summer, referring the changes to Kazan and Selznick. The rehearsal process began on September 15.

Considerable scholarly attention has been given to the many versions of *Streetcar* preceding the final pre-production script on which Kazan's conception for the production and Mielziner's design for it were based.[15] The manuscripts at the University of Texas are as yet uncatalogued and mostly undated, but it is possible to date some of them from internal evidence, and it is easy to separate some very early versions from the later ones. Two of these early versions show Williams trying things out, as was his custom, to see what would emerge as the core of the play.

One is the "Italian version" set in Chicago, in which the characters are called Bianca, Rosa, and Lucio. Several of the central elements in *Streetcar* are present here in addition to the core plot of the older sister who is living with the younger couple and anxious about her relations with the man she hopes to marry. (The surviving fragment corresponds to scene 4 of *Streetcar*.) The expressive element of color is central to the description of the characters here, as it is in the final version. Lucio wears a silk bowling shirt, with the name of his team, "The Busy Beavers," embroidered in scarlet. Bianca wears a vivid silk robe as the curtain rises and is later to change into a white linen suit. Bianca is several years older than Rosa, and is more delicate in every respect. A major difference from the final version, however, is the character of Lucio, who is described as nearly effeminate.[16]

The version called "The Primary Colors," set in Atlanta, moves the characters closer to their final transformations. They are called Ralph Stanley, Stella, and Blanche. Stella exhibits "a certain bovine placidity," while Blanche "is charged with plenty of that blue juice which is the doves of Aphrodite's or anyone's car." Ralph is "a healthy Irish peasant type with urban modifications and a keen sense of the fact that he is one man in a house with two women." Mitch appears here as a character called "Howdy."[17] In this version, however, Blanche is much livelier and more colloquial than she was to become; she engages in a great deal of banter with Ralph, to whom she is clearly attracted from the beginning.

The main problems for Williams in working with the script seem to have been how to portray the relationship between Blanche and Stanley and how to end the play. A surviving fragment of "The Passion of a Moth" depicts an early solution to the problem. Here Blanche and Stanley seem to have made love with mutual attraction. Like Alma in *Summer and Smoke*, which Williams was working on concurrently, Blanche tells Stanley she will go on to Mobile and meet a stranger. She also talks of bearing Stanley's son, who will wash them all clean.[18] At the end of the play, Blanche is alone on stage saying that she has to get packed and be going.

In a version of "The Poker Night" containing a good deal of dialogue that is identical to that in the published versions, Blanche has become a helpless victim in the final scene. She sits staring out the window and is called catatonic by the doctor. Later she crouches in a grotesque, twisted position, screaming. The people from the asylum put a straitjacket on her before they take her away. Williams removed this and other heavy-handed touches, such as Stanley's selling mortuary goods, in revision and softened Mitch's character from that of a "wolf" to the "mama's boy" of the published version.

In a revision of the final scene that Williams sent to Kazan in August, Stella tells Eunice directly that Blanche claims Stanley has raped her. Stella displays Stanley's pajama top, which has been ripped to shreds, and says that his shoulders and back are covered with scratches. All he will say in his defense, she says, is that Blanche is crazy. This made Stella more culpable for deserting Blanche than she is in the final version, and gave a much more emphatic cast to her line, "I couldn't believe her story and go on living with Stanley."[19] This version ends with Stanley still playing cards while Stella elevates her baby to the sky, and then draws it toward her and hides her face in its blanket, an image of the helpless dependence on Stanley that has been sealed by Stella's maternity. In this version, Williams also fleshed out the Shep Huntleigh story in scenes 4 and 10, making it slightly more believable. In previous versions Blanche's millionaire had been anonymous.

In mid September, Kazan began work with Williams on the pre-production version of the script, which was dated October 6, 1947. Although there are more than a hundred differences in lines or staging between the two, this version is fundamentally the same as the reading version published by New Directions. The most significant differences between the script that went into rehearsals and the one that Williams published as the reading version are related to the play's staging, Blanche's dialogue, the music, Blanche's scene with the paper boy, and the characters of Stella and Mitch.

Williams's original plan for the staging was to use a scrim or transparent drop made of gauze rather than canvas, exactly as Jo Mielziner had used it in *The Glass Menagerie*. The face of the building would be painted on gauze, and when Blanche entered the apartment the interior would be lit with blue light while the exterior light would dim out, making the gauze transparent and allowing the audience to see the action inside the apartment. The scrim would be lifted into the wings during the first scene as it was in the earlier play, and it would descend at certain times, such as at the end of scene 2 when Blanche and Stella leave the apartment and in scene 3 when Stanley goes outside to yell for Stella. Eventually, however, Mielziner's more complex lighting plan for this play dispensed with the need to raise and lower the scrim, accomplishing these changes with light alone. The pre-production script also indicates curtains between scenes, where it was eventually decided to use blackouts and musical interludes instead.

Between them Elia Kazan and Alex North were to revise Williams's original plans for the music in *Streetcar* radically, so that the music of the production differed greatly from that even of the reading version. In the pre-production script, Williams was going to use the "Varsouviana," the polka music that signifies Blanche's dissociation from reality, at the end of scenes 8 and 9 and have Blanche sing a nonsense song to herself at the end of scene 8 to suggest that her mind was disintegrating. In this version the polka tune was concentrated at the end of the play, indicating a progressive dissociation from reality, and the blue piano was played more often than is indicated in the reading version.

Blanche was a more sympathetic character in the pre-production script than she finally became. The most important instance of the change was the cutting of a line indicating that the seventeen-year-old boy Blanche had been involved with in Laurel was blackmailing her into having sex with him because he knew about one of her secrets from the past. Cutting this line made Blanche fully responsible for this most telling instance of her "degeneracy."[20]

Both Mitch and Stella were originally more in harmony with the other characters in the French Quarter than they appear in the reading version. Stella's relationship with Eunice is warmer and more intimate in the earlier version, and when Blanche makes fun of the women in the Quarter, Stella says that they are good-hearted and easy to get along with.[21] For his part, Mitch was more "one of the boys." For example, when the men return from bowling in scene 1, Stanley and Mitch in unison provide the punch line to a dirty joke that Steve is telling, while they all bellow with laughter. The subtexts of tension between Mitch and Stanley and between Stella and Stanley's way of life were developed during rehearsals.

The director's concept

Because selections from Elia Kazan's director's notes for *Streetcar* have been published and reprinted several times, his conception of the play and its major characters is more widely known than is usually the case, and has received a good deal of critical attention.[22] Esther Jackson maintains that, in his notes, "Kazan demonstrates his technique in developing a subordinate system of plastic symbols, a linguistic scheme for the explication of the text" that "represents the effective transliteration of Williams' text into acting, staging patterns, music, sound effects, and scenic design."[23]

Kazan's work was more than the production of a subordinate system, however. It was he who formulated and articulated the concept through which all the elements of the stage language were integrated. His conception of the play molded Williams's dialogue; the actors' vocal articulation, gesture and movement; Mielziner's design and lighting; Ballard's costumes; and North's music into a complete and harmonious aesthetic entity, the production. As he describes it, his understanding of the play's essential dynamic came from a letter he received from Williams during the negotiations over the play. Concerned that Kazan thought the play's meaning was not clear, Williams set about trying to clarify it:

> I think its best quality is its authenticity or its fidelity to life. There are no "good" or "bad" people. Some are a little better or a little worse but all are activated more by misunderstanding than malice. A blindness to what is going on in each other's hearts. Stanley sees Blanche not as a desperate, driven creature backed into a last corner to make a last desperate stand – but as a calculating bitch with "round heels" . . . Nobody sees anybody truly but all through the flaws of their own egos . . . Naturally a play of this kind does not present a theme or score a point unless it is the point or theme of human understanding . . . It is a tragedy with the classic aim of producing a catharsis of pity and terror and in order to do that, Blanche must finally have the understanding and compassion of the audience. This without creating a black-dyed villain in Stanley. It is a thing (Misunderstanding) not a person (Stanley) that destroys her in the end. In the end you should feel – "If only they all had known about each other." (L 329–30)

For Kazan this letter "became the key to the production" (L 330). Placing Blanche at its center, he tried to build around her a tragedy of misunderstanding without creating a "black-dyed villain" in Stanley. He expected the audience to be "with Brando at first, as they were closer in their values to Stanley than to Blanche" (L 343). Then, slowly, he would try to bring them around to Blanche's side and an understanding that they had been prejudiced and insensitive (L 343). In conceiving this scheme for the play's basic dynamic, Kazan showed his affinity with melodrama. He had to be reminded by Williams during the rehearsal process that "Blanche is not an angel without a flaw and Stanley's not evil. I know you're used to clearly stated themes, but this play should not be loaded one way or the other. Don't try to simplify things . . . Don't take sides or try to present a moral" (L 346). With Williams's urging, Kazan overcame his natural tendency to moralize. The play developed as a tragedy of subjectivity, a failure of each of the characters to see how differently they each perceived the same reality.

Kazan also took his cue from Williams about the style of the production. In his letter Williams had said that the director had to "bring this play to life exactly as if it were happening in life," adding "I don't necessarily mean 'realism'; sometimes a living quality is caught better by expressionism than what is supposed to be realistic treatment" (L 330). From his days in the Group Theatre, Kazan was used to working in what the Group called "stylized realism."[24] In his notebook, he wrote that a stylized production was necessary for *Streetcar* because "a subjective factor – Blanche's memories, inner life, emotions, are a real factor. We cannot really understand her behavior unless we see the effect of her past on her present behavior."[25] The basis of his stylization for the production was the objectification of this subjective reality, the encoding of Blanche's memories, inner life, and emotions in the stage language. Kazan agreed with Williams's opinion that conventional realism would be inadequate for this play, but he did not oppose realism simply to expressionism as Williams did. Instead, Kazan was to find a middle ground between the epistemological assumption that the action on stage was empirical fact and the assumption that it was a character's subjective perception. As a production of the Group Theatre and the Stanislavsky-inspired Method, Kazan saw character in essentially naturalistic terms. To him a character's actions were motivated by psychology, which was in turn a product of personal experience and social forces. The character's subjectivity was thus the product of "real" conditions within the representational construct of the play. Objectifying Blanche's subjectivity in the stage language meant bringing the elements of her constructed psychology – a set of experiences and motivations created for her by the director – into action and behavior. For Kazan these experiences and motivations originated primarily in the society that produced Blanche. As he wrote:

The style – the real deep style – consists of one thing only: to find behavior that's truly social, significantly typical, at each moment. It's not so much what Blanche has done – it's how she does it – with such style, grace, manners, old-world trappings and effects, props, tricks, swirls, etc., that they seem anything but vulgar . . . Because this image of herself cannot be accomplished in reality, certainly not in the South of our day and time, it is her effort and practice to *accomplish it in fantasy*. Everything that she does in *reality* too is colored by this necessity, this compulsion to be *special*. So, in fact, *reality becomes fantasy too*. She makes it so! (N 366–67)

It was Blanche's social type, "the emblem of a dying civilization, making its last curlicued and romantic exit," that Kazan used as "the source of the play's stylization and the production's style and color" (N 365). He saw

Stanley's behavior as social too: "It is the basic animal cynicism of today. 'Get what's coming to you! Don't waste a day! Eat, drink, get yours!'" (N 365). In the Group tradition, however, he hoped to convey his naturalistic concepts of the characters through stylization. Stanley's animal cynicism, he wrote, "is the basis of his stylization, of the choice of his props. All props should be stylized: they should have a color, shape and weight that spell: style" (N 365). Kazan encoded what he called a "Don Quixote character" for each actor in keeping with what he saw as the "poetic" nature of this tragedy as opposed to simple realism or naturalism (N 366), inventing behavior, costumes, and props to express the idea that each was to represent. But he reminded himself at the outset not to overdo the stylization or allow the rest of his collaborators to overdo it. "Stylized acting and direction is to realistic acting and direction as poetry is to prose," he wrote, "the acting must be styled, not in the obvious sense. (Say nothing about it to the producer and actors.) But you will fail unless you find this kind of poetic realization for the behavior of these people" (N 366).

While Kazan was "in retreat" at his house in Connecticut working on his conception for the play, Mielziner was beginning to work with his staff on the design they had discussed. He had been given the cue for the design from Williams's early script, but the cue was limited. The opening stage directions said only that the building contained two flats, upstairs and down. Faded white stairs were to ascend to the entrances of both, on whichever side the designer chose for the corner side of the building.[26] As mentioned earlier, the script also indicated that a transparent scrim should be used in the same way it was used in *The Glass Menagerie*, with blue lights coming up in the apartment as Blanche entered it and the scrim ascending and descending during the course of the play. Wishing to build on his experience with *Menagerie* rather than repeat it, however, Mielziner conceived a design that used light and transparent scenery in a more complex and subtle way than the earlier one had.

The design for *Streetcar* consisted of a backdrop with a stylized view of the street behind the apartment and a series of walls made of gauze and black duck to produce varying degrees of opacity in front of the backdrop. The rear wall of the apartment was made of gauze with appliqués to represent windows, fanlights, and shutters. From a series of lights mounted behind the proscenium, this drop could be lighted from the front, displaying only the apartment's interior wall. For an exterior scene such as Blanche's departure at the end of the play, the lights were brought up behind the translucent scrim, revealing the actors who stood behind it "on the street" as well as the backdrop (see plate 2). The combination of lighting and scenery helped to produce the stylized effect that Kazan was after, neither conventional realism nor expressionism, but a new visual environment. As Mielziner described it, "throughout the play the brooding atmosphere is like an impressionistic X-ray. We are always conscious of the skeleton of this house of terror, even though we have peripheral impressions, like the chant of the Mexican woman which forms a background to a solo scene of Stella in her bedroom downstage."[27]

The real artistry of the design scheme lay in the juxtaposition of this impressionistic background with detailed realism in props and costumes, achieving precisely the contrast Kazan was looking for in his "Don Quixote characters" and their stark social reality. The notes from Mielziner's conferences during July and August indicate that he was as concerned with the realism of the overstuffed armchair with one arm knocked off, the L-shaped bench, and the dirty, grey thunderbird blankets as he was with the thickness of the gauze and the gluing of the appliqués.[28] By October 16, the major props had been collected and sent off to be painted or sprayed down to keep them from reflecting the light too much. These included a suitably beat-up ice chest and cabinet, the poker table with four mismatched chairs, a threefold gilt screen to go around the iron bed, a gilt oval frame with a metal mirror, a backless side chair, a dressing table, and a metal bathroom sink. These were supplemented by a dark, neutral bed throw for the first scene – to be replaced by a brighter cover in scene 7, after Blanche started fixing up the place – an old green billiard cloth with a torn edge, a crocheted cover with a pink ribbon run through it for the dresser, and cheap fancy pillows.[29] These large props were of course surrounded with the realistic illusion created by genuine liquor bottles, playing cards, birthday candles, a beat-up coffee pot, a bag of peppermint patties, a bowl of fruit, and several displays of Blanche's clothes and jewels.

The realistic props served several functions in the context of the stage language. Their insistent and sometimes jarring iconic realism helped to re-emphasize the friction between the subjective and the objective, between the world as Blanche saw it and the "real" world the characters lived in. They also performed the function common to setting and props in conventionally realistic plays, serving as metonymic material signifiers of the characters' way of life and their tastes and values, a function Mielziner understood well. The torn poker-table cover and the dirty thunderbird blankets encoded Stanley's values and personality as effectively as the cheap fancy pillows and the bright chintz slipcover encoded Blanche's. The displacement of Stanley's things by Blanche's in the apartment signified materially the threat that Stanley feels from Blanche. Because this play was avowedly "poetic," the props also encoded another layer of meaning. Blanche's clothes and jewelry, the focus for the action in scene 2 and the major scenic element in scene 10, are not only metonymic signifiers of Blanche's concern with her appearance and her dependence on material things for security, they are also symbolic of a whole set of abstract values that Kazan conceptualized as "the tradition." If the presence of these things on stage did not signify more to the audience than they do to Stanley, the production would not be realizing the play fully.

Within the technical resources available to these artists in the forties, the new stage language of subjective realism was by no means easy to create. Lighting was of course the central element of the new stage language. It was also the most difficult scenic element to produce and control. Shortly after the Broadway opening of *Streetcar*, *Variety* reported that the production required five large electrical switchboards and seven auxiliaries, five electricians, and five stage managers, only three of whom received program credit.[30] Robert Downing, the production stage manager, noted that the eleven scenes of *Streetcar* had more than sixty light cues, "many of them occurring simultaneously or in rapid succession, and all of them important to the spirit of the play."[31] A newspaper piece done during rehearsals gives a good sense of how complicated it could be to create the effects desired by Williams, Kazan, and Mielziner:

The backstage area looks like the cave of a black octopus family. From a half dozen huge instrument boards, the heavy dark cables wind in an endless maze up into the air and all over the set to provide the Mielziner aura . . . one of the electricians is gradually operating four separate dimmers with his hands and another one with one knee. The fact that the set is really three different scenes demands further light manipulation. The room's wall is visible when lighted from the front, but dissolves into the street outside under spots there. This, too, can disappear with different lights which bring up a railroad bridge in the far background.[32]

For *Streetcar*, Mielziner used sixteen stationary Leko follow-spots to light several areas of the stage softly and precisely with blue light during the scenes in the bedroom and to create a soft play of light and shadow in the exterior scenes, as well as for specific effects such as the street light outside the building.[33] One Leko was also used as a follow-spot on Blanche in either blue or amber, depending on whether the light supposedly derived from daylight, moonlight, or candlelight.[34] This follow-spot was an important element in the stage language because it emphasized the production's focus on Blanche and foregrounded her subjectivity at every moment of the play. The audience was constantly aware of both the action on stage and Blanche's perception of it.

The production of the musical effects for the play was also unusually complicated. The "Varsouviana," a purely subjective effect that was supposed to be heard only by Blanche, was produced by a primitive version of a synthesizer called a Novachord. The rest of the music, which, ostensibly coming from the Four Deuces Bar, was objectively real within the construct of the play's action, was produced not by a single "blue piano," as Williams implies in his opening stage directions for the reading version, but by a four-piece jazz band composed of piano, clarinet, trumpet, and drums. The jazz band played somewhat raucous, sexy tunes to emphasize the present reality while the weird sound of the "Varsouviana" played on the Novachord signified Blanche's subjectivity. The Novachord was operated from backstage, but the arrangements for the jazz band were somewhat more complicated. Although the music was live, the band played in a broadcasting booth on the theatre's upper floor, which was equipped with a microphone, cue lights, a warning buzzer, and an intercom that kept the band in touch with an assistant stage manager who watched the play from the wings. The transmission of sound to the audience was controlled by the stage manager from carefully indicated cues to fade in and out, or to bring the volume up or down.[35]

The orchestra was the central element in Kazan's reinterpretation of the play's music. As was mentioned earlier, Kazan used the polka tune more often at the beginning of the play than Williams had indicated in the pre-production script, thus making the division between the polka tune's subjectivity and the jazz music's objectivity less sharp, and distributing the suggestion of Blanche's disintegrating psyche throughout the play rather than placing it in one expressionistic climax. He also cut the use of the blue piano significantly, simply removing it from the opening scene, from Blanche's speech to Stanley about Belle Reve and death, from the end of scene 4, from the end of scene 5, and from the rape scene. He replaced it with the orchestra at the beginning of scene 2, during the last part of scene 3, and at the end of scene 9. In scene 3, when Williams's pre-production script indicated dissonant brass and piano sounds while Stanley was calling for Stella rather than "Paper Doll," as the reading version indicates, Kazan substituted "F. B. Blues," with the orchestra directed to slide into it, medium swing, and milk it plaintively, and for the clarinet to come up on Stanley's climactic cry for Stella.[36] At the end of the play, as Blanche is led away, Kazan replaced the swelling music of the blue piano and the trumpet with the Novachord playing the "Varsouviana," directing the audience's final attention to Blanche's rather than to Stanley's version of reality.

Kazan also cut the orchestra music from Blanche's scene with the paper boy and from the birthday-party scene, at the point where Stanley goes out on the porch to smoke a cigarette after he has destroyed the crockery. He cut the "Varsouviana" from Blanche's first appearance in the last scene and from the point where she realizes that the doctor is not Shep

Huntleigh up until Stella cries "Blanche, Blanche, Blanche!" Kazan also changed the points at which the "Varsouviana" started and stopped in scenes 6 and 9 to allow it to build up for a slightly longer time during Blanche's speeches.

Making these changes was part of an overall plan that Kazan developed for the music in conjunction with Alex North, a plan that intensified the shifting moods of the play and emphasized its emotional climaxes. A good example is Blanche's first entrance, when she encountered a sailor on the street (a change from the pre-production script, where Williams indicated that she met the flower vendor). The orchestra had been playing "Claremont Breakdown" since the scene's opening, and a trumpet solo came up as Blanche entered. The sailor approached Blanche and asked her a question, which the audience did not hear because of the music. Blanche looked bewildered, unable to answer. Together, the hot trumpet and the incident with the sailor created a stronger contrast between the moth-like Blanche and the raunchy world of the Quarter than the pre-production script had indicated.

The trumpet, with its direct expression of sexuality, later encoded an intense ironic subtext when Blanche tried to escape her own desire. In scene 2, the orchestra began to play "Sundown" on Blanche's line about Stanley's "big, capable hands" (29), and the trumpet came up as the tamale vendor was heard calling "Red-hot!" (30). At the end of scene 5, when Blanche moved from the paper boy to her "Rosenkavalier" Mitch, the orchestra played "Woke Up Blues." The clarinet led and the trumpet filled, muted and "dirty." At the end of scene 7, when Blanche realizes that something has happened to her relationship with Mitch, the refrain of "Claremont Breakdown" was heard again, with ironic reference to the opening scene, the clarinet and trumpet leading a "nasty stomp." A lighter statement of the same theme occurred when the piano played "Sugar Blues" at Blanche's line "I have – old-fashioned ideals" (65) in scene 6. The most obvious encoding of sexuality in the music, however, was the orchestra's playing "Wang Wang Blues" at the end of scene 10, and playing through the blackout while the rape supposedly occurred.

While he was more original with his use of the orchestra, Kazan also integrated the "Varsouviana" into his musical code. Beside the cuts already mentioned, he brought the Novachord up at the very end of scene 1, rather than a few lines earlier as indicated in the pre-production script. Rather than sinking down on the steps with her head falling on her arms, Blanche sat trying to deny the sound as the music grew more insistent. Then, while the music reached a crescendo, she suddenly leapt to her feet, "pressing her hands against her ears" (19). During the blackout, the "Varsouviana" segued into "Winin' Boy" played by the orchestra, which faded at Stanley's first line in scene 2.

The association of the "Varsouviana" theme with Blanche's painful memories of Allan Gray established, Kazan introduced it again in scene 2, when Stanley snatched up Blanche's love letters, ending it when she sat down to go through her box of papers about Belle Reve. In scene 6, when Blanche tells Mitch about Allan, Kazan had the Novachord begin earlier than Williams had indicated, in the middle of the speech rather than at the end. He also had the Novachord cut off sharply when Mitch and Blanche kissed rather than fading out as Williams had first indicated, signifying the importance of her relationship with Mitch in maintaining her connection with reality. Kazan also brought the "Varsouviana" in earlier in scene 9 than Williams had indicated, beginning it when Blanche encountered the flower vendor and playing it through the entire *flores para los muertos* scene. At the end of scene 9, the orchestra played "Morningside Blues," and segued during the blackout into the Novachord playing "Good Night Ladies" as scene 10 opened with Blanche's drunken fantasy. In general, Kazan made more consistent use of the "Varsouviana" to signify Blanche's disintegrating subjective state than Williams had first suggested, and he integrated it more with North's jazz score, embedding the play's juxtaposition of subjectivity and objectivity in the production's musical code.

One of the most interesting uses of sound in the production was the scoring of the series of street cries that was added during rehearsals to the end of scene 3 and the blackout between scenes 3 and 4. As carefully recorded by the stage manager, the rhythm and pitch of each cry and the order of the cries were encoded to evoke the spirit of the French Quarter aurally. They were to sound as follows:

1. 1st man (L) Young Fryers! — __ —
2. 2nd Man (L) Blackberries, 10 Cents a Quart! — __ — - - - -⌐
3. 1st Woman (R) Nice Fresh Roas'n Ears — — - - __
4. 3rd Man (R) Water-Melons! — __ — __
5. 4th Man (L) Irish Potatoes - - - - __ __
6. 2nd Woman (R) Tender Young Snap Beans __ __ ⌐‿ ⌐
7. 5th Man (R) Fresh Country Eggs! — — — __⌐

The criers were to repeat their cries throughout the blackout, each waiting to hear the previous crier, and each maintaining his or her set pattern. This quaint presentation of the inviting abundance of the Quarter was juxtaposed with Blanche's fear of her alien environment as she seeks and seems to have found her temporary haven in Mitch at the end of scene 3.

Much has been made of the colors Williams used for the costumes in *Streetcar*. While the signification of Stanley's aggressive masculinity through the "bold primary colors" of Van Gogh's "The Night Cafe" is obvious in the play, critics have also analyzed the three major colors of

Blanche's costumes as Williams described them in the reading version: the "white suit with a fluffy bodice, necklace and earrings of pearl, white gloves and hat" (ND 5) that she arrives in; the red satin robe that she wears when she tries to attract Mitch in scene 3 and after Stanley has raped her in scene 11; and the jacket she puts on in scene 11 to leave the apartment, which is "Della Robbia blue. The blue of the robe in the old Madonna pictures" (ND 169).[37] Williams filled out most of this vestimentary code after the production, for the pre-production script does not describe the color of Blanche's clothes when she enters, although it does mention a dark-red satin robe and the Della-Robbia blue jacket. In production, Kazan, Mielziner, and Lucinda Ballard developed their own vestimentary code based on the notion of the primary colors. The most significant departure from the script was the decision to use a lavender dress and jacket for Blanche in the final scene, and to cut the line about Della-Robbia blue. Blanche also did not wear white when she first appeared in Elysian Fields. She wore the same lavender dress she wore at the end of the play. Generally, Blanche's costumes were light and filmy shades of delicate pastels, effective material signifiers of her mothlike fragility. The satin robe was described as rose or pink rather than deep red, dissociating her both from simple desire and from Stanley.

Stanley wore for the most part nondescript clothes – blue pants and drab T-shirts, a dark suit, and some greasy seersucker pants. This served to emphasize the bold primary colors of his bright silk bowling shirt and jacket and the red silk pajamas he wore in the rape scene. Stella was associated with Stanley rather than with Blanche through her costumes. In the opening scene the primary colors of her yellow skirt, blue blouse, and red shoes contrasted with Blanche's filmy lavender outfit. In scene 2 she wore a red print dress in contrast to Blanche's blue lace. She wore a vivid blue robe in scene 3 and a yellow skirt and white blouse in scene 11. In short the costumes encoded Kazan's conception of the play as a conflict between the two social realities of Blanche and Stanley, implying greater strength in the aggressively bright and simple primary colors of Stanley's world than in the delicate shades and filmy materials of Blanche's. Stella's bright blue and red and yellow re-emphasized her alliance with Stanley.

Kazan made a number of changes in the play's environment to help develop his concept of competing social realities. In general he toned down the expressionistic elements of Williams's script, using fewer visual and sound effects to signify Blanche's state of mind and introducing more naturalistic suggestions of danger in the environment where she finds herself trapped. In order to remind the audience of the general environment of the Quarter, Kazan introduced several bit parts that did not appear in Williams's script. At the opening, a woman wearing a shabby cotton print housecoat and down-at-heel shoes and carrying a shopping-bag full of parcels passed "wearily across the stage" (6) before Stanley and his pals appeared, and the sailor replaced the flower vendor that Williams had originally intended to accost Blanche as she entered. Thus rather than giving the audience a sense that there is something uneasy and a little mysterious in the environment from the outset, Kazan gave them a sense of local color in the poor and somewhat seamy neighborhood of the French Quarter where the play is set. Similarly, in scene 2 a woman wearing a cotton print dress and red bandana turban and carrying a basket followed the men down the street as they came home from work. Kazan added the street cries at the end of scene 3 and beginning of scene 4, and had Mitch and Blanche pass the black neighbor, who was crossing the stage singing a "melancholy tune" (60), as they entered in scene 6.

One of Kazan's major changes was the repositioning of the significant figure of the flower vendor. As mentioned earlier, Williams had first intended her to accost Blanche at the beginning of the play, foreshadowing Blanche's fears of death and the destructive forces she is facing. Instead Kazan used the sailor, a figure associated with desire rather than death. He moved the first appearance of the flower vendor to the beginning of scene 9, when Blanche sits "drinking to escape the sense of disaster closing in on her" (81). The sound of *flores para los muertos* blended with the sound of the "Varsouviana" as the scene opened and Mitch appeared. Blanche's meeting the flower vendor face-to-face at the door was also added during rehearsals. In the pre-production script, Blanche simply hears the cry outside, and it punctuates her dialogue as she talks about death and desire. During rehearsals, Kazan and Williams worked together on the scene, adding to Blanche's line "I didn't lie in my heart" the line "I was true as God in my heart to all of you – *always* – always!" (85–86), and inserting the scene where the vendor comes to the door and Blanche screams "No, no! Not now! Not now!" and runs back in, slamming the door. Williams remembered that, when Kazan asked him to demonstrate his conception of the old Mexican woman, he got up on the rehearsal stage and advanced to the Kowalskis' door, bearing the tin flowers. When Jessica Tandy opened the door, she screamed "Not yet, not yet!" Kazan's response was "That's it, do it just like that" (M 135). The flower vendor's *flores para los muertos* lines were also moved around during rehearsals to emphasize, in Kazanian fashion, the emotional climaxes of Blanche's dialogue. The cries were inserted after Blanche's lines "regrets – recriminations," "legacies," and "Death," and after a new line that was inserted for Blanche, "I lived in a house where dying old women remembered their dead men" (86; compare ND 148).

The most significant change from an expressionistic to a naturalistic use of the environment came in scene 10, when Blanche's sense of being caught in a trap reaches its climax. As Stanley finished his speech attacking Blanche for thinking she is the "Queen of the Nile," the pre-production script, like the reading version, had "*lurid reflections appear on the wall around Blanche. The shadows are of a grotesque and menacing form*" (ND 158–59). Then Stanley went into the bathroom and closed the door while Blanche made her desperate call to Shep Huntleigh. In the middle of the call, Blanche asked the operator to hold on as the action moved into the subjective reality of her terror:

She sets the phone down and crosses warily into the kitchen. The night is filled with inhuman voices like cries in a jungle.

The shadows and lurid reflections move sinuously as flames along the wall spaces.

Through the back wall of the rooms, which have become transparent, can be seen the sidewalk. A prostitute has rolled a drunkard. He pursues her along the walk, overtakes her and there is a struggle. A policeman's whistle breaks it up. The figures disappear.

Some moments later the Negro Woman appears around the corner with a sequined bag which the prostitute had dropped on the walk. She is rooting excitedly through it.

Blanche presses her knuckles to her lips and returns slowly to the phone. She speaks in a hoarse whisper. (ND 159)

Then she gives her frantic message to Western Union, "In desperate, desperate circumstances! Help me! Caught in a trap. Caught in – " (ND 160).

During rehearsals, this was replaced with a scene in which Blanche's menace came not from her psyche, but from the social reality of the environment where the Stanleys of the world hold sway. Instead of the overt indications that the action on the stage took place only in Blanche's disintegrating mind, the new version of the scene represented action that *could* be taking place only in Blanche's desperate imagination, but that also could and did take place often in the world of the Quarter. In the new version, Stanley went into the bathroom and slammed the door after his speech, pushing Blanche aside. At this point, a scream was heard offstage, along with the sound of excited murmuring from the street and the cafe. Terrified at the sounds, Blanche ran to the phone and dialed, while in the street a woman laughed insanely and ran into the street with a purse. A man in a tuxedo followed, protesting, and the woman struck him. He fell. As the noise rose, another man rushed on and attacked the first man from behind. The assailants vanished at the sound of police whistles and a siren (92–3). How much of this action may be assumed by the audience to be objectively real and how much is the subjective phenomenon of Blanche's mind was purposely left vague.

In the scene as it was played, Blanche put down the phone in the middle of her call, trembling, as a man ran into the street, followed by three thugs who attacked him and were joined by another man. There were police whistles. The men exited, and there was "*an excited murmur of their voices*."[38] The wounded man staggered off while Blanche grasped her jewel box and a couple of gowns from her trunk and went out onto the porch, where she came face to face with the muggers, just before they went out (93). Then she ran back into the apartment, knelt beside the phone, and made her desperate call to Western Union. Here not only are Blanche's fears encoded through flesh-and-blood signifiers of the threatening environment of the Quarter, but she confronts them in the objective reality of the play's present. How closely her perception of these events matches what is "really happening" is left ambiguous, leaving the subjective episteme inextricably intertwined with the objective for the audience rather than separating them clearly as expressionism does. The changes in this scene brought it within Kazan's conception of the play as a conflict of social realities without sacrificing the subjectivity that both he and Williams considered central to its nature.

Realizing the characters

Blanche

Kazan conceptualized each character and encoded the characterizations tentatively in stage language during his intense periods with the script in August of 1947. Using his regular plan of attack adapted from the Method, Kazan worked out a "spine" for each character that related him or her to the general concept he had developed for the play. Having established the most important traits that must be encoded in each character's behavior, Kazan went to the script and began to work out the movement and gestures that would signify these traits to the audience. He decided that Blanche's spine was to "find Protection," and that "the tradition of the old South says that it must be through another person" (N 366). In order to secure protection, Blanche had to prove that she was special, which led to her need to create a sustaining fantasy (N 367). The conflict between the aristocratic role that Blanche invented for herself and the reality she confronted was the core of the play's subjective realism.

Kazan believed that "the variety essential to the play . . . demands that [Blanche] be a 'heavy' at the beginning. For instance: contemplate the inner character contradiction: bossy yet helpless, domineering yet shaky, etc." (N 367). He thought the audience should be on Stanley's side at the beginning of the play because it saw Blanche's negative effect on Stella. The change would come after Stanley exposed her:

Gradually, as they see how genuinely in pain, how actually desperate she is, how warm, tender and loving she can be (the Mitch story), how freighted with need she is – then they begin to go with her. They begin to realize that they are sitting in at the death of something extraordinary . . . colorful, varied, passionate, lost, witty, imaginative, of her own integrity . . . and then they feel the tragedy. (N 367)

As Kazan was to find out during the tryout period, making this crucial turn in the audience's sympathies was no mean feat with Brando playing Stanley. But as the director planned the development of Blanche, he worked on bringing out her least sympathetic side for the audience during the early scenes. This included little touches of carelessness and lack of concern for the people around her. In the first scene, for example, after she gets rid of the well-meaning Eunice and sits waiting for Stella to come from the bowling alley, Blanche finds the whiskey bottle, pours herself a stiff drink, and tosses it down. At this point, the pre-production script indicates that she carefully replace the bottle and wash out the tumbler at the sink (ND 10). Kazan revised this business to have Blanche pick up the glass and shake out the last drops of liquor onto the carpet, adding to her need for alcohol and her hypocrisy about it a touch of carelessness and lack of concern for her sister's property.

Kazan also emphasized Blanche's domineering manner toward Stella from the beginning of the play. Kinesically, Kazan made scene 1 a physical expression of Blanche's attempt to assert her old control over Stella and Stella's attempt to evade it. The agon was played out when Blanche examined Stella's figure in order to compare it unfavorably with her own, and Stella, wanting to conceal the fact that she was pregnant, kept trying to stop her. When Blanche says, "You hear me? I said stand up!" (12), the pre-production script had Stella comply reluctantly. Instead Kazan had Blanche pull Stella to her feet and fuss with her sister's clothes and hair, complaining about Stella's having spilled something on her collar and about her haircut, and examining Stella's hands as she commented on the fact that the Kowalskis didn't have a maid. Each kinesic nuance went to make Blanche seem more domineering and less sympathetic to the audience.

In scene 2, when Blanche has her first confrontation with Stanley, Kazan encoded both Blanche's vanity and her practiced flirtation in her gestures. He had Blanche take a quick look at the porch to see if Stella was watching before she asked Stanley to do up her buttons. She also took a cigarette from behind Stanley's ear and had him light it for her. When Stanley asked her about the white fur pieces, she draped herself in them and posed for him, and she touched his shoulder when she said, "My sister has married a man!" (27). To support this, Kazan made Stanley seem less physically threatening than attracted to Blanche. When he seized her wrist after she sprayed him with the perfume bottle, for example, he held her in place for a moment, attracted to her, before he released her hands, and his manner in the interrogation about Belle Reve was described as insistent, rather than brutal.

Given Blanche's need for protection and what Kazan considered "the tradition of *woman* (or all women) [who] can only live through the strength of someone else," the director concluded that what makes the play universal is "Blanche's special relation to all women . . . that she is at that critical point where *the one thing above all that she is dependent on: her attraction for men, is beginning to go.* Blanche is like all women, dependent on a man, looking for one to hang onto: only *more so !*" (N 370). Although Kazan's analysis of the plight of "all women" reads as not only simplistic but clearly timebound a mere forty years later, his interpretation of Blanche's tragedy works precisely because he emphasized her predicament as an individual caught in a sociocultural nexus that he called "the tradition," the overtly patriarchal system of the old South where a woman's survival was dependent on her ability to attract and hold a male protector. Within the context, Kazan noted,

her past is chasing her, catching up with her. Is it any wonder that she tries to attract each and every man she meets. She'll even take that protected feeling, that needed feeling, that superior feeling, for a moment. Because, at least for a moment, that anxiety, the hurt and the pain will be quenched. The sex act is the opposite of loneliness. (N 370)

To convey her belief that protection can only be found through men, and men can only be acquired through sexual attractiveness, Blanche's near obsession with her appearance needed to be obvious to the audience.

Williams had signified this obsession in his dialogic references to Blanche's constant bathing, her washing and combing her hair, and her concern about her clothes and figure. Kazan encoded these characteristics kinesically and added others, such as a penchant for looking in the mirror as she discussed her appearance or as she gauged her chances for the future. In scene 10, while Blanche and Stanley discussed her fantastic plans with Shep Huntleigh, she retired to the bedroom, draping her torn veil about her and casting sidelong glances at herself in the mirror for reassurance (90).

Perhaps the most effective means by which Kazan encoded Blanche's concern with her appearance was the material signification of props. Scene 2 opens with Stella alone on stage while Blanche takes one of her baths. Blanche's presence, however, is asserted by her open trunk, which "*offers a view of some rather impressive, if gaudy, wardrobe*" (19) and a heart-shaped jewel box full of costume jewelry. The trunk contained, from front to rear, a green jacket, a mauve dress, a chartreuse dress, a light-blue skirt, a blue silk jersey dress, a gold dress, and the notorious white fox furs that arouse Stanley's jealousy and that Blanche later poses in to try to attract him. The prop chart also mentioned various pieces of "Lucinda Ballardry," which made use of the designer's particular talents to signify Blanche's taste and her concern with her appearance.[39] Kazan built the whole scene around the trunk and its contents, using this material signifier of Blanche's need to be attractive as the battleground between Stanley's desire not to be swindled and Stella's desire to protect her sister and the DuBois values from Stanley (see plate 3).

As Stanley attacked the trunk, throwing the dresses on the couch, Stella gathered them up, and as he held up the gold dress and the fox furs, Stella took them from him, putting everything back into the trunk. The same thing happened with the jewels. As Stanley grabbed fistfuls of costume jewelry and tossed them on the table, Stella rescued the jewelry and put it back into the box. The whole business was repeated as Stanley went back to the trunk with his line, "Here's your plantation or what was left of it, here!" (24). Again he pulled the clothes out, and again Stella took them from him and stuffed them back in the trunk as she said, "You have no idea how stupid and horrid you're being" (24).

Through these props, a battle was fought over Blanche that did not require Blanche's physical presence. Instead, the tradition as signified by its material accoutrements became the site of the physical struggle between Stella's loyalty and protectiveness and Stanley's resentment and selfishness. This scene foreshadowed scene 10, which began with a repetition of the visual statement of the trunk. As Blanche stood before the dressing table, drink in hand, arrayed in her crumpled white satin ball gown and rhinestone tiara, she was surrounded by "*a goodly amount of her fancy clothing . . . Beds, armchair, trunk are covered with finery*" (88). This material representation of the tradition, an irritating reminder for Stanley of what he considers Blanche's airs and pretensions, reminded the audience of their earlier confrontation, but in this scene the stakes were higher and the mild flirtation of scene 2 was replaced with Stanley's rape of Blanche.

Kazan found another significance in Blanche's obsessive concern with her appearance, the maintenance of what he called her "social mask . . . *the High-Bred Genteel Lady in Distress*" (N 371). While she seeks protection from the people around her, Blanche also protects her inner being by hiding behind this mask. Kazan considered this the key to her physical behavior, and he noted that "the mask never breaks down" (N 371). A good example of the mask is Blanche's first approach to Stanley when she meets him in scene 1. When Stanley comes into the apartment, he notices the package of meat that Stella has left on the table and puts it in the icebox. According to the stage manager's script, Kazan then had Blanche move to the curtains between the rooms, looking at Stanley, while she prepared to meet him. He stared at her, and she drew back from his stare, withdrawing behind her mask as she said with traditional, artificial sociability, "You must be Stanley. I'm Blanche" (17). Although fighting hysteria throughout the scene, Blanche managed to suppress her fears by maintaining the mask of the Southern belle, dabbing her face with cologne and acting the good guest while Stanley talked to her, yelled for Stella, removed his shirt, and imitated the cat outside when he discovered it upset her. This pattern of Blanche vainly trying to hold onto her mask while Stanley tried constant little gambits to strip it away formed a kinesic paradigm for the action in the scenes between them throughout the play.

In the production, the weakness and dependency in Blanche's nature were encoded materially through her dependence on particular physical objects. In the first scene, when Stanley started removing his shirt, Blanche started moving toward her purse in the living room. Once she had it, she started looking through it for her compact and cologne. She often carried the purse with her as she walked around the apartment, keeping her protective props close by her side. In scene 5, when Stanley came in as Blanche was writing her letter to Shep Huntleigh, she immediately tucked it into her purse. Then she took out the cologne and dabbed her handkerchief with it, putting the cologne carefully back in her purse as they discussed their astrological signs. Later in the scene, as Blanche moved toward Stella for protection from Stanley's implications about her past in Laurel, she kept her purse on her arm. While the purse represented the security of the tradition's props for Blanche, she could also manipulate it to signify her weakness in order to obtain men's sympathy. When the paper boy arrived in scene 5, Blanche went to her purse and made a show of looking through it while she told him she didn't have a dime for the paper, and she took out a cigarette and holder so she could continue her flirtation with him. At the beginning of scene 6, when Blanche and Mitch returned from the amusement park, she looked ineffectually through her purse for her key, and then handed the purse to Mitch so he could look, a gesture both of helplessness and of intimacy.

The cologne and powder in the purse served much the same purposes of signifying Blanche's refinement and her dependence on the security of the tradition. Blanche's dabbing her face with cologne was presented as a reflex response to Stanley's aggression. She also used it as a nostalgic gesture to evoke the world of Belle Reve, as when Stella says, "I like to wait on you, Blanche. It makes it seem more like home" (56), and Blanche replies, "I must admit I love to be waited on" (56). Powdering her face was the most obvious gesture that signified both Blanche's concern with and her insecurity about her appearance. Williams had established the gesture when Blanche asks Stella to stop so she can powder her face before they go in to the apartment during the poker game. In the first meeting with Stanley, Kazan had Blanche look in her purse on the line "I haven't washed or even powdered" (18) and not be able to find her compact, this gesture of unprotectedness increasing her general uneasiness when first confronted with Stanley.

In general, Kazan and Tandy used the props and gestures associated with the tradition to encode the downward cycle of Blanche's attempt to find protection through sexual attractiveness, and its progressive failure, a cycle that repeated what had taken place in Laurel before the play's action commences. Blanche's first attempt to attract a protector is in scene 2, when she tries to get Stanley's interest by having him do up her buttons, asking for a drag on his cigarette, spraying him with the perfume atomizer, draping herself in the furs, and posing for him. This of course does not work very well. She succeeds in attracting Stanley sexually but does not arouse any protective feelings in him. And her flirtatious pursuit of Stanley is mirrored in Stanley's "relentless" pursuit of her in scene 10.

The most obvious object for Blanche's attentions is of course Mitch, and many of the gestures she uses to attract him are indicated in Williams's early scripts. Kazan and Tandy made additions, however. In scene 3, as Mitch started tying his tie, putting his shoes on, and eating Sen-Sen in preparation for meeting her, Blanche arranged her chair in the light and began combing her hair seductively. Then, when Mitch came through the curtains with his awkward pretence of needing to use the bathroom again, and she detained him with the old reliable game of asking him for a cigarette and a light, Blanche dazzled Mitch by waving her cigarette holder around, fitting the cigarette into it, and taking a light from him with aristocratic elegance.

Later Kazan had Karl Malden, who played Mitch, rest his hand on the back of Blanche's chair. As they laughed together, she put her hand on his, and he, suddenly discovering his hand on her chair, stepped back and muttered "excuse me" (39). The gestures signified to the audience a calculating Blanche out to manipulate a bumbling and ingenuous Mitch, precisely the sense Kazan wanted to convey of his "heavy" Blanche at the beginning of the play. This effect changed after the pivotal scene 5, in which, as Williams wrote, "*the important values are the ones that characterize Blanche: [the scene's] function is to give her dimension as a character and to suggest the intense inner life which makes her a person of greater magnitude than she appears on the surface*" (52).

In scene 6, when Blanche has decided that Mitch is her last hope, her gestures in the production became less sexual and more dependent and tender. She buried her face in Mitch's shoulder, and she patted his cheek when he asked if she was laughing at him. Throughout the scene, however, Kazan had Blanche handle Mitch very carefully, as though she knew he was her last chance. She rose for inspection when Mitch asked how much she weighed, a subject about which she had complete confidence, and she daintily extended her arms, allowing him to lift her and whirl her around. She let him keep his hands on her waist until he tried to kiss her, and then she gave him her line about having "old-fashioned ideals" (65). She held him at arm's length through the rest of the scene, increasing the intensity for both Mitch and the audience of the final moment when they embraced and kissed.

The pathos of Blanche's descent was intensified by the irony when in scene 9 it was she whose tender advances were rebuffed. When she said that Mitch seemed to be gentle, "a cleft in the rock of the world that [she] could hide in" (85), Blanche crossed to him and touched him, and he drew back from her, rejecting her tenderness as he now rejected the pretences of her tradition. What Mitch finally offered in this scene was what the others had offered Blanche in the past – the momentary respite from loneliness in sex – and Kazan had her nearly succumb to her need for it. When Mitch put his arms around her waist and turned her towards him after she told the story of the young soldiers, she at first responded sexually: "*At first she takes him, passionately, then pushes him away. He seizes her roughly – grasping a few strands of her hair in his L. hand*" (87). Then, when Mitch made it clear that he had no intention of marrying her, she escaped from danger with her hysterical screaming of "*Fire! Fire! Fire!*" (87).

The incident with the paper boy at the end of scene 5 reenacts what happened with the seventeen-year-old student in Laurel. In its final version, it gives the audience some understanding of how the earlier incident could have happened and thus some sympathy for Blanche. While she takes the same basic approach to attracting the young man that she takes with Stanley and Mitch, even using the same trick with the cigarette to get his attention, her attitude is different. She does not try to manipulate him into giving her protection, but tries to create a fantasy around them where they can achieve a moment of happiness together.

This change of motive was important in Williams's characterization of Blanche as he revised the scene several times during rehearsals with Kazan's collaboration. In the pre-production version, Blanche appears predatory and the young man her victim. The young man clears his throat and looks yearningly toward the door as Blanche talks about not knowing what to do with the long afternoons in the Quarter. Rather than enticing him to come to her to be kissed, Blanche crosses to him, and he simply stares at her and goes down the steps with a dazed look after she presses her lips to his. In a second version, the mood was changed from sexuality to romantic fantasy. Blanche touches the young man's coat when she asks if he got caught in the rain, and she takes a Spanish shawl from the trunk and drapes it about her shoulders. Williams added the line "Come on over here like I told you" (60), and indicated that the young man should obey like a child. Blanche grips him in her arms and looks him in the face with the most *"ineffable sweetness"* (60). Finally, when the young man goes to the door, Blanche says goodbye and waves to him as he smiles like a child who has had a happy dream.

The mood of the actual performance was lighter than those of the earlier versions, although it retained the general romantic tone of the second. The young man was more prosaic and less dazed than in earlier versions. Kazan situated the encounter within the objective reality of the Quarter by having the young man enter and walk along the street, checking the houses for likely addresses. He paused in front of the building, looking up the spiral stair as he checked the address of the Kowalski apartment. The young man got into the spirit of Blanche's flirtation early in the scene. When she thanked him for lighting her cigarette, he came back with "Thank *you*" (59), and he looked toward Blanche rather than away when she told him he looked like a young prince from the Arabian Nights. He did not stare at Blanche when she kissed him, but went, rather dazed, to the door, and as Blanche waved and called "Adios" to him, he turned on the porch and waved back to her, going out *"like a child who has had a happy dream"* (60). Blanche's role was also treated more lightly in performance. Her laughing at the notion of the cherry soda was added, and the fantastic Spanish shawl was changed to a delicate gossamer scarf. The actual performance was thus a mixture of the sexuality in the first version and the fantasy in the second, integrated through a lightly romantic tone.

The incident with the paper boy not only gave the audience some understanding of what had happened to Blanche in Laurel, it also encoded the idea that Blanche seeks to attract every man she meets. The young man is the proof that she is still attractive and that her fantasy may still be enacted. On the other hand, Blanche's behavior with the Doctor at the end of the play signifies her need for protection at its most intense. At first rejecting the Doctor because he is not Shep Huntleigh, she quickly accepts him as a substitute when he shows her the small kindness of telling the nurse to let her go. Kazan emphasized Blanche's pathetic dependence on this last male protector by having her mood change from desperate fear to flirtation after the Doctor helped her to her feet. She looked at him, wavering at first, and then smiled *"as she would at a new beau."* She looked triumphantly at the nurse, and then back to the doctor *"with a radiant smile"* (102). Thus Kazan suggested kinesically that Blanche's final pathos lies in the fulfillment of her drive to seek protection. By retreating completely into her fantasy, she wins protection and the belief that she has triumphed according to the code of her tradition. Kazan intensified the irony by weighting the objective reality that Blanche has lost rather heavily to the negative. As Blanche departed on her protector's arm, Stella was sobbing *"with inhuman abandon,"* Stanley was trying to comfort his wife by speaking *"voluptuously"* to her, and the poker game was going right on with seven-card stud (103). Blanche's attempt to find protection in men was shown up in this scene as a truly pathetic fantasy, and the sympathies of the audience were clearly directed toward her rather than toward Stanley, who had become the "heavy" by this time.

Stella was treated in the production as Blanche's obvious source of protection, necessary to her, although less desirable to her than a male protector. Kazan wrote that Blanche, as a woman of "the tradition," had come expecting protection from Stella and her husband (N 368). Blanche's relationship to her sister is evident in scene 1, when she immediately tries to reassert the dominance she had over Stella at home, and in the way she makes use of her to provide drinks and lemon cokes and towels throughout the play. The climax of Blanche's attempt to enlist Stella in her service rather than in Stanley's comes with her long speech at the end of scene 4 when she pleads with her sister not to hang back with the brutes, but to join her in the struggle for new light and tenderer feelings. In the production, when Stanley slammed the front door to announce his presence, the sisters exchanged a long look. Blanche tried to restrain Stella from getting up and going to the curtains between the two rooms to look at Stanley. Kazan had Stella run to Stanley and throw herself fiercely at him in full view of Blanche while Stanley swung her up with his body, a clear statement of Stella's loyalties and their passionate source (51).

While Stella continues to defend Blanche from Stanley in minor ways after scene 4, it is clear that she will not be Blanche's last refuge against him. Stella is in fact ready to acquiesce when Stanley plans to send Blanche back to Laurel on the Greyhound on Tuesday, although she puts up a token argument that Blanche wouldn't go on a bus. In the production, Kazan had Blanche turn and look accusingly at Stella after Stanley gave her the bus ticket for her birthday, and he had her repeat this look in the closing scene when she realized that the man who had come for her was not Shep Huntleigh. The sense of betrayal Blanche conveyed in this look sent Stella sobbing into Eunice's arms in the final scene. The strategy of Blanche's relationship with Stella followed Kazan's general plan of turning the audience's sympathy away from its natural object, the young wife being put upon by her difficult older sister, to Blanche, who is betrayed for the sake of Stella's own apparent need to seek protection in a man as well as her passion for Stanley.

In writing of Blanche, Kazan spoke of a "tragic flaw":

the need to be superior, special (or *her* need for protection and what it means to her), the "tradition." This creates an apartness so intense, a loneliness so gnawing that only a complete breakdown, a refusal, as it were, to contemplate what she's doing, a *binge* as it were, a destruction of all her standards, a desperate violent ride on the Streetcar Named Desire can break through the walls of her tradition. The tragic flaw creates the circumstances, inevitably, that destroy her. (N 368–69)

From Kazan's point of view, the elements of Blanche's psychic disintegration were in her at the beginning of the play, and indeed long before it. His Blanche was constantly just on the edge of losing control, on the way to a breakdown made inevitable by her own needs and actions. Kazan kept the audience aware of Blanche's state by encoding it in small bits of business throughout the play. In scene 4, for example, when Blanche complains that her purse contains only sixty-five cents, Kazan had Tandy fling the coins under the dressing table, emphasizing her desperation and her barely controlled volatility. In the birthday scene, Tandy pounded on the table and screamed at the top of her voice when she told Stanley that she has said she was sorry about the steam in the bathroom three times, signifying that her control was giving out at the fear of losing Mitch. Later in the scene, when Blanche realized that Stanley's birthday gift was a ticket back to Laurel, the process of her trying to escape from her fear through the comforting mask of the tradition and her inability to maintain it was encoded sequentially. Blanche tried to smile, then to laugh. Giving up both, she turned accusingly to Stella. Then, her control gone, she ran suddenly into the bedroom, sobbing sharply. She paused in the middle of the bedroom, not knowing which way to run, and finally ran into the bathroom with shaking sobs, slamming the door shut (79).

When Mitch arrived at the beginning of scene 9, Kazan indicated that this hysteria, with an added component of alcohol, had completely taken hold of Blanche. She darted about the apartment frantically, hiding the bottle, then rushed to the dressing table to attend to her appearance, "*by now quite beside herself, shaking and muttering*" (81). Her mounting hysteria was intensified by the added incident of meeting the flower vendor at the door and by the climactic moment at the end of the scene when she stood in the door screaming "*Fire! Fire! Fire!*" after Mitch had told her she was not clean enough to bring in the house with his mother. In scene 10 Blanche's complete submission to her terror was encoded kinesically as she ran into the street with her gowns and jewels, was confronted with the muggers, and ran back in to try to call Western Union, "*clutching her possessions*," the only protection she had left. Kazan made it clear that Blanche had lost her balance when Stanley raped her.

Blanche's psychological decline was encoded in other ways as well. Her inability to decide on a course of action was made clear in scene 3, after Stella had come down to Stanley on the poker night. Kazan had Tandy come tentatively down the spiral stair and enter the apartment hesitantly, recoil from seeing Stella with Stanley, and dart back to the porch, closing the door behind her. She stood on the porch and looked about, distraught, considered going back upstairs, turned to Stella's door, and finally leaned against it with a troubled sigh, paralyzed until Mitch came along and rescued her. Her decline was also encoded in small bits of action, as when she sat on the floor staring into space in scene 5 after she had revealed her worries about Mitch to Stella. In general, Kazan added to the scenes in which Williams indicates Blanche's disintegration a series of actions, uses of vocal pitch, facial expressions, and gestures that intensified this for the audience.

Kazan was concerned, however, that the positive sides of Blanche's character be encoded both dialogically and kinesically as well. He wrote that "she has worth too – she is better than Stella . . . she, alone and abandoned in the crude society of New Orleans back streets, is the *only voice of light*. It is flickering and, in the course of the play, goes out. But it is valuable because it is unique" (N 369). To soften the edges of Blanche's character, any suggestion of crudeness was taken out of the dialogue during rehearsal. In her line, "All right; now, Mr. Kowalski, let us proceed without any more double-talk" (ND 40), "double talk" was changed to "digression." A significant change in this scene was the cutting of a line in which Blanche said she liked artists who painted in strong, bold colors and disliked pinks and creams as well as evasions and ambiguities. This statement would have associated Blanche with Stanley's brand of sexuality rather than her own view of sex as a means of securing protection. Her pragmatic line to Stella about Stanley, "Oh, I guess he's just not the type that goes for jasmine perfume, but maybe he's what we need to mix with our blood now that we've lost Belle Reve" (ND 45) was cut, and her line "one that's picked a few days" when Stella tells her she looks "fresh as a daisy" (ND 49) was changed to "What nonsense." The lines in scene 8 when she lies baldly about her age, claiming to be twenty-seven (ND 135), were also cut.

As we have seen, however, crucial lines that made the character of Blanche fundamentally more appealing to an audience, such as those containing the information that she was blackmailed into sex with the seventeen-year-old boy in Laurel, were also cut from the pre-production script. In the production Kazan encoded Blanche's character as he thought Williams had developed it, without supplying mitigating circumstances for behavior that was inevitable for her, but in a way that made the audience as sympathetic and understanding as possible toward her behavior and its motivations. The consummate Method director, he treated the character as a psychologically complete entity, providing human explanations and motives for her behavior wherever he could.

Stella

Stella is a simpler character than Blanche in many ways, but Kazan found several contradictions in her nature that he encoded in the stage language. Kazan believed that, at her core, Stella was more like her sister than she appeared on the surface. Like Blanche, Stella sought protection in a man, Stanley, and Kazan phrased her spine as simply to "hold onto Stanley . . . *Stella would have been Blanche except for Stanley.* She now knows what, how much Stanley means to her health . . . no matter what Stanley does . . . she must cling to him, as she does to life itself. To return to Blanche would be to return to the subjugation of the tradition" (N 372). In this desperate need to hang on to Stanley, Stella's antagonist is Blanche, and Kazan conceptualized the play as a triangle, with Stella at the apex, being fought over by Stanley and Blanche. One complicating factor, however, was Stella's own attitude toward Blanche:

Blanche in effect in Sc. 1 *Resubjugates* Stella. Stella loves her, hates her, fears her, pities her, is really through with her. Finally rejects her for Stanley.
All this of course Stella is aware of only unconsciously. It becomes a matter of conscious choice only in Sc. 11 . . . the climax of the play as it is the climax of the triangle story. (N 372)

Kazan was careful in scene 1 to encode this relationship kinesically. As Blanche criticizes the apartment and asks Stella why she didn't write to let her know she was living "in these conditions" (11), Kazan had Blanche slowly close in on Stella one step at a time. Stella rose, put down her glass, and walked over to Blanche before she said her line, "Aren't you being a little intense about it? It's not that bad at all! New Orleans isn't like other cities" (11), making a definite point of her stand against Blanche's values. As Blanche tried to manipulate her, "*restraining Stella with her voice*" as she said, "You're all I've got in the world, and you're not glad to see me!" (11), Stella began avoiding her through evasive kinesic patterns. While Blanche talked about the situation in Laurel, Stella moved around the apartment, picking up the fan, the magazine, and the candy from the armchair where she had been sitting earlier and taking them into the bedroom, picking up the clothes that were scattered around and putting them in the closet. Stella submitted reluctantly to Blanche's fussing with her as she commented on her appearance, and she began to soften toward

Blanche and embraced her as she saw that her sister was "a little bit nervous or overwrought or something" (14). During Blanche's speech about the deaths at Belle Reve, Stella moved away several times, with Blanche pursuing and holding her until she finally broke loose and ran into the bathroom crying.

By the beginning of scene 2, Stella's guilt and remorse had been well established, along with the underlying resistance to Blanche's dominance that made for even more upsetting unconscious resentment toward her. Stella's treating Blanche as a delicate invalid because of the ordeal she has been through and going to the drugstore to fetch lemon cokes was easily understood as compensation for feeling that she had failed Blanche in the past. Kazan indicated that Stella's complex feelings were buried in this compensatory behavior. In scene 4, he had a little of Stella's hostility come out as Blanche went on with her fantastic plans to have Shep Huntleigh get them both out of Stanley's house. Kazan had Stella slam the powder box down on the dressing table, and the neutral line "You take for granted that I am in something that I want to get out of" (ND 80) was changed to the challenge, "Will you stop taking it for granted that I am in something I want to get out of?" (49).

On the other hand, Stella's love and sympathy for Blanche were made warmer and more active in performance, and Kazan made it clear that she still held onto some of the values of the tradition. In scene 3, as the two sisters laughed about Eunice and the plaster cracking, Blanche was in Stella's arms while she nearly collapsed with laughter. Stella applauded as Blanche and Mitch danced to the radio during the poker game, and she slipped half of her spending money into Blanche's purse in scene 4 when Blanche said dramatically that she would have to take to the streets to support herself. In typical Kazanian style, the relationship between sisters was also made more physical than it had been in Williams's earlier scripts. Stella embraced Blanche six times in the production where there was no indication for it in the pre-production script, including three times in scene 5, when Blanche is at her most vulnerable and most sympathetic. The general effect of the physical action was to encode Stella's conflict between Blanche and Stanley concretely on stage, bringing both Stella's resentment of Blanche's dominance and her love and concern for her sister to the surface.

One of the most difficult aspects of Stella's character to encode in the production proved to be what Williams referred to as her "narcotized" quality. At the beginning of scene 4, after the events of the poker night, Stella is described as having on her eyes and lips *"that almost narcotized tranquility that is in the faces of eastern idols"* (43), a key to her character that Kazan used in creating his own interpretation. He found the source of this quality not in any particular sensuality in Stella's nature, but in her attempt to deny the things she would rather not face about her relationship with Stanley:

Stella is a refined girl who has found a kind of salvation or realization, *but at a terrific price.* She keeps her eyes closed, even stays in bed as much as possible so that she won't realize, won't *feel* the pain of this terrific price. She walks around as if narcotized, as if sleepy, as if in a daze . . . She's waiting for the dark where Stanley makes her feel *only him* and she has no reminder of the price she is paying. She wants no intrusion from the other world. She is drugged, trapped . . . Her entire attention is to make herself pretty and attractive for Stanley, kill time till night. (N 372–73)

Getting this quality out of Kim Hunter's performance proved to be more easily said than done. During early rehearsals, Williams wrote a note to Kazan complaining that Hunter was "bouncing around in a way that suggests a co-ed on a benzedrine kick" in the first scene (N 374), but Kazan did what he could to give her the "narcotized business." Stella's lethargy was in fact the opening message of the play for the audience. The curtain rose on the scene of Stella lounging in a rickety armchair, fanning herself with a palm-leaf fan, reading a movie magazine, and eating peppermint patties from a paper bag. When Stanley disturbed her repose by calling her to come and catch his package of meat, she jumped up to go to him, but when he left, she slipped back into her languorous movements, leaving the meat package on the table in the living room rather than putting it away in the icebox, taking a look at herself in the mirror, and then stepping over a broom on the floor of the kitchen as she went out to the porch.

In this short series of movements, a great deal about Stella's character, her relationship with Stanley, and her attitude toward her life was encoded before Blanche appeared on the scene, and long before she began complaining about Stella's "Chinese philosophy" (46). This languorous indifference was also in Stella's movements in scene 4, as she slowly cleaned up the debris from the poker game while Blanche tried urgently to convince her that the two of them had to get some money so they could get out of there together. Kazan blocked these movements carefully, having Hunter slowly pick up the cards and put them down again, pick up the broom and twirl it so that she irritated Blanche, pick up the cards again, and put them away, pick up some bottles and take them to the kitchen cabinet, pull the table into position and take off the green baize cover, put the beer case away, and move slowly into the bedroom to make the bed. With all of this slow, indifferent movement, Stella was doing menial tasks that Blanche considered far beneath either of them while Blanche concocted her fantasy about getting Shep Huntleigh to set them up in a shop, an eloquent kinesic statement of the responses the two sisters had made to the failure of the tradition and the psychological adjustments by which they coped with the effects of their choices.

While the contrast was made most evident, Kazan developed a kinesic subtext that encoded the similarities between the sisters as well. Stella's concern with her appearance, for example, while not nearly so obsessive as Blanche's, derived from the same source in Kazan's interpretation, the need to attract and hold her protector. Stella wants to stay "pretty and attractive for Stanley." Kazan suggested that like Blanche, Stella looks in mirrors, as in the opening scene when she glances in the mirror to check her appearance before she goes to watch Stanley bowl. Kazan emphasized the identity between the sisters in scene 4, when Stella knelt in the armchair and looked in the mirror as she tried to explain that the violence of the night before "wasn't anything as serious as you seem to take it" (44). Kazan had Blanche rise and come to the armchair, leaning over it to look into the mirror as well, establishing the visual irony of both sisters' regarding their physical appearances with concern while they did their best to avoid true self-knowledge at all costs.

It was the truth about Stella's relationship with Stanley that Kazan felt she was evading through her "narcotized" behavior. "Stella," he wrote, "at the beginning of the play, won't face a *hostility* (concealed from herself and unrecognized) toward Stanley. She is *so* dependent on him, so compulsively compliant. She is giving up so much of herself, quieting so many voices of protest . . . Latent in Stella is rebellion. Blanche arouses it" (N 374). And aside from Blanche's influence, Kazan thought that "Stella herself cannot live narcotized forever. There is more to her. She begins to feel, even in the sex act, *taken*, unfulfilled – not recognized . . . and besides she's deeper, needs more variety . . . Blanche has succeeded in calling Stella's attention to her own 'sell-out' . . . she never sees Stanley the same again – or their relationship" (N 373). At the same time, however, "Stella is plain out of her head about Stanley. She has to keep herself from constantly touching him. She can hardly keep her hands off him. She is setting little traps all the time to conquer his act of indifference (he talks differently at night, in bed)" (N 374). Kazan thought it was Blanche who brought out the conflicting needs in Stella's character, her passionate need for Stanley as lover and protector and her need to be something more than one of Stanley's pleasures. To encode this conflict in the stage language, he had to keep both sides of Stella before the audience.

Stella's near adoration of Stanley was encoded in her handling of his picture in scene 1, before Blanche has even seen him. A true icon in the Kowalski household, the framed photo of Stanley had *"a place of honor"* (14) on the table. Stella handed it to Blanche to look at, but took it back from her when she said "I can hardly stand it when he's away for a night" (14) and held it while she talked about her passionate love for Stanley. She left it, significantly, on the bed when she listened to Blanche's tale of death and the loss of Belle Reve. Stella's reverent handling of Stanley's picture was as eloquent a statement of her feelings for him as the hugging and kissing she did when he was around. The passionate embraces when she came down to him on the poker night and when she ran to him and threw herself "*fiercely at him in full view of* BLANCHE" (51) after Blanche's plea not to hang back with the brutes were more emphatic, however, and left no doubt of Stella's passion for Stanley.

The dynamics of Stella's conflict between Blanche and Stanley was played out in scene 4, as Blanche tried to bring Stella over to her side with the plea for art and light and tender feelings. Blanche sat with her arm around Stella, and when Stanley called for Stella, Blanche tried to restrain her from going to him. Stella, who had "*listened gravely to BLANCHE*" (51), had no doubt at this point where her loyalties lay. She went directly to Stanley and jumped into his arms.

In the final scene, however, Stella's loyalty to Stanley was portrayed as much less firm. When Blanche looked at Stella with her sense of betrayal that the Doctor was not Shep Huntleigh, Stella turned not to Stanley but to Eunice for comfort, while Stanley stood behind Eunice and kissed Stella's hand. When Blanche ran back into the apartment, Stella started to go in after her, but Stanley restrained her, and she went back to Eunice's arms. Stella tried to break from Eunice but was restrained as the full force of her choice of Stanley's lie over Blanche's truth broke on her and she said, "What have I done to my sister! Oh, God, what have I done to my sister!" (102). Finally she stood passively sobbing as Stanley tried to comfort her with his voluptuous murmuring. As Kazan presented it kinesically, the play's outcome was clearly a loss for Stella as well as for Blanche. Confronted with her own choices and the compromises that resulted from them, the convulsively sobbing Stella was a very different character from the narcotized young woman at the beginning of the play. As Kazan said, once Blanche had opened her eyes to him, Stella could never again worship Stanley with the single-minded devotion he demanded.

The process of Stella's shift from unwavering loyalty toward Stanley to the anguished guilt she feels at the end of the play was encoded throughout the performance. When Stanley first abused Blanche to Stella, over the loss of Belle Reve and the Napoleonic code, Stella tried to shut him out by occupying herself evasively with her preparations to go out with Blanche. She turned away from him, fixing her dress, and when he grabbed her arm, she broke free and went to sit at the dressing table, powdering her face. While Stanley went on about the Napoleonic code, Stella persisted in using the powder puff until he took it from her, and she evaded the whole issue by pretending not to understand him with the line, "My head is swimming!" (22). Later in the scene, Stella parried Stanley's invasion of Blanche's wardrobe, the metonymic signifier of the tradition's values and pretensions, by rescuing each piece as he threw it somewhere and putting it back in the trunk.

Kazan added some business to scene 5 which clearly indicated the shift in Stella's loyalties that had taken place during her discussion with Blanche about her fears and her relationship with Mitch, a shift that Kazan hoped the audience would make as well. As Stanley and Stella left for their night out with Steve and Eunice, Stanley engaged in some horseplay with the other couple, and then grabbed Stella as she came onto the porch, saying "Hiyah fatty!" (58). Refusing to respond as he expected her to, Stella shrugged free and coolly went out. Kazan made this into a crucial moment in the rising hostility between Stanley and Blanche: "STANLEY, *bewildered, looks after her. Then turns and looks back toward apartment, thinking of* BLANCHE *and her effect on his life. Soberly, he goes out*" (58).

In scene 7, as Stanley tried to convince Stella of the charges his supply-man at the plant had made against Blanche, Stella's evasive behavior recalled her attempts to evade Blanche's domination in scene 1. Telling him at first that she didn't want to hear what he had to say and trying to distract herself by fussing with the birthday cake and the party favors, she finally decided it was best to listen. As Stanley began to tell her the story, a plea for her to join him, she at first sat and listened to him, but she soon got up and started moving away from him as he pursued her, forcing her to listen. Finally, closing him out, she turned to him and said "Stanley, I don't want to hear any more!" (71), while he continued relentlessly with the story. When Blanche interrupted from the bathroom, Stella responded warmly to her while she explained to Stanley what had happened with Allan Gray, and she avoided looking at Stanley by fussing with the decorations for the party and putting the candles in the cake. Stanley watched Stella carefully throughout the scene to see whether his plea for her to join him against Blanche was having any effect. When it became clear that his having told Mitch the story and bought Blanche the bus ticket back to Laurel had further alienated Stella, his smoldering anger showed in his rough treatment of her and his slamming the bathroom door on Blanche.

The mood established in scene 7 prepared for the explosion in scene 8, as Stella, having come temporarily over to Blanche's side, says that Stanley is making a pig of himself and that he is disgustingly greasy (76).

Stanley's anger and frustration at Stella's defection came out in his smashing of the dishes as he said, "Don't ever talk that way to me! 'Pig – Polack – disgusting – vulgar – greasy!' Them kind of words have been on your tongue and your sister's too much around here! What do you two think you are? A pair of queens? . . . I am the king around here, so don't you forget it" (76–77). In the production, Stella stared unflinchingly at Stanley through this tirade and reached out to protect the rest of the dishes when he made a move to grab them, refusing to give in to his attack on Blanche and the tradition. She spoke reproachfully to Stanley when she went out onto the porch, but then took his arm and led him back inside after he made his little plea to her about the colored lights. Stella's anger at Stanley reached its peak when he callously handed Blanche her bus ticket back to Laurel. Finally giving up her evasive movements, Stella followed Stanley as she said that "Nobody, nobody, was tender and trusting as [Blanche] was. But people like you abused her, and forced her to change" (79). She grabbed his shirt and tore it when he prepared to go bowling. She delivered the line "I want to know why! Tell me why!" "*wildly*" (80), in emphatic contrast to the narcotized state she usually maintained in her daylight life with Stanley. When Stanley forced her back against a chair, handling her roughly as he spoke his lines about pulling her down off the columns, she pulled away from him and leaned against the ice box until she became aware that the pain she felt was from contractions and allowed Stanley to lead her away to the hospital.

Stella reveals the final choice she has made when she tells Eunice in the final scene that she couldn't believe Blanche's story and go on living with Stanley, but Kazan kept her behavior toward Stanley noncommital up to the end. All of the tenderness Stella showed in the last scene was for Blanche and the baby. While she submitted to Stanley's attempts to comfort her at the end, she did not respond to them, but remained sobbing for Blanche and her own betrayal of her sister. Kazan clearly conveyed that Stella's sympathies were with Blanche during the second half of the play, as the audience's should be, but that Stella was caught in a trap as unyielding as Blanche's. She is helplessly dependent on Stanley, and the baby only makes her more so. While she hates both Stanley and herself for doing it, she acquiesces first in his forcing Blanche out with the bus ticket and then in his version of the rape story that necessitates committing Blanche to the asylum. This is too much to deny through her narcotized sensuality. Stella knows what her marriage has made her at the end of the play, and that she has condemned herself to a future of the same. As Kazan wrote in his notes, "her only hope is her children and, like so many women, she will begin to live more and more for her children" (N 373).

Stanley

Kazan saw Stanley's spine as being to "keep things his way" (N 374). He is threatened by Blanche because he has a great need to bring everyone else down to what he feels is his level:

> It's as if he said: "I know I haven't got much, but no one has more and no one's going to have more." It's the hoodlum aristocrat. He's deeply dissatisfied, deeply hopeless, deeply cynical . . . the physical immediate pleasures, if they come in a steady enough stream, quiet this *as long as no one gets more* . . . then his bitterness comes forth and he tears down the pretender. But Blanche he can't seem to do anything with. She can't come down to his level so he levels her with his sex. He brings her right down to his level, beneath him. (N 375)

Kazan saw this weakness as a chink in the armor of Stanley's carefully nursed hedonism: "He's got it all figured out, what fits, what doesn't. The pleasure scheme. He has all the confidence of resurgent flesh" (N 375). To convey this sense of hedonism on stage, the use of objects and props was very important. Stanley "sucks on a cigar all day because he can't suck a teat. Fruit, food, etc . . . the things he loves and prizes: all sensuous and sensual – the shirt, the cigar, the beer (how it's poured and nursed, etc.) . . . Nature gave him a fine sensory apparatus . . . he enjoys! The main thing the actor has to do in the early scenes is make the physical environment of Stanley, the *props* come to life" (N 375–76).

Marlon Brando, of course, used physical objects masterfully in expressing this aspect of Stanley Kowalski on the stage. The notion of the cigar was dropped, but Stanley was constantly putting things in his mouth throughout the production – beer, cigarettes, meat, pretzels, even his greasy fingers. The association of Stanley with gross hedonism was made at his first appearance, as the Negro Woman laughed heartily at Stanley's calling Stella to come and catch his meat. Kazan made further use of this visual signification when Stella heedlessly left the package of meat on the table and Stanley carefully put it in the icebox when he came in, protecting his pleasures. It was alluded to again when Stanley picked up the plate of cold meat Stella had left for his supper in scene 2 and ate it with his fingers while they talked about her taking Blanche out to supper at Galatoire's. Stanley's simple pique at being deprived of his supper clearly contributed to his initial resentment of Blanche that Stella aggravated by telling him to be nice to her and cater to all the airs and pretensions that were precisely what he resented about Blanche.

When he smoked cigarettes in the production, Brando took two out of the pack and put one behind his ear, making sure the next one was right there so he wouldn't have to wait for it. He also was very protective of his liquor, holding it up to the light to check its depletion when he first suspected Blanche of drinking it and sucking on the bottle as he drank his beer. He ate pretzels out of a bag and showered himself with beer when he came back from the hospital while Stella was still in labor, and he methodically licked each finger twice between pork chops during the birthday-party scene.

Kazan was careful to indicate that Stanley's hedonism was not limited to sex, food, and drink. Stanley took a sensuous pleasure in his clothes, particularly his silk pajamas, which he wiped his face with before he put them on in scene 11. He put his clean shirts away in scene 5, as he did the meat and his lunch pail, taking good care of his things. He even started to pick up the debris from his plate-smashing frenzy after he had calmed down in scene 8, just as he took the radio to be repaired after he had smashed it in scene 3. While Stanley seemed at times to be a demonic figure of disorder, Kazan and Brando took pains to show that he also loved his possessions and had a fundamental instinct to preserve what was his, whether it be his wife or his next dinner.

Kazan thought that a related aspect of Stanley's character was his fundamental indifference to the people and things around him: "Stanley is interested in his own pleasures. He is completely self-absorbed to the point of fascination. To physicalize this: he has a most annoying way of being preoccupied – or of busying himself with something else while people are talking with him, at him it becomes. Example, first couple of pages of Scene 2" (N 376). At the opening of scene 2, Stella explains to Stanley that she is taking Blanche out because of the poker game and because Blanche is upset over the loss of Belle Reve. Kazan objectified Stanley's indifference to Stella's and Blanche's feelings by having Stanley come in and pat Stella's behind after she kissed him. His first response to the news that Stella was going out being to ask, "How about my supper, huh? I ain't going to no Galatoire's for supper" (20), he went to the icebox and took out the cold plate, eating the meat as Stella tried to explain that Blanche was upset. Then he walked around the bedroom as Stella tried to get him to be nice to Blanche, his attention fixing on the information that Belle Reve was lost and beginning to form the idea that he has been cheated. Similarly, while he questioned Blanche about living at the Hotel Flamingo in scene 5, he only half paid attention to her answers while he moved about getting dressed, clearly more interested in making his accusations and upsetting Blanche than in Blanche's answers.

Probably the most memorable aspect of Stanley's character as played by Marlon Brando was his explosive violence. In Kazan's conception of the character, the violence had its root in the same deep dissatisfaction with his life as Stanley's desire to drown himself in sensual pleasures: "Usually his frustration is worked off by eating a lot, drinking a lot, gambling a lot, fornicating a lot. He's going to get very fat later. He's desperately trying to squeeze out happiness by living by *ball and jowl* . . . and it really doesn't work . . . because it simply stores up violence and stores up violence until every *bar in the nation is full of Stanleys ready to explode*" (N 377). This could hardly have been encoded more effectively in action than Marlon Brando did it, with the sudden, unexpected explosions of violence during the poker game, when he leaped up and threw the radio out the window, and during the birthday-party scene, when he jumped up and started hurling the crockery to the floor (see plate 4). Kazan also saw to it that Stanley's partially repressed violence was constantly present for the audience, as Brando slammed the perfume atomizer down in scene 2, or grabbed Hunter roughly and hit her in scene 3, or slammed the drawers in scene 5. The overwhelming characterization of Stanley was that of a dangerous man about to explode.

The fact that the audience understood this characterization was used very effectively in the rape scene, to build up the sense of menace as Stanley indulged in casual violence toward Blanche before he actually began stalking her for the rape. Having been angered by Blanche's fantastic stories about being invited on a cruise of the Caribbean with Shep Huntleigh and about Mitch's having come with a bouquet of roses to apologize, Stanley grabbed the train from Blanche's ball gown and threw it at her, attacking her "lies and conceit and tricks" (92; see plate 5). Then Stanley swept the rhinestone tiara off Blanche's head and tossed it upstage, as she fled from him in terror. Pursuing her into the bedroom, he finally grabbed and held her, accusing her of "sitting on [her] throne and swilling down [his] liquor" (92) as she nearly fainted in his grasp. Blanche's well-grounded fear of Stanley was thus emphatically established before the scenes of violence in the Quarter that followed, combining with them to give the audience the sense that Blanche really was "caught in a trap" when Stanley appeared in his red pajamas and began closing in on her. Using the realistic scenes of street violence rather than the purely expressionistic effects that Williams had originally called for emphasized Blanche's physical danger from Stanley, who was identified with the life of the Quarter that threatened her from all sides.

The violence in Stanley's sexuality had also been well prepared for. As Kazan saw it, "in Stanley sex goes under a disguise . . . Sex equals domination . . . anything that challenges him – like calling him 'common' – arouses him sexually. . . . Sex equals sadism. It is his 'equalizer'" (N 377). As Kazan developed the last scene, he had Brando play Stanley as ready to make peace with Blanche until she puts on airs and tells him the lies about Shep Huntleigh and Mitch, which arouse simultaneously his anger and his desire to conquer her. The need to dominate sexually was also encoded throughout the production. As mentioned earlier, in response to Blanche's flirtation with the perfume atomizer, he seized her wrist and held her in place, attracted to her, then he pushed her aside when he said he'd get ideas about her if she weren't his wife's sister.

The element of dominance was also encoded in Stanley's sexual relationship with Stella as early as scene 2, during their argument about Belle Reve. When she resisted his talk about the Napoleonic code, refusing at the outset to join in his attack on Blanche, Stanley grabbed Stella's arm to get her attention, and then pulled her into the living room as he started to pull apart Blanche's trunk. They enacted the typical scenario of abusive husband and battered wife on the poker night. When Stanley hit Stella, she staggered out, saying, "I want to go away, I want to go away!" (40), but she returned when he called her, forgiving him as she had done more than once before. Kazan brought the elements of violence and sexuality together at the end of scene 8, when Stanley handled the pregnant Stella roughly and threw her against a chair while he talked about pulling her down off the columns "and how [she] loved it" (80). Added to this hint of sado-masochism were a number of gestures that simply indicated Stanley's joy at his conquest in the physical possession of Stella. In addition to Williams's original indication of his slapping Stella on the thigh during the poker game, Stanley's "Hello Stella, tutti frutti" line at the beginning of scene 2 was added during rehearsals as was his patting of Stella on the behind.

Despite the highly negative aspects of Stanley's character, Kazan was keenly aware of Williams's warning not to see him as a "black-dyed villain." Kazan wrote that "as a character Stanley is most interesting in his 'contradictions,' his 'soft' moments, his sudden pathetic little-tough-boy tenderness toward Stella" (N 377). He noted that Stanley cries like a baby in scene 3, and that he almost makes it up with Blanche in scene 8. In a crucial interpretation of scene 10, Kazan wrote that Stanley "*does* try to make it up with her – and except for her doing the one thing that most arouses him, both in anger and sex, he might have" (N 377). Kazan also added some subtle indications that there was more to Stanley and Stella's relationship than is apparent from the dialogue. When Stella first asked Stanley to try to understand Blanche and be nice to her, Kazan added a revealing bit of business – "*A look passes between* STANLEY *and* STELLA" (21) – indicating that there are areas of unspoken understanding in their relationship. As noted earlier, Stanley's speech about Blanche's past in scene 7 was delivered as a plea for Stella to join him against her. More importantly, Kazan softened Stanley's behavior in the final scene. Rather than sitting passively at the poker table while Blanche was being brought out, Stanley answered the door and spoke to the doctor. When Blanche ran back into the apartment, Stanley stopped Stella gently from running after her, putting her in Eunice's arms. His final comforting of Stella was also less overtly sexual than Williams had indicated in the pre-production script, since he didn't reach inside her blouse.

The change in the last scene also served another strong element in Stanley's character as Kazan saw it, the desire to control, to have things his way. Rather than sitting passively as Stella and Eunice dispose of Blanche, Stanley had an active role, indicating that the decision was a mutual one, and not Stella's alone. Stanley stood and faced Blanche as she started to come out through the curtains, holding out to the end in doing what he thought was his right, protecting his life, having things his way.

Mitch

In developing Mitch, Kazan started with the spine to "get away from his mother . . . Mitch is the end product of a matriarchy . . . his mother has robbed him of all daring, initiative, self-reliance. He does not face his own needs" (N 378). Kazan thought the complexity of Mitch's character arose from the fundamental conflict of his feelings toward his mother, which naturally complicated his feelings toward all women: "Mitch, in his guts, hates his Mother. He loves her in a way – partially out of *early habit*, partially because she is clever – but much more fundamentally he *hates her*. It is a tragedy for him when he returns to her absolute sovereignty at the end. He will never meet another woman who will need him as much as Blanche and will need him to be a man as much as Blanche" (N 379). Kazan and Karl Malden worked the character of Mitch up from this fundamental Freudian insight. In an interview, Malden explained that Kazan had conveyed the core of Mitch's character to him through the reading of the single line when Blanche asks him if he loves his mother very much and Mitch replies, "Yes" (ND 113). Malden could do nothing with the line until Kazan explained, "you hate your bloody mother. Sure, you have to say you love her – you even have to think you do. But deep inside you know she's got a double nelson on all your emotions and she's the reason why you can't develop and mature." Malden said, "As soon as I understood that, I'd licked not only the line, but the whole character."[40] Mitch's line was finally reduced in performance to a miserable nod, and other changes were made to set him apart from the other men, make him seem less "one of the boys." He no longer joined in with Steve's dirty joke, and he wore a jacket and tie to the poker game when the others wore T-shirts and sports shirts.

Mitch's feelings toward women assumed importance in the play mainly because of the way they made him relate to Blanche. Kazan wrote that

Mitch is Blanche's ideal in a comic form, 150 years late. He is big, tough, burly, has a rough southern voice and a manner of homespun, coarse, awkward, overgrown boy, with a heart of mush . . . He is straight out of Mack Sennett comedy – but Malden has to create the reality of it, the truth behind that corny image . . . the reason he's so clumsy with women is that he's so damn full of violent desire for them. (N 378)

Kazan and Malden worked on business that would make Mitch's awkwardness appear both funny and touching, particularly in the scene when he first meets Blanche. After he came out of the bathroom, and Stella introduced him to Blanche in the bedroom, Mitch started to move past the women but couldn't get by. Saying "Excuse me, please" (33), he made his way past, stumbling over Stella, while the women turned to watch him, "*smiling at his confusion*" (33). At the door he realized that he was still clutching the towel from the bathroom, and, overcome with embarrassment, he stepped back into the bedroom and handed it to Stella. Then he quickly returned to the game, tying his tie and putting his shoes back on while the women giggled in the bedroom. As the game continued, Mitch laced his shoes and put his jacket on, ate some Sen-Sen, and then told the men to deal him out so he could "go to the 'head'" (36). On his way to the bedroom, he ate some more Sen-Sen. When Mitch returned to Blanche in the bedroom, she began her usual flirtation by asking him for a cigarette, and he showed her the silver case with the inscription from his dead girlfriend. When Blanche asked him to fix the lantern, he fussed with it clumsily before he put it over the light. Unconsciously, his hand found the back of Blanche's chair, but he drew back and muttered "excuse me" when she put her hand on his. When Stella came out of the bathroom, Mitch turned around foolishly to get out of her way, nearly bumping into Stella and then nearly backing into Blanche. When Blanche started waltzing, he swayed to the music like a dancing bear.

To encode the connection between Mitch's awkwardness and his sexual desire, awkward gestures and movements were emphasized at potentially romantic moments, making Mitch appear tentative about his masculinity, as when Blanche forced him to bow to her and present his flowers like her "Rosenkavalier." When Mitch brought Blanche home from their date, Williams had specified that he carry a Mae West doll he had supposedly won at the amusement park, but this was changed in performance to a silly Raggedy Andy doll (see plate 6).[41] Mitch looked away, embarrassed by his own feelings when he looked into the bedroom after he and Blanche had come inside the apartment, and he handled Blanche clumsily when he tried to kiss her. When Blanche said she had "old-fashioned ideals," Mitch released his hold on her and went to the door, standing with one foot up on the porch to cool off.

The violence of Mitch's desire broke through his reticence in scene 9, when he comes to see Blanche after Stanley has told him about her past, and he has had a few drinks. Kazan encoded the danger of violence that lies just below the surface in Mitch at this point by having him break through the door to get in and prowl restlessly around the apartment while Blanche searched for liquor and tried to talk to him as though nothing had happened. In a pattern that was to be repeated by Stanley in scene 11, Mitch circled about the apartment, and then closed in on Blanche while she tried to move away, with a greater and greater sense that she was being menaced, until she dropped to her knees while he tore the lantern off the light bulb. Then he pulled her to her feet and shoved her face into the light.

Mitch's guilt and confusion still fighting his violent desire, he dropped back from Blanche after this show of force, listening dumbly for the most part while she talked about her past, until she told him about the young soldiers. This story aroused him so that he came up behind her and put his arms around her waist, turning her to face him. When Blanche, realizing that he was not going to marry her and only wanted "what [he had] been missing all summer" (87), told him to go away, he had already backed up toward the door before she started screaming fire, and had hurried out the door and up the alley before she got to the porch.

In the final scene, Kazan indicated the feeling for Blanche that remained with Mitch despite the combined forces of his mother and Stanley. Mitch's behavior toward Stanley had an edge of hostility throughout the scene, and he stared into space, nearly dropping his cards when he heard Blanche's voice. As Stanley tore the lantern off the light bulb and went after Blanche, asking her if she wanted it, Mitch rushed him, shouting "You! You done this, all a your God-damn rutting with things you – " (102), but when the men subdued him, he collapsed in a chair, head in arms, sobbing (102). The kinesic statement was that Mitch's sensitive nature, like Blanche's, had been violated by Stanley, that his hopes for happiness were as defeated as hers, that perhaps they could have saved each other if it hadn't been for Stanley's interference.

Steve and Eunice

During the rehearsal period, Kazan developed the relationship of Steve and Eunice into a comic mirror for that of Stanley and Stella. Eunice's nagging at Steve for not telling her he was going bowling was a less attractive version of Stella's following Stanley around and going to watch him bowl. During the poker fight, Eunice expressed her objections to Steve more effectively if less delicately than Stella did hers to Stanley. When Eunice shouted down to Steve from her apartment, Steve muttered "Oh–oh!" and hurried upstairs (41). Kazan extended the fight between Steve and Eunice in scene 5 kinesically to show the kind of behavior Stanley expects from women. After their initial exchange about Steve's "going up" at the four deuces, Eunice appeared on the steps, a comic figure, "*rubbing her backside*" (53). When she returned with Steve from the Four Deuces after Stanley's initial accusation of Blanche, Eunice was sobbing, with Steve's arm around her, comforted by Steve's ludicrous explanation of why he saw other women: "You know I don't love those girls . . . I love you. You know I love you. I only do that with other girls because I love you" (55).

Later in scene 5, as Steve and Eunice came out to meet Stanley, Kazan had Eunice race down the steps, bellowing "Come on, lover boy. Come on" (58) and shouting with laughter, Steve in hot pursuit. Stanley grabbed Eunice as she went by him, and she eluded him with delighted shrieks. When Stella shrugged out of Stanley's grasp a moment later and walked coolly down the street, the contrast between the two women heightened Stanley's anger at the effect Blanche was having on his heretofore adoring and sensual wife. Kazan also encoded a reminder of the kind of relationship Stanley was missing in scene 8 after his explosion about the airs his women were putting on and his destruction of the dishes. As Stanley and Stella stood outside on the porch while Blanche tried to telephone Mitch, the audience heard "*laughter, at first quiet and intimate – and soon boisterous and downright dirty, between* EUNICE *and* STEVE *in the apartment above*" (77). It was at this point that Stanley made his plea to Stella that it was "gonna be all right again between you and me the way it was . . . God, honey, it's gonna be sweet when we can make noise in the night the way that we used to and get the colored lights going with nobody's sister behind the curtains to hear us" (77–78).

Kazan also strengthened and dignified Eunice's character in some scenes, however, and emphasized her ties to Stella, partly to convey the extent to which Stella has become accustomed to the life of the Quarter and partly to encode a quality of natural human decency in the final scene. The play's opening scenic image of Stella sitting in the armchair eating candy from a paper bag, fanning herself, and reading a movie magazine, was mirrored in Eunice's sitting on the porch, eating peanuts and reading a confession magazine. The visual suggestion in this opening scene was that Stella was like any woman in the Quarter at this point. Eunice's casual intimacy with and loyalty to Stella was indicated in the first scene as she moved about the Kowalskis' apartment, putting away Stella's clothes and straightening up the beds, to defend her from Blanche's obvious disapproval. In the final scene Eunice was given additional dialogue to emphasize her and Stella's shared concern for Stella's baby, and it was she who held Stella in her arms and comforted her throughout the whole ordeal of Blanche's removal. Cutting Stella's line about the women of the Quarter being good-hearted and easy to get along with further tipped the balance of humanity in Eunice's favor. She is kind and loyal to Stella while Stella is disdainful and catty about her behind her back, at least when she is under Blanche's influence. Eunice may have appeared gross and ridiculous at times during the performance, but it was clear that she was the most decent person on the stage during the final scene.

In every case, Kazan's work with the actors served his basic purpose of objectifying the subjective, bringing the characters' individual perceptions of reality out in their behavior. It was at once the natural approach for a Method director to take toward actors and the appropriate direction for the subjective realism of *Streetcar*. As Williams said, the play was about the failure to communicate because of each character's failure to understand how the others saw the world. The tragic failure in the play was Chekhovian, the failure of four people to get beyond their subjective visions of the events both in the present and in the past so they can understand their significance to the others. Kazan's kinesic expression of that failure was the behavior of four people living out four separate visions of these events, their significance, and their consequences on the stage.

Rehearsals and try-outs

Kazan has written that "the rehearsals of *Streetcar* were a joy – which wasn't what I expected" (L 342). He was afraid that the classically trained English actress Jessica Tandy would have difficulty acting with the young Brando, who "had mannerisms that would have annoyed hell out of me if I'd been playing with him. He'd not respond directly when spoken to, make his own time lapses, sometimes leaving the other actors hung up" (L 342–43). Tandy, the consummate professional, never complained, despite the fact that Brando's spontaneity wreaked havoc on her own technique of carefully working out each moment of each scene and then setting it for the performance. In Kazan's mind, "the contrast in acting styles helped create the contrast between the cultured woman from Belle Reve and the New Orleans 'Quarter' redneck. There was one door in Jessie's performance I could never unlock, but I wasn't sure I wanted to. The character of Blanche should have certain inhibitions, no? She was, wasn't she, bound by her tradition?" (L 344).

With Brando and the rest of the cast, trained in the same Method technique he was, Kazan was more comfortable, and was able to make use of the shorthand of the Actors Studio as he did with Karl Malden's portrayal of Mitch. He noted how helpful it was to have the Method in common with Brando in explaining the significance of Stanley's telephone call about the bowling team during the birthday-party scene:

On the phone he lays down the law as to where he will and will not bowl. At first sight the phone conversation seemed to be an interruption, even an irrelevancy, but a little examination revealed that during the talk about the bowling the man made up his mind decisively about his argument with the women. In fact, the speech on the phone had to be read with direct dramatic reference to the scene with the women. The import of the speech was not in the writing but in the acting. So I was happy that night, as I looked at this page of Tennessee Williams, that Marlon Brando was trained in a certain way and would know what I was talking about.[42]

Williams was rather diffident in his first rehearsal period with Kazan. Unlike the later plays they worked on together, there was little rewriting of *Streetcar* to do during rehearsals, and Williams generally came by in the afternoon, once he had finished his other work for the day. One anecdote that survives in several versions will serve to convey Williams's reticence during this first production:

During a rehearsal of "Streetcar" Williams had an idea for the production that he wanted to offer to the director, Elia Kazan. He turned to a colleague beside him, explained what his idea was and asked him whether it would be all right to speak to Kazan about it. His companion, who had never encountered such diffidence in a successful playwright, said, "Of course." Williams nevertheless waited for a break before approaching Kazan.[43]

During the rehearsals and tryouts of *Streetcar*, Kazan came to a realization about the play which disturbed him at first, but then led to an insight about Tennessee Williams that was to prove essential to their work together. In his memoirs, Kazan reports that he was concerned all through this period that the audiences seemed to have too much sympathy for Stanley, even at the play's end. Although Williams reminded him that Blanche was not flawless and Stanley was not evil, Kazan was disturbed that the audience's loyalty was not more clearly with Blanche. Thinking at first that the fault was in his direction or perhaps in Brando's upstaging Tandy, he finally came to realize that he had after all been oversimplifying Williams's play in his directorial scheme: "Was the play an affirmation of spiritual values over the brutish ones? Certainly. But that simple? No" (L 349). Partly through more personal experience with Williams and partly through more experience with the play, Kazan gradually came to realize that the audience's conflict, the division in sympathies, was the essence of the play as Williams had written it: "Blanche is attracted by the man who is going to destroy her. I understood the play by this formula of ambivalence. Only then, it seemed to me, would I think of it as Tennessee meant it to be understood: with fidelity to life as he – not all us groundlings, but he – had experienced it" (L 351).[44]

3 Realism and fantasy: *Camino Real*

The long road to Camino Real

In an interview published on the day before the premiere of *Camino Real*, Williams explained the experience that had provided the germ for the play. Seeing people in costumes carrying torches lined up along the railroad tracks in Mexico had made him fear "dying in an unknown place," but he couldn't help thinking, "what a beautiful play this would make."[1] Williams went on to say in the interview that he had written the play first as an "original sketch" in two months, adding, "I was advised not to go on with it. It was too fantastic."[2]

Later on, Williams was inclined to lay the blame for his abandoning the original one-act version of *Ten Blocks on the Camino Real* on Audrey Wood. In *Memoirs* he recalled writing the play in New Orleans during the winter of 1945–46 and sending it off to Wood. He remembered being chilled by the telephone call that conveyed her response: "'About that play you sent me,' she said stridently, 'put it away, don't let anybody see it.'"[3] Actually the communication between writer and agent had been neither so dramatic nor so one-sided as Williams remembered. Williams had first sent a copy of what he called "the Mexican poetic fantasy" to Wood on February 27, 1946. Two weeks later, he was writing to her about revising the play, noting that the only good scene in the first version was the one at the Gypsy's.[4] This was a fairly accurate assessment, and the scene at the Gypsy's, Block 7 of *Ten Blocks*, was to remain without substantial changes throughout the many revisions of the manuscript to become Block 12 of *Camino Real*.

Williams published a revised *Ten Blocks* as one of the five short plays in *American Blues* (1948), where Elia Kazan found it. Kazan began using it for some exercises in his class at the Actors Studio in the fall of 1949. After Kazan had worked with Eli Wallach and other young actors on the fiesta scene for about two months, he staged it for Williams, who immediately agreed to enlarge the one-act into a full-length play.[5] Fired up by the work at the studio and by Kazan's interest, Williams began to work on the script

64

again. On November 11, 1949 he sent Audrey Wood a revision of the section being done at the Studio, and he sent her another set of revisions later in the month, writing enthusiastically about his hopes for the production and suggesting that they might get Gene Kelly for Kilroy. This possibility appears to have been pursued seriously throughout the period when *Ten Blocks* was being planned as half of a double bill, probably with *27 Wagons Full of Cotton,* which eventually became the basis for the film *Baby Doll.* Several press releases from the fall of 1951 indicated that efforts were being made to get Kelly released from his movie contract in order to act in the play. Wallach may also have been considered a possibility for the role of Kilroy early on. Williams wrote to Wood on August 28 that he hoped the one-acts would not go into production until January because he hoped to have Wallach available.[6] In November, Williams reported to his friend Maria Britneva that they were "suspended in air, waiting breathlessly for Marlon Brando to make up his mind. He is the only one that seems right to play the male lead in both short plays, and he is interested but claims that he needs a week in which to consult his analyst about it and make the proper spiritual adjustment."[7]

Meanwhile, Kazan continued to communicate with Williams about the script, but was unwilling to enter into a contractual agreement to direct. Williams's recent experience with Kazan on *The Rose Tattoo* made him worry. After showing interest in the early versions of *Tattoo,* and giving Williams a good deal of advice on its revisions, Kazan had decided not to direct it. By his own account, Williams was devastated when he received Kazan's letter telling the playwright that he couldn't direct *The Rose Tattoo* because he was too deeply involved in his next two film projects.[8] One of these was *The Hook,* a screenplay by Arthur Miller about the Brooklyn waterfront, which, through various creative, personal, and political convolutions, evolved into Miller's play *A View from the Bridge* and Kazan's film *On the Waterfront,* with a screenplay by Budd Schulberg.

Williams resented Kazan's apparent choice of Miller's unfinished screenplay over his own play. He has confessed that he battled a certain professional jealousy toward other playwrights throughout his life, and no playwright was more threatening to him at that moment than the author of the season's greatest artistic and popular success, *Death of a Salesman.*[9] Shortly after *Salesman*'s opening, Williams complained to friends that he had received in one day five complete sets of Arthur Miller notices – more than he had ever received for any play of his own.[10] He tried hard to make an exception for Miller, the contemporary he most admired both personally and artistically. But when it came to Kazan, what seemed to Williams as a clear choice of Miller over him still rankled.

Audrey Wood continued to register some understandable anxiety about securing a contract with Kazan to direct the one-act plays, despite her efforts throughout the fall of 1951.[11] As he wrote to Wood from Rome on October 27, however, Williams was dismayed and frightened by what he considered the rapid progress on the plans for the production. Worried that he did not know exactly what Kazan wanted done with the script, he expressed his hope that he and Kazan could sail back to New York from Europe together and discuss the play fully. At this point there also arose from Williams a hint of resentment at the involvement in his writing that he both needed and sought from Kazan. He wrote to Wood that he hoped Kazan did not expect to collaborate with him in the actual writing of the script. Noting that the director had a very creative mind, he said that he thought Kazan's views would be stimulating – provided his demands were not overwhelming and his ideas were compatible with Williams's.[12]

This letter provides a hint of the tremendous complexity of Williams's relationship with Kazan. On the one hand, Williams considered Kazan's contribution essential to the creation of his plays. He valued both Kazan's imagination and his ability to define an order and a forward momentum in the sometimes disordered products of Williams's creative strivings. He believed that Kazan's direction was absolutely crucial to the full realization of his plays on the stage. But he also sensed a tendency in his collaborator to seek creative control of whatever he was working on, a tendency Kazan has discussed frankly in his autobiography. This early in their career together, Williams was already drawing clear boundaries. Whatever contributions or suggestions Kazan might make, the script was his, and Kazan was shortly to demonstrate his firm acceptance of Williams's position.

Williams did sail back from Europe with Kazan, reporting happily to his friend Maria Britneva that the director was "in a good mood and full of enthusiasm for the project" (St. Just 48). Immediate events were to prove that Williams's and Wood's anxiety about the contract was justified, however. Kazan decided to direct George Tabori's *Flight Into Egypt* before he did the Williams plays. In late December it was announced that the idea of the double bill had been dropped, and that Williams planned to. expand *Camino Real* into a full-length play with music and choreography.[13] *Flight Into Egypt* opened on March 18, 1952, closing after only forty-two performances. Williams wrote to Maria Britneva that "Gadg [Kazan] and the actors did a bad job on it. It was a good play, but it was over-produced. The scenes were played too hard and heavy, so that the simple truth was lost in a lot of highly virtuoso theatricality. You couldn't see the characters for the staging! That's the sort of mistake that very good directors sometimes make – they get too imaginative for their material" (St. Just 54).

But Kazan faced more disturbing events in the spring of 1952. Like many of the thirties leftists in the theatre, Kazan was subpoenaed by the House Un-American Activities Committee and questioned about his political activities and his former membership in the Communist Party. After a closed hearing on January 19, Kazan requested an open hearing on April 10, at which he testified about his eighteen-month membership in the Party twenty years earlier and his reasons for leaving it. He also performed the ritualistic act required by the Committee in order to avoid blacklisting – "naming names," listing his colleagues in the Group Theatre who had also been party members in the mid thirties. As might be expected, the first six months of 1952 were among the most difficult in Kazan's life as he agonized over his moral and political convictions, his testimony, and the intensely negative reaction to it, both public and personal.[14]

While Kazan was going through his difficult spring, Williams was hard at work on the script of *Camino Real* and recording his progress in letters to Cheryl Crawford, who hoped to produce the play. On February 10, he wrote that he had read the unabridged memoirs of Casanova (twelve volumes) and the Dumas novel *La Dame aux Camellias* to make sure Casanova and Marguerite would ring true.[15] On June 29, Williams told Crawford that he had prepared a revised draft he wanted her to read, noting that Kazan had been pleased with the first draft and wanted to go into rehearsal with it in late October. He also took the occasion to counteract what he considered Crawford's Yankee thriftiness, reminding her that, while both he and Kazan wanted her to produce the play, she would have to understand that it would require a lavish and liberally budgeted production.[16] Crawford was very pleased to accept the job of producing *Camino Real*, and she worked hard to serve the artistic values of this, in 1953, very unusual play on Broadway, but subsequent events were to prove Williams's worries about her penny-pinching correct.[17]

Probably the most important artistic issue at this point was the choice of a designer, always important, but especially crucial for this play in which the visual elements of the stage language conveyed so much of the meaning. The first choice of both Williams and Kazan was of course Jo Mielziner. When approached about *Camino Real*, Mielziner was critical of the script at first. As he wrote later, "the manuscript made heavy demands on the director, the actors, and the designer, and some of the fleeting, short-lived scenes called for bulky scenery and properties."[18] He warmed to the project after some preliminary discussion with Kazan, however, and he wrote to Williams on August 26 that he "felt like an ungrateful dog to criticize a script that is so packed with excitement and beauty."[19] Mielziner suggested several abstract concepts that he thought would serve the artistic expression of the play:

Perhaps the basic set might take a physical form which suggested some sort of a bear pit, as though Kilroy were trapped in a place where there is no obvious physical escape. Perhaps some sort of a "labyrinth." I hope we could find ways of using projected images and patterns and colors to fulfill your suggestion of the constant changes in the various blocks. Of course, physical props that actors dealt with would have to be three-dimensional, but I am convinced that some style in physical production must unite these ten blocks.[20]

Somewhat reassured by this letter, Williams wrote to Kazan that Mielziner now seemed enthusiastic about the production, but the playwright was concerned that Cheryl Crawford considered the designer's fee too high.[21] Williams urged Kazan to return to New York to fight the money battle with his old Group Theatre and Actors Studio colleague Crawford.

Eventually Lemuel Ayers, an old friend of Williams's from his days at the University of Iowa, and the designer of *Oklahoma!*, was chosen to design the set, the costumes, and the lighting for *Camino Real*. The heavy realistic set that Ayers eventually designed for the production differed greatly from Mielziner's fluid, imagistic sketches. Mielziner's drawings call the audience's attention to the stage as a performance space and create the Camino Real for the spectator as a subjective realm unrelated to time and place. By contrast the realism of Ayers's stark grey walls and heavily constructed buildings insisted ironically on the Camino Real's relation to an objective reality recognizable to the audience. The Siete Mares was a recognizable resort hotel. The pawn shop, the Ritz Men Only, and the Bucket of Blood cantina called attention to themselves as recognizable caricatures of typical Skid Row establishments. The set made a witty statement about a milieu familiar to the audience before the action began, creating an expectation for the production that simply was not appropriate to the play (see plate 7).

For her part, Cheryl Crawford maintained that the set for *Camino Real* "never pleased" her, assigning the responsibility for its artistic short-comings to Kazan rather than to Ayers:

Kazan chose to have dark, forbidding stone walls enclose the action, and they made the play even more chilling. I would have preferred a set with the off-white adobe walls one sees in the Southwest and Mexico, where the angle of the sun creates mysterious blue-black shadows and rattan blinds or ancient canvas make pools of deep shade. When Kilroy goes, I wanted the set to become transparent so that we would see him leaving the plaza to wander in an empty desert of sand stretching endlessly toward nothing.[22]

The effect Crawford sought called for the combination of transparent scenery and lighting of which Mielziner was already the acknowledged master in 1952. The producer was much more likely to have gotten it from him than from Ayers.

Kazan also blamed himself for the design's failure to support the artistic values of the rest of the production, but for different reasons. "I wanted a production that had the bizarre fantasy of the Mexican primitive artist Posada," he wrote. "It happens in the topography inside the author's head. What it needed was the vision of the right artistic collaborators . . . Posada! Sounds great, doesn't it? . . . But something beyond talk is required, in this case the right help from the right designer."[23] Kazan's description of his collaboration with Ayers suggests that his error was a failure to live up to his self-disciplined responsibility as director by insisting on a single artistic vision throughout the production:

I wrote the designer we'd chosen a long note explaining what I hoped for in the set. I didn't get it; what I got was a lugubrious realistic setting that was, in a word, heavy-handed. And too real. It made the fantasies that took place inside it seem silly. I should have ordered a new setting, but I didn't. I betrayed myself by not sticking to my guns. I'd buried my original – and I believe correct – intention in talk. And good fellowship. The designer was a friend.[24]

As Kazan tells it, this incident illustrates the chief danger inherent in the dynamics of collaborative art, the failure to communicate aesthetically. There is no doubt that the realistic set was out of harmony with Williams's timeless fantasy and with the stylized costumes and choreographed movement that encoded it in Kazan's production.

Williams had begun to discuss casting, as well as designers, with Crawford during the early fall, and he wrote to Kazan that she had a list of possible actors. Kazan, however, had other ideas, probably originating in his conviction as a member of the Group Theatre that the best thing for a play is an ensemble of actors rather than a group of "stars." Since Williams had been so pleased with the work that had been done at Actors Studio, Kazan recalls, he cast the play from among Studio members. Unfortunately, while Eli Wallach gave a brilliant performance as Kilroy, Kazan came to see that "many of them, dear and good people, were . . . not up to the needs of their parts." He noted that "they were trained in a more realistic technique. So was I."[25] While not all of the actors actually came from the Studio, the technique that dominated the production, both directing and acting, was very much the Method as practiced at Actors Studio. The attempt to interpret the subjective fantasy of Tennessee Williams through the stylized but naturalistic psychological realism of the Stanislavsky-influenced Method technique was the major aesthetic challenge that Kazan faced in this production.

Meanwhile, Williams and Kazan were involved in an intense reworking of the script through the international mails. During the summer of 1952, Williams wrote from Rome of his search to find a proper balance in the play's form and structure, and what he referred to as a dance-like rhythm and movement.[26] As summer faded into fall, Williams evinced a good deal of uneasiness in his communications before he received Kazan's response to his revised script. He wrote that he was very disturbed when Kazan told him he had not yet read the script but that Molly Kazan and actor Frederic March had reacted to it unfavourably.[27]

On November 17, 1952, Kazan sent Williams exactly what he had been asking for, a 3,500-word letter outlining what Kazan thought Williams needed to do in his final revision of the script. Kazan had two major points to make in his letter, related to the play's meaning and its structure. The major problem with the play, he said, was that Williams needed to clarify whether it had an immediate social statement to make, as was implied by the Survivor scene, or whether he was aiming for a more universal statement. Kazan thought the Survivor scene suggested a social theme of class exploitation, while later scenes suggested a more universal theme of the existential confrontation with death.

Reacting to the play as if it were allegory, Kazan asked a number of the kinds of questions that Williams had already encountered from Audrey Wood. He wanted to know what specifically was represented by each of the characters, whether walking through the arch leading to Terra Incognita was meant to represent death literally, why Don Quixote was brought in as a savior at the end. Suggesting that Don Quixote represented the spirit of romanticism, Kazan suggested an overall thematic statement that became the key to the production for him, and the key to the play for many. Enumerating a colorful list of what he considered the romantic outcasts, the rebels, and the Bohemians of the fifties, Kazan suggested to Williams that his play was a defense of this fast-disappearing breed. As an afterthought, Kazan suggested that a list of these types should appear somewhere in the play, suggesting that Esmeralda pray for them on the roof before she retires.[28] This was the origin of Esmeralda's prayer in Block 16, the passage most often quoted by critics to explain the play:

God bless all con men and hustlers and pitch-men who hawk their hearts on the street, all two-time losers who're likely to lose once more, the courtesan who made the mistake of love, the greatest of lovers crowned with the longest horns, the poet who wandered far from his heart's green country and possibly will and possibly won't be able to find his way back, look down with a smile tonight on the lost cavaliers, the ones with the rusty armor and soiled white plumes, and visit with understanding and something that's almost tender those fading legends that come and go in this plaza like songs not clearly remembered, oh, sometime and somewhere, let there be something to mean the word *honor* again![29]

Williams worked hard on this speech, revising it several times during the rehearsal period and again between the production and the revised version of the script that was finally published. Like Kazan and the critics, he saw it as the crucial statement of the play's meaning.

Kazan also wanted to make clear from the start that he considered *Camino Real*'s thematic statement neither social nor "universal," but personal and subjective. He and Williams, Kazan asserted, would be speaking for themselves in this play. If its hero was the arch-romantic, the misfit, it was equally clear to Kazan who the antagonist was: Gutman, the archetypal American businessman who called the shots and was out to exterminate the romantics and the rebels. Having learned from his experience with Stanley Kowalski, however, Kazan realized that Gutman was not the simple villain of melodrama. There was something attractive, or at least entertaining, about him. The schematic complement for Gutman, Kazan noted, was the Gypsy. While Gutman preyed on the people facing the end of the line and death, the Gypsy exploited love and the future. But touched with the romantic spirit of anarchy, she too had her attractive side.

Kazan's directing concept for *Camino Real* was based on his view of Gutman. Noting that men had made great profits from finding the places where elephants went to die and selling off their deposits of ivory, Kazan suggested that the Camino Real was a burying ground for society's last surviving romantics, and Gutman was preying on them. The strength of this metaphor, however, was to come from the style with which it was treated. Kazan saw the play as a lively comedy. His view was in keeping with a note that Williams had placed at the beginning of Block 7 in the published version of *Ten Blocks*:

In this scene I am trying to catch the quality of really "tough" Americana of the comic sheets, the skid-row bars, cat-houses, Grade B movies, street-Arabs, vagrants, drunks, pitch-men, gamblers, whores, all the rootless, unstable and highly spirited life beneath the middle-class social level in the States.[30]

Williams continued to believe in the importance of this style throughout the many versions of the script. Two weeks after the play opened in New York, in fact, he was writing to Brooks Atkinson that he felt the play's dominant element was grotesque comedy traceable to the American comic strip and animated cartoon.[31]

The difficult aspect of this comic-strip style for Kazan was maintaining its consistency without slighting the pathos that Williams was trying to achieve through the Jacques Casanova–Marguerite Gautier (Camille) story line. He hoped to establish a delicately poignant humor with the suggestion that Casanova and Camille were playing roles they had outlived. Kazan hoped that he could get a similarly mixed effect of pathos, humor, and brave defiance from the music. He thought the band should be world-weary, but capable at times of an off-beat vigor that flourished in resistance to middle-class propriety.

Kazan's second major concern was the play's structure. He did not like the two-act structure that Williams had conceived for it, with the break in the middle of the fiesta (Block 11 in the published play). In keeping with his Stanislavskian view of dramatic structure, Kazan looked for a continuous action or spine in the sixteen blocks and a clear protagonist with whose motive or objective the audience could identify. He suggested to Williams that they conceive of the play as two-act structure based on Kilroy's experience, with the first act composed of Kilroy's arrival on the Camino Real, his realizing what that meant, and his trying to get out, finally, by stowing away on the *Fugitivo*. The first act would end with Kilroy's being thrown off the *Fugitivo*. Establishing in the first act that there was no exit from the Camino Real would give the action in the second act a clear structure unified by the existential question of how to face death. Kazan thought that his more organic structure would help him to construct a unified action for the production, using, as a good Method director should, Kilroy's desires – to escape in the first act, and to learn how to die in the second – as the spine of the play.

There was a problem with this strategy, however. While Kilroy had been the clear protagonist of *Ten Blocks*, Williams had dissipated the focus of interest a good deal with the material he had added to make the full-length play. Minor characters like Lord Byron and the Baron de Charlus now were the subjects of fully developed scenes. More importantly, the Jacques–Marguerite material now amounted to a second story line, only tenuously connected to Kilroy's. The most substantial change Kazan wanted Williams to make was to reunify the action by refocusing it on Kilroy and integrating the Jacques–Marguerite story more fully with Kilroy's. He feared that he and Williams would be frantically trying to integrate Kilroy into the long middle section of the play from which he was now absent during the last few rehearsals, and pleaded with Williams to do it now while he could do it effectively. Kilroy should be a guide throughout the play for the audience, he suggested, providing it with someone to identify with during its whole bewildering experience of the Camino Real.

For several single-spaced pages, Kazan then laid out carefully how this might be done, basing the scenes on material in the script before him or in earlier versions, and following the spine or through-line for the action outlined earlier. Much of the action he described, such as having Kilroy try to raise money for a bus ticket by serving Gutman and carrying baggage, was eventually incorporated into the script. The bell-hop business formed the basis for Kilroy's enforced role as Gutman's patsy and his active participation in Blocks 3, 4, 5, and 6 of the script as published. Kilroy also played a major role in Block 9, the *Fugitivo* scene, as choreographed for the production. After the incident in which Kilroy tried to stow away, Kazan suggested a climactic curtain with the crash of the *Fugitivo*. In production, it was decided to stay with Williams's original curtain, in the middle of the fiesta. At first, this was the single curtain in a two-act play, but later an act break was added at the end of what is Block 6 in the published script, after the climactic chase scene when Kilroy is caught and forced into the role of patsy. Although Kazan went along with Williams's original choice in this rather than insisting on the structure he developed, the director found a way to make the act breaks meaningful within his interpretation of the action. In the first, Kilroy's frenetic attempt to escape is defeated, the climax coming when he is caught and forced into the patsy's role; in the second, as Eli Wallach noted, Kilroy competes by dancing at the Fiesta and wins the Gypsy's daughter, a temporary reversal of fortunes before his death in Act 3.

Kazan suggested that the Kilroy–Esmeralda scene (Block 12 as published) remain as written, but outlined two scenes leading up to it, which are essentially Blocks 10 and 11 as published. Then he outlined the scene in which Kilroy shows his love for Jacques by offering him his last dollar and carrying his luggage over to the flophouse. This became Block 13 in the published script. Kazan also suggested that Kilroy's speech about the "warmness"[33] of a loved one be moved from his opening scene to his dying scene with Marguerite and that the Gypsy be brought into Block 16 to emphasize the image of Esmeralda as a captive bird, both ideas that Williams acted on very effectively.

Kazan also made two suggestions that Williams did not act on. He disliked the figure of the Dreamer, which he found pretentious, and he found the figure of Lord Mulligan, the iron-and-steel man from Cobh, somewhat of an anomaly among the romantic outcasts. He urged Williams to give the Dreamer's *hermano* speech to Kilroy or to find a substitute character that was more in keeping with the play's exuberant mood and to reveal after Lord Mulligan's death that he was a closet romantic. Williams chose to leave his dreamer and his iron-and-steel man alone, and his resistance to these two suggestions is an interesting indication of the nature of the creative collaboration between the two men.

Although he was willing to make use of his collaborator's ideas in shaping his plays, Williams was also, as we have seen, very protective of his role as author. Kazan's enthusiastic participation in what he saw as Williams's artistic statement could prove both heartening and threatening. It is evident in Kazan's letter, for instance, that the director was already thinking of the play as a joint artistic property. Several times, he used "we" when referring to the need to express the play's meaning clearly. By this time, the play was in his mind a joint artistic property that would express the feelings of both men about the fate of the romantic in the repressive world of the fifties.

Of course this was partly reassuring rhetoric – we're in this together against the philistines who don't understand us – but there was also an unconscious note of ownership that was typical of Kazan's desire to attain artistic control of everything he worked on. While Williams very much needed Kazan's great directorial strengths – his clear-headed vision of what the playwright seemed to understand only instinctively and imagistically, his gift for objectifying ideas and personalities through action, and his vital creative imagination – the author was wary of what he had hinted to Audrey Wood was the director's desire to take over the script. Williams respected and trusted Kazan's advice more than anyone else's, and he almost always followed it in spirit, but there was a point at which he simply stuck to his guns. If the Dreamer and the iron-and-steel man from Cobh seemed right to him the way they were, he was not about to change them to fit Kazan's scheme for the play, no matter how brilliant it was.

In fact, Williams at first resisted making the substantial changes that were being asked of him. At what Kazan referred to as a historic meeting between Williams, Kazan, and Crawford early in December, Williams exploded, letting Kazan know that he felt his interference with the script was too great, his suggestions too specific.[34] On December 9, Molly Kazan felt she had to intervene before the two men became seriously alienated from each other. "A misunderstanding is going to make us all trouble in the end, whatever happens with the play," she wrote to Williams, "never before with you and never with any writer have I seen so desperate and absolute an identification. It's dangerous. If you lose the sense that you are more *than* anything you write, you lose your power to SEE it and you lose the power to bring it to its own full realization."[35] On December 10, Kazan wrote in a conciliatory vein. Somewhat chastened by Williams's outbreak, he said that he would refrain from making any more specific suggestions for change, at least for the time being, and he assured Williams that he was right to do things his way or not at all.[36] Kazan continued to urge Williams to rewrite the first act with a through-action motivated by Kilroy, and to have it state the author's meaning clearly in the author's terms, but he made it clear that he realized the meaning might not be the one he had laid out in his earlier letter.

In the end, both before and during the rehearsal period, which began on January 29, 1953, Williams revised the script substantially along the lines Kazan had suggested. Kazan had established a precedent of influencing the development of a play's meaning and structure in his work with Williams which was to hold for the rest of their work together.

Revising the script

Williams restructured the action of *Camino Real* along the lines Kazan had outlined. Through the efforts of both Williams in revision and Kazan in rehearsal, Kilroy was woven through the action of the play, having some function on stage during almost every one of the sixteen blocks. Still, the play clearly had two overlapping story lines in the Jacques–Marguerite sequence and the Kilroy sequence. Williams once referred to *Camino Real* as a "mutilated play,"[37] and he remarked several times that it would have been more unified if he had written it all at once rather than in spurts separated by years of work on other things.

Beginning rehearsals with what both playwright and director considered a workable script, Williams continued to revise at a feverish pace. On the second day of rehearsals, the production stage manager wrote in his private notes that he was struggling to keep pace on the typewriter with the flood of rewriting that Williams was doing. He referred to whole new scenes being written and long passages being torn out of the script or inserted into it.[38] By this time, Williams was working in the spirit of Kazan's vision of the play, and much of his work during the rehearsal period went toward making the romantic characters more admirable and more sympathetic to the audience – encouraging its identification with Kilroy, Jacques, and Marguerite and distancing it from Gutman. If the romantic characters were to bring Williams's subjective statement of his romantic credo directly to the audience, it was important that the audience be drawn into sympathy with them.

Kilroy

Williams smoothed Kilroy's rough edges to make the audience's identification with him easier. For example, in the earlier *Ten Blocks*, Kilroy shows the photograph of his "one true woman" not to Marguerite as he is dying, but to Jacques in a scene where the two Casanovas compare conquests. Before he takes out the picture of his wife in that scene, Kilroy shows Jacques pictures of "a cookie [he] used to cut in San Antone" (70), "a seventeen-year-old Ginny [he] had in L. A." (70), and "Betsy Lou and Martha Jane Thompkins, identical twins, in Omaha, Nebraska" (71). This attitude was more appropriate to the rough-and-ready comic strip milieu in which Williams first conceived of Kilroy than to the sentimental mood of the scene with Marguerite that Williams wrote during rehearsals (85).

Similarly a speech that Williams had written for Kilroy about the advantage to one's health of staying drunk all the time was eliminated during rehearsals, presumably because it was not in keeping with the character of "all-American boy" that Kilroy was becoming.

Another important element in the transformation of Kilroy was the conception of his role as patsy. At first Williams had thought of fulfilling Kazan's suggestion to weave Kilroy through the action by making him a shill. The role of patsy, however, had the advantage of making Kilroy a sympathetic and somewhat pathetic character at the same time as it increased the possibilities for humorous action and made use of the plastic talents of a versatile actor like Eli Wallach. In a note for the first rehearsal script, Williams pointed out that various pantomime clown-bits could be worked out for Kilroy throughout the second act, including the *Fugitivo* scene where he would work as a comic red cap.[39] Williams also suggested a pantomime sequence for the *Fugitivo* scene that would carry out Kazan's suggestion for Kilroy's involvement and help to develop the comic pathos that was becoming the dominant mood of the play's second half. At the final whistle of the *Fugitivo* (a ship in the early scripts), Kilroy would throw off his fright wig and nose and run to catch it. Missing it, he would return, looking disconsolately back at the departing ship and putting the nose and wig back on. As Marguerite wandered downstage murmuring "Lost," Kilroy would light his nose, becoming only an intermittent light in the dimness. Kilroy's patsy costume also contributed to the mood. Originally it included huge slap-soled shoes and white cotton gloves with padded fingers as well as the fright wig, clown pants and red flashing nose, but the shoes and gloves were eliminated, presumably to give Wallach more freedom of movement.

Most important to the audience's sympathy for Kilroy as patsy was the climactic chase scene in which Kilroy vaults from the stage and rushes up and down the aisles of the theatre, frantically trying to escape while Esmeralda cheers him on, a dramatic expression of the last youthful hopes of the characters to free themselves before they are enslaved by the forces of Gutman and the Gypsy. This scene was worked out collaboratively during rehearsals, with Kazan choreographing the action and Williams supplying the dialogue. Its combined visual and aural elements encoded one of the play's most effective statements of the defeat of youthful innocence and hopes for freedom by the cynical forces of greed, selfishness, and cruelty.

The addition of direct appeals to the audience provided the simplest, most efficient way to enlist its identification with Kilroy. In the early stages of rehearsals, Williams added in answer to the prostitute's offer of "*Love?*," Kilroy's lines "Sorry – I don't feature that. (*To audience*) [No, thanks,] I have ideals." (28), inviting the audience's collusion. Kazan later cut the line "I have ideals," presumably because he considered it too "corny," an effect he carefully avoided in this play. A little later in the scene, when his wallet was stolen, Kilroy turned to the audience and called on it as a witness, again inviting its identification with him. At the end of the scene, Kilroy addressed his final speech directly to the audience, from the edge of the double-apron stage:

What've I got to cash in on? My golden gloves? Never! I'll say that once more, never! The silver-framed photo of my One True Woman? Never! Repeat that! Never! What else have I got of a detachable and negotiable nature? Oh! My ruby-and-emerald studded belt with the word CHAMP on it . . . Sometimes a man has got to hock his sweet used-to-be in order to finance his present situation. [You know what I mean?] (31)

This direct appeal confronted the audience with Kilroy's situation, and forced it to consider the dilemma he faced as a question presented to it rather than as an incident passively observed, as would have been the case if the illusion of the fourth wall had been preserved. Kazan's kinesics and Williams's dialogue intensified Williams's statement in what Kazan considered "the most direct subjective play of our time."[40] In a joint interview with Williams given shortly before the play opened, Kazan explained, "it's Tennessee speaking personally and lyrically right to you. That's one reason we've pulled the audience inside the fourth wall by having the actors frequently speak directly to the spectator and by having some of the exits and entrances made through the aisles of the theatre."[41] Both playwright and director were acutely aware that the success of this technique depended on the degree of sympathy between the audience and the characters who presented it with Williams's message. These included Jacques and Marguerite as well as Kilroy.

Jacques

Jacques was less kind and long-suffering toward Marguerite in the earlier versions of the script than in the final one. He teased her about her obsession with the *Fugitivo*, telling her that the sound she heard was not a distant plane, but a mosquito. After the plane had departed without her, he did not simply comfort her as he does in the published script, but argued with her about her papers and belittled her for trying to use his. As Marguerite berated him hysterically for not helping her to get on the plane without her papers, he reminded her that the papers had been stolen while she was visiting the decadent establishments on the wrong side of town. The earlier Casanova also took a more active part in the sordid life of the Camino Real. After he was thrown out of the Siete Mares by

Gutman, he was stalked by Lobo, the knife-wielding low-life who had killed the Baron. Jacques whipped a steel blade from his cane, sending Lobo back into the shadow of the arch. The fact that Jacques had his dangerous side made the fact of his sentiment more poignant, but in rehearsal it was decided to forego the contrast in order to make him more sympathetic to the audience.

As they did with Kilroy, Williams and Kazan worked to increase the feeling of pathos that Jacques inspired in the audience. The scene where he is crowned King of the Cuckolds after Marguerite leaves him to look for a gigolo, Block 11 in the published script, was added during rehearsals, and the incident where his remittances are cut off was lengthened and made more poignant. In *Ten Blocks* he simply is brought a wire by a waiter, reads it, and drops his head in his hands. When Marguerite asks him what the matter is he says, "my remittances are cut off" (55). Marguerite asks, "Completely?" and he says "Yes" (55). For the pre-production script, Williams had developed this incident in Block 7 further, having Gutman take the letter and hold it to the light, telling Jacques that it must be his remittances. Jacques asked him to put it in his pocket, saying that he would open it when he had recovered his strength. This created suspense and prepared the audience for the scene in Block 13 when Jacques finds out that the remittances are discontinued and Gutman heaves his portmanteau with its "fragile mementoes" out of the second-story window. During rehearsals, the incident with the letter was moved to what is Block 7 in the published version, allowing the relationship between Jacques and Marguerite to be developed in one scene. The incident in Block 13 was elaborated with the presence of the Bum and A. Ratt, and with Jacques's reaction to Gutman, "And so at last it has come, the distinguished thing!" (83).

Jacques was also made more timid about stating his opinion of conditions on the Camino Real, less the "old hawk" and more the aging Bohemian at the end of his rope who has acquired the skill of discretion to get along in enemy territory. In the pre-production version of the script Jacques made veiled criticisms of the state of affairs directly to Gutman, suggesting that perhaps his check had been delayed by the "state of emergency" in the country. In the final version, Jacques's disapproval was reduced to the description, confided secretly to Kilroy, of what happens to corpses on the Camino Real, a clearly powerless and pathetic act of rebellion. In general, the revisions in Jacques's role tended to change him from a fading but still gallant man of the world to a figure of powerless romantic endurance. The traces of active resistance to Lobo, to Gutman, and to Marguerite were removed from his character, leaving his nobility to arise from the dignity with which he bore his defeat and his ability to make love overcome betrayal.

Marguerite

Perhaps the greatest change was in the character of Marguerite Gautier, which Williams seemed to rethink completely in the process of revision. His earlier versions focused rather melodramatically on her role as Camille the prostitute. She was a hard and cynical woman of the world, seeking escape from despair in fading pleasures and willing to do anything to find a permanent escape, even betray the only one who loved her. In revision, Williams softened the character, making her less hard and selfish and emphasizing the side of Camille that he saw as victim, the frail invalid who had every reason to despair. In *Ten Blocks*, for example, Marguerite abandons Jacques in the restaurant when she hears that his remittances have been cut off. In the final version of *Camino Real* she reproaches him for not telling her that he was short of funds so she could help him. Williams removed the incidents from the pre-production version in which Marguerite attacked Jacques for not getting her on the *Fugitivo* and taunted him with his lack of money and fading potency, showing none of the remorse that characterized her in the final version of Block 10. Minor incidents which displayed Marguerite's thoughtless cruelty, such as pushing the old blind La Madrecita, were also removed during revision, and her vices, such as smoking hashish in the bazaar, were made less overt.

Marguerite's sexuality had also been emphasized more in earlier versions. An early version of the crowning of Jacques as King of the Cuckolds had Marguerite brought out to the square to join the male dancers in a game of blind man's buff, in which she was whirled from one to another, falling in "wanton attitudes" among them, laughing breathlessly, until they released her and she staggered dizzily into the center of the Plaza.[42] Most significantly, Marguerite's major speech in *Ten Blocks* is the story of her sexual awakening at the age of fifteen. In the final version, Williams replaced this central speech with the description of "Bide-a-While," the tuberculosis sanitorium, moved from the end to the middle of the play to signify the doom that Marguerite is so desperately trying to escape. Death and despair thus replaced sex and lost youth as Marguerite's central concerns. The frail victim of consumption was a much more sympathetic figure for the audience than the cynical prostitute would have been.

Don Quixote

Like the other romantic characters, Don Quixote was ennobled in revision, the effect of his appearance changed from comic to magical. There was no Prologue in the production. Williams added the frame plot about Don Quixote falling asleep in the Square to make the published version of the play clearer after a storm of criticism complained about its obscurity in production. In the earlier scripts, Don Quixote first appeared in the final block, when he climbed out of a manhole in the fountain, with Sancho following. After an exchange in which he and Don Quixote argued about whether they were on the Camino Real or the Camino Real, Sancho said it was all the same to him and challenged the old knight to fire him and pay his wages. Then he headed for the Bucket of Blood cantina. In the production, Don Quixote first appeared in a misty light at the top of the stairs leading to Terra Incognita. As he descended the stairs, his glittering helmet with its snowy-white plume became visible above the body of what otherwise might have been taken for any old desert rat, and his lance with its tattered blue pennant came into the audience's view. As he approached the dry fountain, it began to flow, signifying the new life that could arise from romantic hopes for the future.

Gutman

The character of Gutman also changed as the play's meaning changed. In *Ten Blocks* he appears as "The Proprietor," a figure of indifference who knows all about the events on the Camino Real and dispenses information about things even to Kilroy. In this version it is he and not Jacques who tells Kilroy about The Way Out and the laboratory where the "stiffs" are taken. He even has a long existential duet with the player of the blue guitar in Block 3, which ends: "There is a moment when we look into ourselves and ask with a wonder which never is lost altogether: Can this be all? Is this it? Is this what the glittering wheels of the heavens turn for?" (51). In the early versions of the long play, Williams made Gutman more actively evil. He inserted the phone call to the "Generalissimo" which makes it clear that Gutman represents the interests of the wealthy who are in league with the government to oppress the poor. Here Gutman treats the word "brother" as a subversive threat and arranges the Gypsy's festival to distract the people when the Survivor dies. Williams also changed him from indifferent to cruel. He taunts Jacques with the threat of spending his last days shut up in a monastery and Marguerite with the prospect of Bide-a-While. A gross representation of the vices of the wealthy, he is revealed at the beginning of Block 13 dancing drunkenly with Violet (Eva in the final version) and drinking from a magnum of champagne.

As he revised the script, Williams reconceived Gutman's character in some substantial ways. In *Ten Blocks* he had used the guitar player to serve as a master of ceremonies, announcing each block with a chord on his guitar. In early versions of the long play, Williams replaced this with a loudspeaker, which announced each block with the hollow resonance of announcements in airports and railroad stations. As the play moved into rehearsal, Williams replaced the loudspeaker with Gutman as narrator, and changed his character accordingly. Gutman thus became more removed from the other characters, less involved in the action. He no longer argued with Jacques about the state of emergency in the country, or taunted him and Marguerite about their impending doom. His function as existential commentator was also reduced considerably. His long speech about life and death was reduced to the few lines at the beginning of Block 7 in the published version, and he did not explain anything about the Camino Real to the characters, becoming the figure that Marguerite describes as "a fat old man who gives sly hints that only bewilder us more" (63). Thus the indifference of the character in *Ten Blocks* was synthesized with the cruelty of the pre-production version to produce the final character of Gutman.

Intensifying Gutman's presence as the cruelly indifferent deity of the Camino Real, Williams removed him further from the action and had him act as director of the pageant. As Marguerite made her entrance, Williams had Gutman step out of the representational frame and call for a follow-spot on the arch, telling everyone to pick up their cues to meet the "legend" who was about to enter the Plaza. At Kazan's urging to give Gutman's introduction of Marguerite more of a mocking tone, Williams rewrote these lines during rehearsal so that Gutman stepped entirely out of the frame and addressed the audience directly:

Ah, there's the music of another legend, one that everyone knows, the legend of the sentimental whore, the courtesan who made the mistake of love. But now you see her coming into this plaza not as she was when she burned with a fever that cast a thin light over Paris, but changed, yes, faded as lanterns and legends fade when they burn into day! (*He turns and shouts:*) Rosita, sell her a flower! (45)

Gutman's metatheatrical role as "director" was repeated several times throughout the play, a reminder to the audience of the indefinite ontological status of the action on stage. Williams made him master of ceremonies at the Fiesta, for example, and had him use his power as director-deity when Kilroy tried to escape: "GUTMAN: Follow-spot on that gringo, light the stairs! (*The light catches Kilroy.*)" (68). During rehearsals, Williams also placed Gutman outside the frame at the play's ending, having him call for a follow-spot on "the face of the ancient knight" (92) and end the play with his direct address to the audience: "The Curtain Line has been spoken! (*To the wings:*) Bring it down! (*He bows with a fat man's grace as – The curtain falls.*)" (93).

The minor characters

Williams also directed a good deal of attention to the minor characters in revision, carefully defining their symbolic functions in the play and developing them more fully as characters when it seemed appropriate. The figure of the Dreamer, which evolved from the player of the blue guitar in *Ten Blocks*, became a symbolic representation of the romantic poet, whose only poem is the single word, *"Hermano"* (brother). Similarly the Survivor, who merely dies in *Ten Blocks*, after gasping that the fountain is empty, was given the speeches about his horse that articulate his romantic spirit in the long version. Before rehearsals began, Williams also introduced the Bum in the window of the Ritz Men Only as a commentator on the action through his snatches of popular songs or "bop-talk." He also developed the proprietor of the Ritz Men Only into the character A. Ratt.

The minor character who received the most substantial development, however, was La Madrecita, developed from a flower vendor in a snow-white rebozo in *Ten Blocks* – who sells *flores para los muertos* like the flower vendor in *Streetcar* – and turned into "La Madrecita des Las Soledadas" for the Laboratory scene in Block 9 of *Camino Real*. Called "La Ciquecita" in early versions of the long play, this character became the blind woman who cradled the dying Survivor and the dying Kilroy in her arms in the attitude of the *pietà*. Prior to rehearsals, Williams gave her the chanting lines –"Rojo està sol! Rojo està el sol de sangre! Blanca està la luna! Blanca està la luna de miedo!" (25) – after the Dreamer spoke the word *hermano*.[43] While Gutman gave his existential speech at the beginning of Block 7, La Madrecita held up glass beads and shell necklaces, calling "Recuerdos, recuerdos?" ("mementoes") (43). Williams thus prepared the audience carefully for La Madrecita's role as archetypal mother in Block 15, which Kazan called the "antiphonal scene," as she sat with the body of Kilroy across her knees and intoned "this was thy son, America – and now mine . . . Yes, blow wind where night thins – for laurel is not everlasting . . . Keen for him, all maimed creatures, deformed and mutilated – his homeless ghost is your own! . . . Rise, ghost! Go! Go bird! 'Humankind cannot bear very much reality'" (87–88; see plate 8).

Cuts and changes

While Williams was giving the characters more definition, he was making the dialogue more poetic and more oblique. As noted earlier, Gutman's long existential speech was cut considerably. In earlier versions, Jacques's speech to Kilroy about the Laboratory had continued with the statement that romance is what divides men from beasts and brings them close to God, and Jacques's description of himself as a "romantic realist." In keeping with the tendency toward obscuring these direct thematic statements, Williams also deleted Gutman's statement that he was operating a side-show of legendary figures, each of which signified something of "cosmic import" on the Camino Real. Overall, the effect was to produce a more poetic play, one whose meaning was conveyed through plurisignifying visual, kinesic, aural, and linguistic codes rather than through denotative statements, but Williams paid for his indirection with the audience's confusion. As one honest newspaper critic said in his review, "'What is this all about?' I dunno."[44]

As he worked out the scenes with Kazan and the actors during rehearsals, Williams made substantial revisions that were retained in the published version of the script. Block 7 in the published version, the scene with Jacques and Marguerite on the terrace, was only about half the length of the version published when rehearsals began. The carnival scene (67–69) began rehearsals as primarily the scene of the *Fugitivo*'s crash, very close to the way Kazan had described it in his letter. After the blind man's buff scene, the pilot and the navigator came panting into the Plaza, disputing in a foreign tongue. Gutman called for a follow-spot on them, noting that something not on the program had occurred. Under questioning they admitted that the *Fugitivo* had flown without them. A loud distant crash and a crimson flare above the Sierras followed, and the crowd carried the pilot and navigator triumphantly toward the cantina on their shoulders.

On the fourth day of rehearsal, the scene that appears in the published version was substituted, exchanging the action and technical effects of the *Fugitivo* crash for the fuller development of the attraction between Kilroy and Esmeralda. Instead of the crash scene, a speech known to the production staff as the "Winchell bit" was substituted. At the beginning of Block 13, when Gutman is inside with Eva, the loudspeaker glowed, and the unctuous voice of a news commentator was heard announcing the crash of the *Fugitivo*. After the play opened, and it received no particularly kind treatment from Walter Winchell, Williams considered cutting this bit to save time for some speeches he wanted to add to clarify the play's meaning. The only reference to it, or to the *Fugitivo*'s crash, in the published version is Nursie's comment to the Gypsy in Block 12 that she has been scooped by Winchell in announcing the crash. The other substantial change to the script that originated in rehearsal was the elaboration of the chase scene in Block 6 of the published script. This was largely Kazan's doing. As he worked out the scene with its complicated dashes up the aisles and into the boxes of the theatre, Williams supplied the dialogue that punctuated it.

Although Williams's revisions of the script were most sweeping in the weeks just prior to rehearsals and during the first two weeks of the rehearsal period, he continued rewriting throughout the whole process of run-throughs and out-of-town tryouts. Production stage manager Seymour Milbert, who was responsible both for keeping up with Williams's revisions and for recording the movements of the actors in the production script, noted that Williams's changes for the staging of one scene required that the scenery be rebuilt on the third day of rehearsals and that, when Kazan was staging the scenes, Williams and Kazan were constantly finding moments in which to improvise new lines and scenes (Milbert, February 2). As the production moved into its tryout phase, however, the changes became less sweeping, and were focused on more subtle elements of rhetorical style and audience response. The director's notes that were recorded during the run-throughs and the Philadelphia and New Haven tryouts show both Kazan and Williams indicating necessary revisions in the dialogue. Most of these were for rhetorical effects, simply to shorten the length of the speeches, to cut out repetition and what Kazan called "corn," and to make sure the lines had the desired emphasis. The presence of the audience also helped to determine which lines simply weren't working and which ones the audience found vulgar or offensive.

Williams cut Marguerite's long speech to Jacques in Block 10 in half, deleting the lines from "What are we sure of?" to "Or under that ominous arch into Terra Incognita" (63). Kazan also asked whether Jacques's long "formaldehyde speech" (36) – the description of what happened after the Streetcleaners took someone away – which Williams had lengthened considerably from the previous version of the script, could not be shortened. Williams disagreed, however, and the speech remained as it was. A week later, Kazan asked Williams to add a line to the speech, noting that it should end with the thought that only the poor were treated this way.[45] In response, Williams added the lines, "There is a charge of admission to this museum. The proceeds go to the maintenance of the military police" (36). Williams also made notes to himself to make revisions as the rehearsals proceeded, often for subtle rhetorical reasons, such as changing the line about "fading legends" in Esmeralda's prayer (91) because the word "country" appeared twice in the speech.

In the interest of avoiding "corn," Kazan cut the Gypsy's line "Fly away on the magic carpet of dreams" (91) as she puts Esmeralda to bed in Block 16, her line "The Camino Real is a funny paper read backwards" (72), and Kilroy's line "I have ideals" (28) when he refuses the prostitute Rosita. He also asked Williams to cut out as much "corny comedy" as possible in the transition from operating table to dance to prayer in Blocks 15 and 16.

Vulgarity or fear of offending the audience was a major concern, not only for Kazan and Williams, but particularly for the producers, who were somewhat nervous about this unorthodox play. Crawford's assistant Ethel Reiner thought that Marguerite's whole speech about the camellias and their reference to her menstrual cycle (45) should be cut because they would be embarrassing to the audience. Williams made a note to himself to change the Bum's line "Boatload of Mother-lovers," noting that it might be offensive, and two days later Kazan cut Marguerite's line, "Don't give me that Dago talk!" in response to Jacques's "Forse, forse, non so!" (57), because it was offensive to the audience and not in keeping with the softer character they had been developing for Marguerite. Kazan also suggested that Williams change Gutman's line "A crown of horns!" in the King of the Cuckolds scene (66) and cut Esmeralda's line "as long as they don't bring the Pope over here and put him in the White House" and the word "God" from the seduction scene (76). Williams had changed the pail of water the Gypsy doused Kilroy with in Block 16 to a slop jar in his preliminary script, but it was changed to a dishpan during rehearsals. These were minor changes, but they were part of an overall effort to reduce gratuitous alienation of a bourgeois Broadway audience that playwright and director hoped to bring into empathy with Williams's Bohemian characters.

Williams was also called upon to come up with new lines as the rehearsal process revealed the need. Kazan was particularly concerned that he come up with "a better gag" for Kilroy's line to A. Ratt in Block 6: "I been in countries where money was not legal tender. I mean it was legal but it wasn't tender" (38). Kazan made his request on March 4 and repeated it on March 12, but Williams either liked the joke or was not able to think of a substitute; it stayed in the script. Williams did, however, take Kazan's suggestion for Gutman's order for Kilroy to put on the patsy suit at the end of the chase scene. At Kazan's request, Williams also added two lines for Gutman in Block 5 and more farewell remarks for Kilroy in Block 11. The revision of the script during the rehearsals and tryouts was clearly a collaborative affair, with suggestions arising from Kazan, from Williams, and even from producers and actors. But it is also clear that the final word on dialogue was Williams's.

Directing the rehearsal process

The undisputed authority over the production itself was Elia Kazan. That he was treated with a marked deference even by the producers was evident from the ceremonial first reading when the cast gathered with the production's "brass" in front of the press to begin its work. An interesting sense of the pecking order from the production staff's viewpoint emerges from stage manager Seymour Milbert's description of that first day:

Tennessee Williams arrived. Walter Chrysler Jr. The Lieblings [Audrey Wood and her husband William Liebling], he as dour and inscrutable as ever: there as Williams' play agent. Kazan enters. A small hush. People start to settle. He flings off his over-coat and strides to the center table. Greets some of the people. His air is one of unusual power, concentrated force, directness. Directness over everything: there is no latitude for anything but the most simple and meaningful communication. (Milbert, January 29)

Allowing for the hyperbole of an admiring young stage manager, this description clearly suggests that Kazan was the center of the production, and his position was confirmed proxemically when, sitting at the center of the center table with Williams on one side and choreographer Anna Sokolow on the other, he delivered his opening remarks to the cast. In good Method style, Kazan told the actors to read simply, talking directly to the actor to whom the lines were addressed, and not to try to give a performance. When called upon to address the audience, he told the actors, find one person in it and talk to him. He also set the stage for his Method treatment of this poetic fantasy: "This is a profound, emotionally charged play, with philosophically written lines, and poetry. Treat the philosophy and the poetry with reality, as simply meaning" (Milbert, January 29).

When the company returned for the second reading that afternoon, "the brass" had left, and Kazan was together with Williams, the actors, and the production staff. Milbert noted that no producer was welcome in the theatre at any time, particularly during rehearsals, and although it was part of his job to convey the ideas of Cheryl Crawford and Ethel Reiner to Kazan, neither of the producers had any significant influence over the play's artistic development. Kazan did collaborate fully with the rest of the production staff as well as Williams, however, and he gave a surprising degree of freedom and authority to Anna Sokolow, who was to direct the dance-like movement of the street people. This movement was to serve as a constant kinesic and visual environment for the main action of the play, providing the pace and tempo of life on the Camino Real as well as the mood that Kazan hoped to derive from their visual model for the play, Mexican artist José Guadalupe Posada. In the four weeks of rehearsal time available to them, it would have been impossible for Kazan alone to achieve the stylized movement that he hoped for from his chorus of street people and still elicit effective performances from his largely Method-trained cast, unfamiliar as they were with the acting demands of non-realistic plays.

Milbert noted that he had never seen such a delegation of responsibility to a co-worker as Kazan's to Anna Sokolow. Sokolow directed the street people in all of the large crowd scenes, the crucial *Fugitivo* and fiesta scenes, and the parts of scenes calling for stylization and movement to music by the crowd. Meanwhile Kazan was "revealing the life and meaning of the play, coaching the actors, creating the mood and spirit of it. Controlling the 'ham' in the actor, restraining him until his own creative processes reveal[ed] the true life of the play" (Milbert, January 31).

While Sokolow rehearsed the street people on the stage, Kazan was up on the mezzanine having intense, private sessions with individual actors, or rehearsing scenes with two or three principal actors. Meanwhile, Williams was in one of the aisles with his typewriter turning out revisions, some of which were suggested by Kazan's meeting with the actors upstairs. On the third day of rehearsals, for example, Kazan began the morning with a private session with Jo Van Fleet, who played Marguerite, while Sokolow rehearsed the street people for the Survivor scene. Then everyone came together as Kazan rehearsed the whole company in the Survivor and *Fugitivo* scenes. Kazan began the afternoon with Hurd Hatfield, who played Lord Byron, and then Van Fleet and Joseph Anthony – Marguerite and Casanova. Meanwhile Sokolow rehearsed the street people for the Fiesta scene. Then Kazan worked with groups of the principal actors on the seduction scene and the Baron scene, and then with Eli Wallach alone on the character of Kilroy. While this was going on around him, Williams was rewriting the whole Gypsy scene, the second half of Block 11 in the published version, which was given to the actors the next day.

As Kazan saw it, his major work during the early days of the rehearsal period was to communicate his concept of the play to the actors, to establish the overall approach that would unify all of their efforts into a meaningful realization of Williams's play. The Stanislavskian background that Kazan shared with most of the actors made for a unique interpretation of Williams's poetic play. In the tradition of the Group Theatre, he developed a style for the play that would help to integrate their efforts. He recalled his approach in an interview twenty years later:

I tried to produce *Camino Real* in the style of the Mexican-Indian figures of death, the candy skulls and the little wooden, dancing skeletons; I took a lot from a Mexican artist named Posada who is a sort of primitive and influenced Diego Rivera a lot; and I used some of his works, like his dance of death. Williams approved of all this.[46]

In rehearsal, however, Kazan also worked with the reality of Mexican life. He brought out photographic histories and scenes of life in Central America for Sokolow and the actors so they could work on appropriate bodily movements, attitudes, and costumes. It was the juxtaposition of realism and fantasy that gave the production its unique aesthetic character.

Actors

In a similarly delicate balance with the stylized fantasy of the crowd scenes and the carefully choreographed movement of all the actors was a psychologically realistic approach to the acting of the roles, based on the orthodox Method principles of identification with the role, the honest expression of emotions derived from the actor's own experience, and communication among the actors on stage. When Kazan talked to the actors about the meaning of fantasy on the first day of rehearsal, he told them to play simply, to avoid being sententious or philosophical. As he had in *Streetcar*, he avoided making any suggestion to the actors that the play should be stylized. He helped them to develop their roles just as he would in any realistic play.

For each scene, Kazan made sure the actors understood the "spines" of their characters as he conceived them, and he worked at getting them to feel the motivations for all of the characters' behavior. Thus, he told the street people in the first scene that they were engaged in a desperate struggle for existence. They had no time to feel sorry for themselves, much less the Survivor when he died in front of them. To Frank Silvera he emphasized the spine of Gutman's character. As the owner of the hotel, he was the only one of the characters who was free from the physical struggle for existence. His job was to keep the hotel running smoothly. This formed the primary motive for the brisk pace at which he introduced each Block and moved the action along – Gutman's desire was to keep things going. As a businessman whose only concern was his business, Gutman's attitude was to be a distillation of matter-of-factness. Similarly, his mirror image A. Ratt, the proprietor of the flophouse, was simply Gutman without money. He was to be completely blasé about the events in his hotel, complying with the Baron's request for an iron bed with chains with the same insouciance with which he filled a bed immediately after one of his guests had died in it. These things happened every day. His desire was to keep his business running smoothly.

Kazan used his own experience to explain the determination with which the Loan Shark tried to persuade Kilroy to hock his golden gloves. Telling him about the indignant cry of "Bring out the books!" whenever a customer faltered on a sale in his father's carpet business, Kazan explained to actor Salem Ludwig: "Yours is the honest indignation [of] all, *all* businessmen who can't understand why he won't sell. Your mind is made up – he *owes* you those gloves – what right has he to keep them? Your business is bad – your rent is high – he has *got* to sell them to you" (Milbert, January 30).

Kazan explained to Wallach that Kilroy's primary motivations throughout the first act were his fear and his strong sense of justice. He asked Wallach if he had ever been in a strange town with no money in his pocket, and reminded him that in some southern states a man who was picked up for vagrancy was put in a chain gang for six months. He asked Wallach to concentrate on this fear. Competing with his fear was Kilroy's sense of justice. It was this, Kazan said, that made Kilroy so angry about having his wallet stolen. He really expects the others to feel the same outrage that he does. In discussing the Festival scene, when Kilroy is made the Chosen Hero and Esmeralda keeps calling him "Champ," Kazan reminded Wallach that Kilroy was a prize fighter. The excitement of the chase and Esmeralda's shouts could bring him back to the old days of his triumph when people wanted his autograph and bought him drinks in all the bars on Eighth Avenue. This could make him feel that he really might begin to live again.

Kazan developed a whole history for Esmeralda to bring her up to the moment of the fiesta when she tries to break out and go after Kilroy in search of freedom. Kazan told Barbara Baxley that she was a prisoner at the Gypsy's, and Nursie was her guard. Esmeralda was not really the Gypsy's daughter, but someone she had found as a child and raised "in the business." Kazan told her about young girls he had seen in Munich the summer before, who offered themselves to Americans for money. They were not really prostitutes, he said, "They're just kids, they want some fun, some joy, some escape from confinement, and what do they get? There is no fun for them. So they sell themselves. It's really very tragic" (Milbert, February 1). It was this sense of confinement that Esmeralda was fighting when she tried to break away and go after Kilroy, Kazan said, and he told Baxley to fight hard to get away, to kick at Nursie, desperate to escape.

For Jennie Goldstein, who played the Gypsy, Kazan domesticated the role, putting it in terms of the Jewish mother that Goldstein, a veteran of the Yiddish theatre, knew well. He asked her to imagine how she would feel if she were a Jewish mother whose daughter had not only married a "Goy," but a real bum, a bum from the South. This was how she should feel when Esmeralda picked Kilroy for the Chosen Hero. But the Gypsy is a business woman, and, disgusted as she is, she decides that "business is business, so what the hell" (Milbert, February 1).

As he worked on encoding the play's meaning kinesically and vocally, Kazan aimed at a consistent development of the germs he had provided for each of the characters. The Gypsy was to combine the hardened practicality of the "business is business" approach to life she shared with Gutman, A. Ratt, and the Loan Shark with a gross sexuality and a flair for the dramatic that produced moments of grotesque comedy. When she tried for a moment to seduce Kilroy, beginning with the line, "Have you ever been attracted by an older woman" (72), she was to be "truly lecherous, a sagging, down to earth, dirty, dirty approach" (Milbert, February 1). When she went to change her money at Walgreen's, Kazan wanted her to go out with a lecherous walk. Trying this in rehearsal, Goldstein came out with a few bars of "Give 'em a Tango" as she moved. Kazan, sensing the rightness of this touch, insisted that she sing both when she exited and when she returned at the end of the scene.

Kazan also worked with Barbara Baxley to encode the subtext of Esmeralda's lines in the seduction scene with Kilroy. Telling her that she should be working "against, and 'beneath' the meaning of her lines" in the scene, he emphasized that all of her effort should really be directed at seducing Kilroy (Milbert, February 1). Together they worked out a scene in which Baxley delivered her lines about the stabilization of currency, the dialectics of the class struggle, and the "Bolsheviskies" while doing a kind of belly dance. This gave a whole new play of significance to Kilroy's line, "This is not what I mean by a quiet conversation" (76).

The scenic environment

While he was drawing felt emotions and carefully developed realistic motives out of his actors, Kazan was also staging the scenic environment that would provide the play's fantastic stylization. Given Ayers's realistic set, the fantasy had to be encoded through movement, costume, make-up, and the incidents that surrounded the characters. To signify fantasy as the production began, Kazan had three life-sized dolls seated at one of the tables in front of the Siete Mares as the curtain went up. One of the actresses was to emerge from the hotel and talk to one of these figures as Gutman announced "Block One on the Camino Real," setting the stage for the arrival of the Survivor. As the scene of the Survivor's death went on, the two sides of the street were to encode contrasting visual representations of life on the Camino Real. The hotel guests, holding cocktail glasses and occasionally commenting to each other on the action, would peer out at the disturbance from behind the curtains. The street people were to use their garments as protection, watching the action from behind rebozos, shawls, and hats, and providing the background for the stylized movements of La Madrecita and the Dreamer. Through costume, kinesics, and pictorial composition, the existential condition of the Camino Real was thus encoded: the rich and the poor watching from opposite sides of the street the doom they know will be theirs, but, with the exception of the dreamy poet and the blind mother, too concerned with their own efforts at escaping their common fate to express their common humanity by helping the dying man. Kazan used the "human environment" to signify the qualities of universal fear and universal indifference throughout the play, a reminder of the life the romantic outcasts are trying to escape.

Kazan continued to work with the actors on developing their characters throughout the period of the run-throughs and the out-of-town tryouts. Some required a good deal more help than others, for, as Kazan admitted in his autobiography, some of the actors he had cast from the Studio simply were not up to the demands of their parts.[47] The director worked just as hard to develop and deepen the characterizations of the major actors as he did to draw credible performances from the weaker ones, however. Frank Silvera, for example, had a tendency to play Gutman a little more vulgarly than Kazan thought the suave hotel owner should be played. Kazan told Silvera not to "fan his parts" in Block 5 and to make his grunt when he was upstairs with Eva less vulgar (Notes, Feb. 21). He also tried to get Silvera to give Gutman a little more range of feeling, noting that he should make the announcement of Block 15, after Kilroy's death, slowly and gently, and that he should show more compassion in his announcement of Block 9, after Marguerite has missed the *Fugitivo*.

Because of his intention to use Kilroy as a sympathetic subjective presence interposed between the Camino Real and the audience, Kazan stressed throughout the rehearsal period that it was important for Kilroy to maintain contact with the audience outside the fourth-wall illusion. Thus he added more asides and direct appeals than were planned originally. After the line about having ideals was cut from his refusal of Rosita, Wallach was told to smile a "no thanks" at her and then "look rather dolefully at audience . . . Oh my God, did you ever see such an awful . . ." (Notes, March 13). He was also told to make his line about having a heart as big as the head of a baby in his first long speech an aside to the audience and to act as if the idea of hocking his "Champ" belt rather than his golden gloves was the suggestion of someone in the audience. Later, when A. Ratt said the bed in Number 7 was free after its occupant had died, Kilroy was to look at the audience, sharing its reaction. During the seduction scene, he was to turn and look at the audience as Esmeralda made her speech about the monetary system, but he was told not to break the fourth-wall illusion on the "I am sincere" speech, keeping his attention on Esmeralda and the audience's attention on believing momentarily in young love. In short Kazan made sure that Kilroy maintained a carefully calibrated intersubjective relationship with the audience throughout the play without sacrificing the representational character of the performance.

Kazan demanded similarly careful control from the Gypsy and Esmeralda. He made use of every opportunity to convey the Gypsy's cool-headed self-interest and hypocrisy beneath her clowning. During Block 2, for example, as she announced the fiesta that would restore her daughter's virginity, the Gypsy was to speak very sweetly into the microphone and very nastily to Esmeralda. The problem for Esmeralda was controlling her sexuality, making it apparent enough that the audience could under-stand Kilroy's weakness in the seduction scene, yet not so grossly explicit as to alienate the Broadway audience. Kazan warned Barbara Baxley that her opening dance in Block 11 might be too vulgar, but he told her to put her hand in her crotch in Block 12.

Kazan also paid careful attention to the statements that were being encoded pictorially and kinesically. Although Anna Sokolow staged the scenes with the street people, Kazan watched them closely during run-throughs and made notes for her on specific details. He noted, for example, that the street people did not seem hungry enough in Block 2 because they weren't fighting hard enough for the coins Kilroy flings to them. He urged Sokolow to choreograph a little dance for the Skid Row people's entrance to music in Block 3. He also made suggestions about specific details of their movement, such as the timing of their looking to the right and left when Gutman announced the fiesta. Kazan also left the actual choreography to Sokolow and did not override her final decisions, but he took an active role in collaborating with her.

Kazan worried over other aspects of movement and composition himself. One point of concern was Esmeralda's entrance. At first he planned to have Esmeralda enter from the cantina in the first Block, before the Survivor appeared, and cross the stage, preparing the audience for her image when the Gypsy announced the fiesta. He was concerned that this entrance slowed down the tempo, however, and he thought about cutting it on February 24. The next day, still not sure whether this was the best thing to do, he decided to discuss the entrance with Williams. On February 26, the entrance was cut. At this point Kazan also had Kilroy kneel down when Esmeralda said her prayer, intensifying the meaning of Williams's words pictorially.

On March 9, Kazan was working carefully to refine his pictorial compositions, noting for example that the "Esmeralda group" should be further center stage for the "We're caught picture" in Block 5 and reminding himself to "set" this scenic image the next day (Notes, March 9; see plate 9). He also made a note to take one of the street people out of the "Abdullah–Jacques picture" in Block 6. Always an extremely visual director, Kazan was particularly concerned about the pictorial code in *Camino Real*, for, with Sokolow's choreographed movement, it carried the main burden of signification of the fantastic that was crucial to the realization of Williams's vision on the stage. Without its juxtaposition with the psychological realism of the acting and the heavy visual realism of Ayers's set, Williams's existential poetry would be only half realized.

Equally important to the production was the pacing of the action. It was the relentless and climactic pace Kazan maintained that was considered the strongest element of his signature on Broadway during the late forties and early fifties. In Eric Bentley's somewhat unflattering estimation,

Mr. Kazan goes to work on the actors' nerves like an egg beater. His orgasmic organization of scenes has become a mannerism time after time, the slow to-and-fro of dialogue works itself up to the frenetic climax. Yet it's no use knowing he is not a good director unless you can also see that he is almost a great one.[48]

While Bentley was overstating this effect, there is no doubt that pacing, tempo, rhythm, tension, and suspense were crucial to any Kazan production. In the rehearsals for *Camino Real*, the director was concerned mainly about keeping things moving quickly, particularly in the first Block. This was why he cut Esmeralda's first entrance, and it was the basis for much of his extensive work with the Survivor scene. To gain some sense of urgency in the long conversation between Jacques and Marguerite (Block 7 in the published version), Kazan went over the whole scene, carefully overlapping the speeches. He did the same thing with La Madrecita's speeches in the "antiphonal scene," Block 15.

The playwright at rehearsal

Williams took an active interest in the shaping of the production throughout the rehearsal period, making notes freely on every aspect. His primary interest, of course, was the dialogue, making sure that the actors said the lines correctly and clearly. He was particularly concerned about the Survivor's "pony speech" and about specific lines that actors had a tendency to transpose, such as the Baron's line, "Nothing in this community does much good" (34), which he corrected several times. He was also concerned about the interpretive function of the actors' intonation of the lines. He noted, for example, that Lord Byron said the words "passion for declivity" in the same tone as what preceded and followed this phrase, noting that it should be marked by some difference in tone. He also disapproved of the way the "Winchell bit" was being delivered, noting that it didn't come across as a news broadcast because it was lost in "the rhubarb" of the fiesta and that the news commentator did not have the proper air of mystery about him (Notes, February 21).

Williams was intensely interested in the other elements of the stage language as well, and he expressed his opinion about them freely. As always, the lighting was a particular concern for him. He made specific criticisms, such as that the lighting on Don Quixote before he stepped into his spotlight was too dark; that the color for the *pêche flambeau* the Mulligans have was not the right shade of blue; and that the light on the screens in the scene on the terrace made them look too white. Williams was equally specific about things like pace and gesture. He noted that there was an unnatural silence after Jacques's line, "What is [this]?" (66) before he was crowned King of the Cuckolds, commenting that the action should be continuous there. He also commented that Jacques and Marguerite held their kiss too long and cautioned Kilroy always to obscure his heart with his hands in Block 16 so that it would never be plainly visible to the audience. Although they were small matters in themselves, Williams was aware that each of these elements encoded his play's meaning, and for that reason they were significant.

The response

Everyone involved in the production of *Camino Real* was aware of the battle it faced in getting the public and the critics to understand and accept the play. Throughout the tryout period, Kazan assigned an assistant to circulate during intermission and report to him on the complaints and confusions of the audience. Several revisions were made to clarify cloudy issues and make the audience more comfortable, but three recurring "big questions" signified the audience's essential unwillingness to accept a play that did not have a logical one-to-one correspondence with a recognizable reality: Where is this? When is this? How did they get there and where do they want to go if they don't even know where they are? (Notes, [March 2]). Williams and Kazan worked hard to prepare both critics and public for the play through interviews and newspaper articles, and Williams even gave a lecture at the Yale School of Drama before the New Haven tryout, but their efforts were unsuccessful.[49] The reviews of *Camino Real* were devastating to Williams, rejecting the play as pretentious, self-indulgent, and incoherent. But the critics who condemned the play had almost unanimous praise for Kazan's direction, Ayers's design, and the actors' work. Ironically, Ayers's set, the most disruptive element in this collaborative effort, received the highest praise for introducing a note of realism into what was seen as Williams's bleakly chaotic world.

Williams tried desperately to save his play, the most personal statement he had yet brought to the stage. He wrote to some of the critics, trying to explain the play to them,[50] and he revised it substantially after it opened on Broadway. On March 31, twelve days after *Camino Real*'s New York opening, Williams told Cheryl Crawford that he was working on a prologue in which Don Quixote arrived down an aisle of the theatre and that he was putting in a ghostly chase scene, almost all in Kilroy's mind, to echo the climactic chase in Block 6 and pick up the action in the final Block. He was hoping to make these changes in the Broadway production and make up for the increased time by cutting the "Winchell bit," and some other unsuccessful lines.[51] Of course this was never done in the Broadway production, but the published script contains the play as revised, with the Don Quixote prologue fully developed to provide a frame for the action, now a "dream play." He also added a new Block 1, in which the characters Prudence and Olympe prepare for Marguerite's entrance, and revised a good deal of the dialogue, notably Esmeralda's prayer.

In June Williams wrote to Brooks Atkinson that he realized the play would not continue much longer, wistfully repeating the thought he had expressed in the Afterword he had written for the play a few days earlier:

> A book is only the shadow of a play and not even a clear shadow of it . . . The printed script of a play is hardly more than an architect's blueprint of a house not yet built or built and destroyed. The color, the grace and levitation, the structural pattern in motion, the quick interplay of live beings, suspended like fitful lightning in a cloud, these things are the play, not words on paper, nor thought and ideas of an author, those shabby things snatched off basement counters at Gimbel's. (8)

Williams also managed to be philosophical about the experience, noting the value of his artistic collaboration with Kazan and the unique spiritual bond that it had created between them. Never once in the two years it had taken to plan and execute the production, nor in the difficult time after it, did either collaborator disappoint or betray the other's faith, he wrote, a truly remarkable thing in the theatre as he knew it.[52]

Despite Williams's initial blow-up over the revision of the script, the production of *Camino Real* marked the point at which Tennessee Williams and Elia Kazan were most closely in tune, both artistically and personally. Williams dedicated the play to Kazan. Kazan has written that he felt especially close to Williams during this time because of his unwavering support after the House Un-American Activities Committee (HUAC) Hearings, when so many of Kazan's old friends turned away. As a result of his sudden demise as the fair-haired boy of Broadway, Kazan also found a deeper understanding of Williams in his role as Bohemian, homosexual, outsider. The two were united both in their mutual understanding and admiration and in the values they shared with each other, values they had tried to express in *Camino Real*.

One of the irritants that was to test this close alliance over the next few years began with Eric Bentley's review of the play. There he presented Kazan's collaboration with Williams in the light most calculated to offend the playwright:

We are told that Mr. Kazan was virtually co-author of *A Streetcar Named Desire* and *Death of a Salesman* even to the extent of changing the character of the leading persons; it is arguable that both plays would have failed without his changes. Still, in these cases, he had to regard a play as a mold into which his ideas could be poured. In *Camino Real* it all looks the other way round. The production seems to be the mold, the script to be fluid.[53]

Knowing Williams's sensitivity on this point, Kazan sent Bentley "a friendly but firm note . . . stating that he had not written one line either of *Streetcar* or *Salesman*."[54]

Williams apparently did not see the review, learning of Bentley's statement only when it was reprinted the next year in *The Dramatic Event*. At this point, Williams drafted a letter in reply to Bentley's statement, angrily affirming Kazan's protest and reasserting that *Streetcar* contained no word not written by Tennessee Williams. He added that the play's interpretation on the stage could not possibly have been more completely the interpretation that the author had intended.[55] In the letter, Williams wrote that the functions of direction and writing in the theatre were wedded, and that when the work was right, they were consummated in the wedding with a "passionate rightness" that was rarely equalled in the relations between two people. Following the letter was a statement intended to be signed by Williams, Miller, and possibly Kazan, denying Bentley's allegation and deploring his irresponsibility in printing it, even with the disclaimer he had appended in a chapter entitled "After-thoughts," where he recorded Kazan's protest, and countered,

I take it Mr. Kazan includes under the heading of authorship only the dialogue. But it seems to me that if a director helps to create the very idea of a character – changing it from what it was in the author's original script – he is co-author – even though the creation and changing has been done without recourse to the dialogue. Dialogue after all is only one of a playwright's means of communication.[56]

The fact that Bentley was stating one of the central principles of what Williams called "the plastic theatre" may be partly responsible for the passion in Williams's response. While he did write every word of the dialogue, he also believed that words were only one of a playwright's means of communication, and he was fully aware that Kazan had encoded a great deal of the play's meaning in the language of the stage. Williams may have been particularly sensitive to Bentley's charge because at some level he felt that it was true. The question was at what level did collaboration become co-authorship? At what point did the author no longer own his play? In 1954 Williams was angrily asserting that *Streetcar* belonged to *him*, and Kazan was supporting his statement fully. Over the next few years, however, this relationship was to see some changes.

1. Irene Selznick, Elia Kazan, and Tennessee Williams at the opening rehearsal for *Streetcar*.

2. Peg Hillias as Eunice, Kim Hunter as Stella, Marlon Brando as Stanley, Karl Malden as Mitch, Ann Dere as Nurse, Rudy Bond as Steve, Nick Dennis as Pablo, Jessica Tandy as Blanche, and Richard Garrick as Doctor in the final scene of *Streetcar*, showing Jo Mielziner's use of scrims and spotlights to achieve the effect of subjective realism.

3. Marlon Brando as Stanley, Kim Hunter as Stella, and Jessica Tandy as Blanche in scene 2 of *Streetcar*.

4. Marlon Brando as Stanley, Jessica Tandy as Blanche, and Kim Hunter as Stella in the birthday-party Scene from *Streetcar*. Stanley is about to smash the crockery as Stella grips the table.

5. Marlon Brando as Stanley and Jessica Tandy as Blanche in scene 10 of *Streetcar*. Preliminary to the rape, Stanley violates Blanche by grabbing at her costume.

6. Karl Malden as Mitch and Jessica Tandy as Blanche in scene 6 of *Streetcar*.
Mitch holds the Raggedy Andy doll he has won at the amusement park.

7. The festival scene from *Camino Real*, showing Lemuel Ayer's set as well as the movement choreographed by Anna Sokolow for the crowd.

8. The pietà image. Vivian Nathan as La Madrecita and Eli Wallach as Kilroy in Block 15 of *Camino Real*.

9. William Lennard as the Second Officer, Eli Wallach as Kilroy, Henry Silva as the First Officer, Ernesto Gonzalez as Abdullah, Jennie Goldstein as The Gypsy, Barbara Baxley as Esmeralda, Salem Ludwig as Nursie, and Frank Silvera as Gutman in the "We're Caught" scene from *Camino Real*.

10. Burl Ives as Big Daddy, Barbara Bel Geddes as Maggie in *Cat*. Big Daddy probes Maggie's body for signs of life in Act 3.

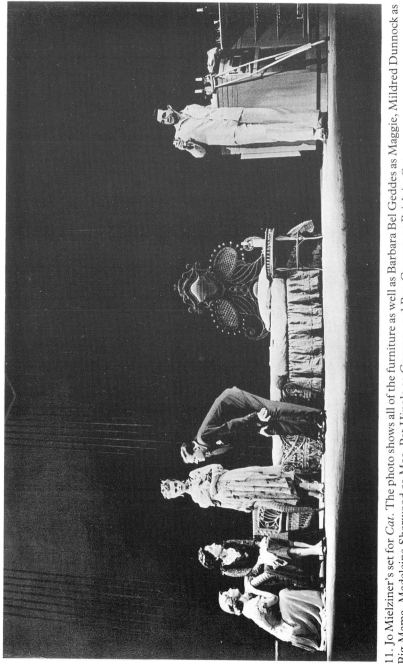

11. Jo Mielziner's set for *Cat*. The photo shows all of the furniture as well as Barbara Bel Geddes as Maggie, Mildred Dunnock as Big Mama, Madeleine Sherwood as Mae, Pat Hingle as Gooper, and Ben Gazzara as Brick in *Cat*.

12. Ben Gazzara as Brick stumbles into the arms of Burl Ives as Big Daddy in *Cat*.

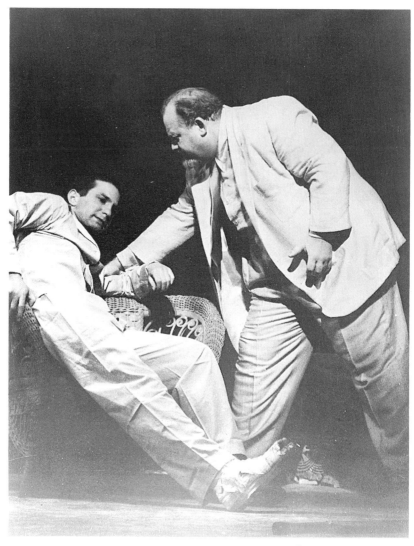

13. Ben Gazzara as Brick struggles to get up out of the chair, while Burl Ives as Big Daddy pushes him back down in Act 2 of *Cat*.

14. Mae leads the No-Neck Monsters in singing to Big Daddy in Act 2 of *Cat*. Madeleine Sherwood as Mae, Burl Ives as Big Daddy, Fred Stewart as Reverend Tooker, Pauline Hahn as Dixie, Darryl Richard as Buster, Seth Edwards as Sonny, Janice Dunn as Trixie, and Mildred Dunnock as Big Mama.

15. Barbara Bel Geddes as Maggie kneels before Burl Ives as Big Daddy in Act 3 of *Cat*.

16. Joe Mielziner's set for the final scene of *Sweet Bird*. Geraldine Page as The Princess, Paul Newman as Chance, Logan Ramsey as George Scudder, John Napier as Hatcher, Duke Farley, Ron Harper, and Kenneth Blake as the Men in Bar, Charles McDaniel as Scotty, James Jeter as Bud, Madeleine Sherwood as Miss Lucy, Charles Tyner as The Heckler, Rip Torn as Tom Junior, Diana Hyland as Heavenly, Sidney Blackmer as Boss Finley, Bruce Dern as Stuff, Monica May as Violet, Hilda Brawner as Edna.

17. The bar scene in *Sweet Bird*, showing Mielziner's use of lighting in combination with Kazan's composition. Madeleine Sherwood as Miss Lucy, Paul Newman as Chance, Charles McDaniel as Scotty.

18. Paul Newman as Chance crouches by the phone while Geraldine Page as the Princess looks on disdainfully in Act 3 of *Sweet Bird*.

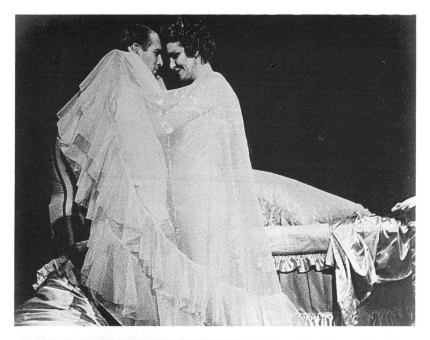

19. Geraldine Page as the Princess spreads her pink butterfly wings over Paul Newman as Chance in Act 1 of *Sweet Bird*.

20. Geraldine Page as the Princess takes a dominant position to Paul Newman as Chance in Act 1 of *Sweet Bird*.

21. Sidney Blackmer as Boss Finley makes a threatening gesture toward Diana Hyland as Heavenly in Act 2, scene 1 of *Sweet Bird*.

4 Presentation and representation: *Cat on a Hot Tin Roof*

In the spring and summer of 1954, Tennessee Williams was trying to interest Elia Kazan in directing a revised version of the hapless *Battle of Angles* called *Orpheus Descending*. He had received some indication of interest from Joseph Mankiewicz, a greatly respected director, but Williams naturally preferred to have Kazan if he could get him. Kazan, having survived the HUAC hearings and the personal anguish that attended them, had accomplished three of his most substantial directorial achievements in the year since *Camino Real* – *Tea and Sympathy*, *On the Waterfront*, and *East of Eden* – the last of which he was going to California to finish in mid September. He told Williams that, for the first time in his life, he felt "quite exhausted. Out of gas. (petrol) No gissum left. Also rather discouraged."[1] He felt that *East of Eden* had not turned out as well as it should have and that he was repeating himself artistically. More fundamentally he felt that he was in a state of depression that kept him from getting up the necessary enthusiasm to start any new project. Essentially he told Williams that if Joseph Mankiewicz was enthusiastic about doing *Orpheus*, Williams should go ahead and give it to him.

Orpheus Descending was eventually directed neither by Kazan nor by Mankiewicz, but by Harold Clurman, and not until 1957. In the meantime, Williams managed to engage Kazan's interest in directing a play about which he had solicited and received the director's advice early in the spring. The play, variously called "A Place of Stone," "The Richest Land This Side of the Valley Nile," and "Cat on a Hot Tin Roof," had grown in Williams's imagination from a short story he had published in 1952 and an old clipping from a small-town Mississippi newspaper. The clipping, still tipped into an early version of the script, contains a portrait photograph of G. D. Perry, his substantial wife, and their nine children, five of them big strapping boys with short necks. The story reads as follows:

> From Manager to Owner of 7,400 Acres in Tunica
> G. D. Perry and family of Hollywood, Miss. Mr. Perry has just closed a deal for one-half interest in the Duke Plantation which consists of 14,800 acres. This gives

97

him 7,400 acres in Tunica County, Miss. He and his wife were reared in Tennessee. He is the son of Marshall Perry, formerly of Madison County, and grandson of Col. G. W. Day of Humboldt. His wife was Miss Sallie Jett Whitley of Mason, Tenn., at which place they were married in 1897. He went to the delta in 1900 as manager for B. F. Duke, better known as Tobe Duke, on this plantation which he has just closed the deal for. He managed for Duke 12 years. After Duke's death he leased this plantation and bought the plantation of W. M. Johnson and C. A. Bar[missing] both of Memphis. Mr. and Mrs. Perry have nine fine children.[2]

From this germ had come Big Daddy and Big Mama, Mae and Gooper's "no-neck monsters," and 28,000 acres of the richest land this side of the Valley Nile. The Maggie–Brick story had its beginnings in Williams's short story, "Three Players of a Summer Game," although the character of Maggie evolved considerably from that of Margaret in "Three Players" – a young Southern woman who became more vigorous, more domineering, and more castrating as her husband simultaneously drank himself into helplessness and failed to extricate himself from his wife's dominance through an affair with a young widow.

The third act controversy

Like any Williams play, *Cat on a Hot Tin Roof* went through many transformations before it reached the stage. What has made its case unusual to critics and scholars was that Williams chose to reveal part of the process through which it was developed when he published the reading version of the play in 1955. As is well known, the reading version contains two third acts, what Williams called the "Broadway Version" taken directly from the stage manager's prompt book with stage directions – such as *"Margaret turns R to door, Gooper XLC a bit"*[3] – just as they were recorded for the actors, and an earlier version of the third act. In a "Note of Explanation" that introduced the "Broadway Version," Williams went out of his way to explain how helpful Kazan's advice had been to him over the years. At the same time, he intimated that the changes he had felt forced to make in order to have Kazan direct *Cat on a Hot Tin Roof* had violated his sense of artistic integrity. Noting the dangers that the influence of "a powerful and highly imaginative director" could have upon the development of a play, before and during production, Williams asserted that "Elia Kazan and I have enjoyed the advantages and avoided the dangers of this highly explosive relationship because of the deepest mutual respect for each other's creative function: we have worked together three times with a phenomenal absence of friction between us and each occasion has increased the trust" (RV 124).

Williams went on to list the three major reservations Kazan had communicated to him in his initial letter about the first typed draft that had been shown him: that Big Daddy was too important a character to disappear from the play after Act 2, that Brick should undergo some change as a result of his conversation with Big Daddy in Act 2, and that Maggie should be more sympathetic to the audience (RV 125). In his note, Williams maintained that, while he had embraced the suggestion about Maggie enthusiastically, he had not agreed with the other two: "I didn't want Big Daddy to reappear in Act Three and I felt that the moral paralysis of Brick was a root thing in his tragedy, and to show a dramatic progression would obscure the meaning of that tragedy in him and because I don't believe that a conversation, however revelatory, ever effects so immediate a change in the heart or even conduct of a person in Brick's state of spiritual disrepair" (RV 125). However, Williams wrote, he had made the changes because he had wanted Kazan to direct the play, and he felt that the play's success justified the revisions because "a failure reaches fewer people, and touches fewer, than does a play that succeeds" (RV 125).

Whether Williams meant to imply it with these words or not, many critics have read the "Note of Explanation" to suggest that Kazan had asked for changes in the script in order to assure the play's commercial success. Several have condemned Williams for violating his artistic integrity by giving in to what they see as a manipulation of his artistic vision for profit. In the first critical book on Williams, Nancy Tischler wrote:

The disturbing thing about this explanation is its implication that the author lacks artistic integrity. This spokesman for an organic theatre that honestly interprets human experience, puts success first and changes his plays to please a director. As a novitiate, deference to others was understandable; but after ten years of comparatively phenomenal success, he should have accepted the responsibility for his work all the way. It is unfair to put the blame on Mr. Kazan. Without intending it, Williams reinforces the general impression that his directors shape his plays for him.[4]

Of course, the interaction between Williams and Kazan on this script had been no different than that on *Camino Real*, or even *The Rose Tattoo*, which Kazan ended up not directing. Williams had shown Kazan an early draft; Kazan had written him a long letter detailing his reactions and making suggestions for revision. But Williams had been uneasy about making the changes in *Cat*, and about his relationship with Kazan, from the beginning of their work together on this play. In May of 1954, before Kazan had actually been contracted to direct, Williams had sent a copy of the revised script to Audrey Wood, explaining that he was sending a copy to Kazan at the same time and noting that he would expect the director to make a definite commitment to the play at a specific time.[5] He also expressed his doubts about the new direction the play was taking at Kazan's suggestion, asking Wood whether she thought Kazan's suggested ending contained an echo of *Tea and Sympathy*. He felt the new ending would change Maggie from a strong woman who achieved her will through dominating a weak man to a generous woman who gave him back his manhood. He also could see no purpose in Big Daddy's return except to soften the story. At this point, Williams thought he might go to Los Angeles, where Kazan was working on *East of Eden*, and confer with him about the new script with the help of Christopher Isherwood, who had read it and liked it. He hoped the three of them might come to an agreement about the disputed changes, but he was not sanguine about the prospect. He even suggested that José Quintero would make a good director for the play if things did not work out with Kazan.

In the end, Williams decided against any of these measures. In October of 1954, he wrote happily to his friend Maria Britneva that Kazan had committed himself verbally to direct *Cat*, starting rehearsals at the beginning of February. Williams added that Kazan was "genuinely enthusiastic about the script but of course he had suggestions which I have been trying to follow and that has kept me busy as a 'Cat on a Hot Tin Roof'!"[6] Writing of the "great tensions and contentions" surrounding the formation of a producing unit on October 17, he stated clearly: "The only thing I want is Kazan" (St. Just 101). Through his usual process of gradual revision, Williams arrived at a pre-production script in early November, 1954, writing to Britneva that he would "soon know if Gadg [Kazan] is sufficiently satisfied with it to go ahead this season. It's getting late. They may want to put it off till the next. I hope not!" (St. Just 106). In the course of the revisions, he restored much of the sense that he felt had been lost in his first attempt to rewrite as Kazan had wanted him to. A good example is the ending, which obviously had been troubling him a good deal at the time that he wrote his letter to Wood. In the early version that Williams called "*Cat* number one," a version that preceded the November pre-production script, Margaret makes a speech that communicates overtly the strength and dominance over Brick that Williams referred to in the letter:

Brick, I used to think that you were stronger than me and I didn't want to be overpowered by you. But now, since you've taken to liquor – you know what? – I guess it's bad, but now I'm stronger than you and I can love you more truly! (RV 122)

In this version, Maggie locks up Brick's liquor, telling him that they will get drunk together after they have conceived a child, and throws his crutch off the gallery. As the play ends, Maggie says: "Oh, you weak people, you weak, beautiful people! – who give up. – What you need is someone to – . . . take hold of you. – Gently, gently, with love! And . . . I *do* love you, Brick, I *do!*" (RV 123). And Brick answers, "*[smiling with charming sadness]:* Wouldn't it be funny if that was true?" (RV 123).

As they get ready for bed in the November pre-production version that followed this one, Maggie asks Brick whether she should put his pillow on the sofa where he has been sleeping, and he shakes his head slightly. Seeing his tentative reaction, Maggie catches her breath, returns the pillow to the bed, and puts out the lights. When Brick hobbles over to the bed, Maggie gives her speech about the weak beautiful people who give up with such grace, adding that she can give Brick's life back to him, for there is nothing more determined than a cat on a hot tin roof. Brick warns her that he might be impotent, and Maggie answers that she is not afraid. In the "Broadway Version," Maggie throws the bottles of whiskey rather than the crutch off the gallery and convinces Brick that the only way he can get more is for Maggie to go for it, which she will do if he helps her to make "that lie [about her being pregnant] come true" (RV 158). When she asks Brick, "What do you say, Baby?" he answers, "I admire you, Maggie," and she ends the play by touching his cheek gently after her speech:

Oh, you weak, beautiful people who give up with such grace. What you need is someone to take hold of you – gently, with love, and hand your life back to you, like something gold you let go of – and I can! I'm determined to do it – and nothing's more determined than a cat on a tin roof – is there? Is there, Baby? (RV 158)

The Maggie of the final version combined the strength and dominance of the earliest Maggie and the gentleness of the intermediate version. She was sympathetic, but she was also strong. This revision resulted from exactly the kind of dialectic process that had occurred in all of Williams's work with Kazan, but he felt much more resistant to it with *Cat* than he had with the earlier plays.

The major change in the play involved the re-introduction of Big Daddy. In his *Memoirs*, Williams wrote that he had seen nothing for Big Daddy to do in Act 3 and that he had not thought it dramatically proper for him to re-enter, but he had given Big Daddy the "elephant story" to tell, dialogue which was later removed because of censorship. Williams wrote that the dialogue he put in its place was always offensive to him.[7] Kazan has explained his point of view as well. He wrote in his autobiography that he felt Big Daddy's final disposition in the story had to be conveyed to the audience, and that bringing him back would strengthen the last act, "by far the weakest of the three," a suggestion that Kazan says "had nothing to do with making the play more commercial."[8] Kazan saw immediately that Williams did not like the scene with the elephant story, and he says he asked the playwright several times if he wanted the scene played the way it had appeared in the earlier script, but Williams wanted it left the way it was. When the elephant story was censored by the Commissioner of Licenses on April 4, *Variety* reported that Williams "says he never liked it very much anyway. He explains that the smoking-car story, to which various playgoers objected, was not only not essential to the drama, but actually distracted from its effectiveness." It also reported that "Elia Kazan, who staged the Playwrights Co. production and reportedly insisted on retaining the bit of dialog during the tryout tour and for the Broadway opening, was not quoted on the subject before sailing over the weekend for Europe."⁹ Clearly the tension over this point had not been resolved happily within the creative process when the play opened.

But this was not Big Daddy's only function in Act 3. More significant were his reception of Maggie's announcement that she was pregnant and his confirmation that she had life in her body, despite the fact that he knew she was lying about the pregnancy. Williams made Big Daddy's celebration of Maggie's role as life-giver a visual as well as a verbal statement in his earliest versions of the scene. His directions told Big Daddy to catch Maggie's shoulders in a fierce grip and turn her facing away from him. Then Big Daddy put his hand over Maggie's stomach, sliding his hand slowly and forcefully over her abdomen while her eyes flitted and closed as she sighed and leaned her head back against his chest. Williams indicated that Big Daddy should slowly, sensually press and prod the softness of Maggie's belly while he announced that she had life in her body. Kazan retained this pictorial and kinesic statement of the dying Big Daddy passing on the power of his life through Maggie in the production, and it became a central element in the production's eloquent pictorial code (see plate 10).

Williams's revision of the third act also defined the characters of Brick and Big Daddy more fully. As Kazan had suggested, Williams made the character of Brick evince a change as a result of his talk with Big Daddy. At the beginning of Act 3, he said, "I didn't lie to Big Daddy. I've lied to nobody, nobody but myself, just lied to myself. The time has come to put me in Rainbow Hill, put me in Rainbow Hill, Maggie, I ought to go there" (RV 127). This speech amounts to a classic moment of recognition, and an indication that Brick intends to change his life. Rainbow Hill is a hospital that specializes in the rehabilitation of alcoholics. Brick's announcement that he wants to go there is his way of saying that he is now ready to give up his crutch of alcohol and start to live with "mendacity," as Big Daddy has told him he must. Throughout the act, small changes in lines provide a growing indication that Brick has changed. Williams cut his line about waiting for the "click" to happen so that he'll be too drunk to care what happens around him and inserted his line, "Take it, Gooper" (RV 134), referring to Big Daddy's estate. When Gooper says that Brick can't stand to be in the same room with him, Williams had Brick say, "That's the truth."

The most important change, however, was the addition of two speeches in which Brick supported Maggie's lie about the pregnancy, further developed by actions that indicated Brick's growing admiration for her and the suggestion that their relationship now has a future. In the earlier version, Brick had remained silent throughout Maggie's announcement and Mae's accusation that it was a lie. In the "Broadway version," when Mae says that Maggie can't possibly be pregnant because Brick will not sleep with her, Brick asks her how she knows that they aren't silent lovers, and that they don't come to some temporary agreement (RV 156). When Mae says she did not believe Brick would sink to Maggie's level, he sits next to Maggie on the couch and asks, "What is your level? Tell me your level so I can sink or rise to it . . . You heard what Big Daddy said. This girl has life in her body" (RV 156). Brick watches *"with growing admiration"* while Maggie takes his pillow and puts it on the bed, and then pitches the bottles of whiskey out onto the lawn. His submission to Maggie at the end of the play is a willing if passive one, suggesting that there is more to the relationship than her dominance of him.

As he did throughout his revision, Williams also softened the character of Maggie in the third act, making her less catty and drawing a distinction between her motives for wanting the family fortune and those of Gooper and Mae. Williams had her tell Brick that he had to come in off the gallery and participate in the family conference in order to protect Big Mama from Gooper and Mae, and he cut two particularly catty speeches. The combination of yearning and domination in Maggie's approach to Brick at the end of the play made her a much more sympathetic figure than she had been in the earliest versions.

The pre-production script

Maggie

There were to be significant changes made in the characters of Maggie, Brick, and Big Daddy even after the pre-production script was established in November. The Maggie of the pre-production version is meaner, more calculating, and more desperate than the Maggie of the Broadway version. She comments, for example, that it's too bad Mae and Gooper's children have no necks because you can't wring their necks if they have none to wring.[10] After remarking that Big Daddy harbors a little unconscious "lech" for her in Act 1, Maggie announces to Brick that she is going to wear her Chinese silk pajamas, without a thing underneath them, for the rest of the party. Then she goes into the closet and proceeds to toss out each of her undergarments as she changes. When she offers Brick a rubdown, she asks him to take off his robe and lie on the bed and let her pour a bottle of eau de cologne on his body and "rub it in good."

In the pre-production version, Maggie's desperation is directly related to her fear of poverty as well as to her sexuality. After she takes the phone call from Miss Sally for Big Mama, she tells the story of her rich old Aunt Cornelia, to whom she used to read the newspaper every night. Commenting on what a mean old woman her aunt was, Maggie complains that all she got when her aunt died was her unexpired subscription to five magazines and the Book of the Month Club and a library full of every dull book ever written. When Brick suggests that she could leave him, she responds that divorcing Brick would leave her with nothing, because he didn't have a cent that didn't come from Big Daddy and Big Daddy was dying of cancer. In the pre-production script, Maggie's view of her situation is pragmatic, to say the least. She says that, although she is sorry Big Daddy is dying, she has to face the facts. It will take money to take care of an alcoholic, and she must defeat Mae and Gooper's plan to freeze them out of the estate. Maggie's desperation made her more vulnerable as well as more determined in the earlier version. When Mae revealed that she and Gooper listened through the walls – "We hear the nightly pleadin' and the nightly refusal" (79) – Maggie uttered a soft cry, shutting her eyes and her lips against her hurt.

Finally, Maggie showed much more overtly in the pre-production version both her understanding and her resentment of Brick's relationship with Skipper than she did in the Broadway script. Her long, revealing speech about their college days was cut for the production. Here she had described Brick and Skipper leaning on each other's shoulders and singing sad songs to the moon because the end of their dreamlike friendship, unstained by anything carnal, was coming with their graduation. She referred to a mysterious fever Skipper had run as graduation approached and to the glamorous jobs both boys had given up in order to keep playing football together after college, remaining adolescents forever. This speech not only had clarified the nature of Brick and Skipper's relationship, it had added a good deal to Maggie's characterization. Understanding precisely the nature of Brick's feeling for Skipper made her feel her own exclusion from his love more desperately. The earlier Maggie was more extreme and more emphatic than the Maggie that eventually emerged in the production. Her emotions were sharply defined and overtly expressed. The reasons for them were also laid clearly before the audience.

Brick

In the pre-production version, the alcoholic Brick alternated between withdrawal from the situation and outbursts of violence when his protective reserve was penetrated. His defining characteristic was the "slow vague smile" that he gave everyone over his drinks. His attack on Maggie in Act 1 was more physically violent than in the final version, however. Rather than swinging his crutch once and falling on the floor as he did in the production, Brick swung at Maggie and missed, shattering the table lamp, then swung and missed twice more before he hurled the crutch at her across the bed and pitched forward onto the floor. This carefully encoded series of movements signified both Brick's fury when Maggie finally penetrated his reserve and his frustrated impotence to do anything about it, extremes of emotion that were toned down in the Broadway version.

When Big Daddy made the tentative comparison between Peter Ochello's love for Jack Straw and Brick's for Skipper in Act 2, Williams indicated that Brick's transformation was volcanic, as he shouted, "YOU THINK SO TOO! . . . You think me an' Skipper did, did, did – *sodomy* – together?" (55). Like Maggie and Big Daddy, Brick talked more bluntly about sex in the pre-production version. After accusing Big Daddy of calling him "a queer" (54), Brick suggested that maybe that was why Big Daddy put him and Maggie in Jack Straw and Peter Ochello's bed, where both of them died. His line that he and Maggie "never got any closer together than two people just get in bed, which is not much closer than two cats on a – fence humping" (RV 91) appeared in the pre-production version, but was cut for the production, as was his closing line about possibly being impotent with Maggie.

As happened with Maggie, Williams's reshaping of Brick's character in Act 3 proceeded dialectically. From the withdrawn but volatile alcoholic in the earliest versions, Williams made Brick into a much more active and interested party in Act 3 of the pre-production version. Brick repeated Maggie's line to Gooper, "You'll be in charge an' dole out remittances, will you?" (74), with a sad grin. And when Gooper brought out his plan for the estate, Brick suddenly laughed and remarked on the fat white envelope Gooper had, saying that Mae looked at it as if she were a robin and it was a fat white worm. He also threatened to hit Mae with his crutch it she didn't stop abusing Maggie.

The biggest difference between the Brick of the pre-production version and the Brick of the production, however, was in his response to Big Daddy, and particularly his reaction to the elephant story. In the Broadway version, Brick sits off to the left and watches while Big Daddy tells the story, responding only when Big Daddy asks him whether his rendering of the story is decent enough. At the end, Big Daddy says, "You didn't laugh at that story, Brick," and Brick responds, "No, sir, I didn't laugh at that story" (RV 152). In the pre-production version, Brick moved across the room, sat beside Big Daddy and rested one hand on his father's shoulder as he began to tell the story. When he chuckled, Brick chuckled with him. When Brick said he was telling the story "too ruttin' decent" (RV 152), they laughed together a moment, and then Brick shifted his hand to Big Daddy's other shoulder and leaned against him. Brick laughed hugely at the completion of the joke. As he had been with Maggie, Williams was a little extreme in the revision of Brick's character the first time around. During rehearsals, he and Kazan made the change in the character less overt, recapturing the quiescence and reserve of the earlier Brick, but indicating the possibility of a change in his attitude toward alcohol and his new admiration for Maggie's tenacious clinging to life.

Big Daddy

The changes in Big Daddy were not as fundamental as those in Brick and Maggie, but in general they went to soften the edges of the character and make him more acceptable to an audience. Big Daddy's language was considerably more graphic in the pre-production version than in the script established for Kazan's production. Although Williams included a note in the script saying that the four-letter words were put in only to give the emotional level of the speeches and need not be used on stage, with the exception of the word "fuck," which he changed to "rut," he restored most of Big Daddy's crude language when he prepared the reading version for publication. Significantly, the reading version for *Cat* was prepared from the pre-production version and an even earlier version of Act 3 rather than from the production script, as the reading version of *Camino Real* had been. Some of the phrases that were cut for production were Big Daddy's remark that Reverend Tooker reminded him of the expression "all hawk and no spit" (RV 55); his retort to Big Mama, "Fuck the goddam preacher" (RV 58); his remark to Brick that he had "*laid* [Big Mama] – regular as a piston" (RV 80); and his remark that he wanted to find a "choice one" and "hump her from hell to breakfast" (RV 72).

Big Daddy was also more overt about his dislike for Mae and Gooper and their brood in the pre-production version. Maggie's story about Big Daddy's not knowing how many children Mae and Gooper had, and the fact that "the news seemed to come as a sort of unpleasant surprise" (RV 20) when he found out there were five with another on the way, was cut for the production, as were two of the three speeches in which he says he hates "that son of a bitch of a Gooper and his wife Mae and those five same screechers out there like parrots in a jungle" (RV 80).

Finally, Big Daddy's admiration for Jack Straw and Peter Ochello was considerably tempered as Williams revised the script for the production. In the version that preceded the pre-production script, Big Daddy had a long speech comparing Brick's rejection of Skipper's love unfavorably to the devotion of Straw and Ochello. After Jack Straw died, Big Daddy said, Peter Ochello expired in a few months because he simply could not live without his lover. Admitting that Straw and Ochello were a pair of "eccentric old sisters," Big Daddy still conveyed his admiration of their having been truly devoted to each other.[11] Williams cut all but the sentence about their being devoted to each other for the pre-production script, and that was cut during rehearsals, leaving only Big Daddy's accusation of Brick: "*You!* – dug the grave of your friend and kicked him in it! – before you'd face the truth with him!" (RV 92).

While the final script retained the sense of Big Daddy's greater tolerance for homosexuality than Brick's, it was missing his standard for judgement. Brick, under the influence of what Williams described as "*the wide and profound reach of the conventional mores he got from the world that crowned him with early laurel*" (RV 89), took a "moral" stance in refusing to listen to Skipper's confession of love and cutting him out of his life. Big Daddy had originally explained to Brick that his son's disgust with himself originated in his failure to live up to the deeper human value of loyalty to Skipper and his knowledge that this failure of love was responsible for Skipper's suicide. Big Daddy's recognition that the love between Straw and Ochello was indeed "higher" than the relationship between Brick and Skipper – which Brick constantly idealizes because it was chaste and pure, lacking any physical involvement – was a clear assertion of the validity of homosexual love on Williams's part. The fact that he deleted the speech even before rehearsals began suggests that he was not quite ready to make such an overt statement on Broadway.

The pre-production script also contained some suggestions for the performance that Kazan built on as he developed the production. Williams suggested that Maggie and Brick would come down to center stage and address the audience when their long speeches became "recitative," an idea that Kazan extended to Big Daddy, and made into a central element of the production's proxemic or spatial code. The juxtaposition of the direct address to the audience and its presentational staging with the chiefly representational mode of the play eventually gave the production its distinctive character. Williams also suggested the use of fireworks in the pre-rehearsal script, although he did not visualize the effect quite as grandly as Jo Mielziner eventually produced it. Williams described it as a *"puff and crackle and the night sky blooms with an eerie greenish glow"* (RV 65). This was to happen several times, with the final effect being green and pink. In the production, Kazan placed the fireworks strategically, and Mielziner developed them carefully to achieve both a spectacular effect and an emphatic signification.

The production

The presentational dynamic

Kazan's interpretation of *Cat on a Hot Tin Roof* was already taking shape as he read the pre-production script that Williams sent to him in the fall of 1954. The title page of the script still bore the alternate title, "A Place of Stone," and the quotation from Yeats that was to be its epigraph:

> Amid a place of stone,
> Be secret and exult,
> Because of all things known
> That is most difficult.[12]

Kazan crossed this quotation out in his copy, and, interestingly, wrote on the title page, "Style! Yes! poetic – some like a Dylan Thomas *reading* words!!"[13] When the play was published, the epigraph was of course the well-known passage from Dylan Thomas:

> And, you, my father, there on the sad height,
> Curse, bless, me now with your fierce tears, I pray.
> Do not go gentle into that good night.
> Rage, rage against the dying of the light![14]

This shift of emphasis went along with the production's general focus on Big Daddy and his death rather than on the Brick–Maggie storyline. His imagination stimulated by Big Daddy's rhetorical power, Kazan developed the production around the impetus of direct communication between the characters and the audience. At the beginning of Act 2, for example, he made a note to himself to have Big Daddy come downstage facing the audience and talk straight out to them while the others remained way upstage, even out on the gallery. Williams agreed with Kazan about the power of Big Daddy's character and the centrality of words in the play. In *Memoirs* he wrote, "in *Cat* I reached beyond myself, in the second act, to a kind of crude eloquence of expression in Big Daddy that I have managed to give no other character of my creation."[15]

Although Williams had incorporated the idea of addressing the audience in the "recitative" speeches of Maggie and Brick in the early scripts, he had not counted on what was in 1955 the radical concept that Kazan devised for the production. As Kazan noted in a later interview, the conventions of representational realism were so entrenched in the Broadway theatre of the fifties that foregrounding the production's theatricality to the extent of having the characters address the audience directly had been considered anathema for many years. The last time he could remember it being done was in the production of *Our Town* in 1938.[16]

Kazan's pride in this rejection of realistic convention and his continuing interest in subjectifying theatrical experience were evident in an interview he gave in the early sixties:

I was busting out of the goddamned proscenium theatre uptown. In *Cat on a Hot Tin Roof* I had everybody address the audience continually. Every time they had one of those long speeches they'd turn and say it to the audience. Nobody thought anything of it once we opened. But there was a hell of a lot of bitching about it before . . . The whole second act of *Cat* was a long address by Burl Ives to the audience. I had him address various members of the audience . . . "what would *you* do?" is implicit in this kind of staging. It sucks the audience into the experience and emotion of that moment.[17]

Kazan wrote in his autobiography that he had to convince Williams to accept his notion of how Burl Ives would play the part of Big Daddy. When Kazan said he was going to bring Ives right down to the edge of the forestage, have him "look the audience right in the eye, and speak it directly to them," Williams protested that *Cat* was a realistic play, and should be kept within the representational conventions. When pressed by Kazan to say whether old cotton planters actually talked that eloquently and that long without interruption, Williams replied that they did. After all, who would dare interrupt them?[18] Nonetheless Kazan pursued his concept for the production in the face of Williams's skepticism, if not his opposition.

The design

When the central dynamic of the production had been established as direct communication between the characters and the audience, it had to imbue all the elements of the stage language. Here Kazan reports that he did run into opposition from Williams, who had a clear idea of what he thought the set should be like, an image that had evolved as he had revised the play. In the notes for the designer he prepared for the script preceding the November pre-rehearsal version, Williams described the basic plan of the set that was eventually used for the production: a bed-sitting room in a Mississippi Delta plantation, opening onto an upstairs gallery and showing white balustrades against a fair summer sky that fades into dusk and night during the course of the play. This is what is needed to support the action of the play which, as Williams was fond of pointing out, observed the unities of time and place, the action of the play being confined to the single set and occupying exactly the amount of time it took to enact on stage. The lighting was obviously crucial for this play, to show the passage of time that is a central thematic concern as well as a structural one.

Beyond this, however, Williams's original image of the set was strikingly different from the set Kazan and Jo Mielziner eventually devised between them. Williams described the room as Victorian, with a touch of the Far East, and poetically haunted by the tender relationship of Jack Straw and Peter Ochello.[19] He noted that the room should not have changed much since Straw and Ochello's time. To suggest the style for the design, Williams referred the designer to the reproduction he had seen of a faded photograph of the verandah of Robert Louis Stevenson's home in Samoa: "there was a quality of tender light on weathered wood, such as porch-furniture made of bamboo and wicker, exposed to tropical suns and tropical rains, which came to mind when I thought about the set for this play" (RV xiii). The photograph, he wrote, also brought to mind "the grace and comfort of light, the reassurance it gives, on a late and fair afternoon in summer, the way that no matter what, even dread of death, is gently touched and soothed by it. For the set is the background for a play that deals with human extremities of emotion and needs that softness behind it" (RV xiii).

Williams described in detail the big, slightly raked, double bed and the "entertainment center" that were the most significant objects in the set, and then he cautioned the designer, lest he feel that the previous description confined him to literal realism. As in the published "Note for the Designer," Williams envisioned that "the set should be far less realistic than I have so far implied in this description of it": the walls should dissolve mysteriously into the air below the ceiling; the set should be roofed by the sky; stars and moon suggested by traces of milky pallor, as if they were observed through a telescope lens out of focus (RV xiv). The original note, however, added the idea that a spiral nebula might be faintly suggested in order to suggest the "mystery of the cosmos," which Williams thought should be a visible presence in the play, almost as present as an actor in it. He also thought that the cloud effects and the sound effects for the windstorm in Act 3 should be as unrealistic as the set. As he revised the script, however, Williams began to reconceptualize the set as well. In November he sent off a rewrite of the scene description suggesting that the room should appear to have been remodelled since Straw and Ochello's time, and now had an open, Japanese effect.[20] The canopied bed, he suggested, could appear to have been removed from an Italian renaissance palazzo when Big Daddy and Big Mama raided Europe a few years previously.[21]

When Kazan and Mielziner began talking about the design, their concept of a production that foregrounded the characters' rhetorical appeals to the audience became the central element in their discussion. Kazan has written:

Jo Mielziner and I had read the play in the same way; we saw its great merit was its brilliant rhetoric and its theatricality. Jo didn't see the play as realistic any more than I did. If it was to be done realistically, I would have to contrive stage business to keep the old man talking those great second-act speeches turned out front and pretend that it was just another day in the life of the Pollitt family. This would, it seemed to me, amount to an apology to the audience for the glory of the author's language. It didn't seem like just another day in the life of a cotton planter's family to Jo or to me; it seemed like the best kind of theatre, the kind we were interested in encouraging, the theatre theatrical, not pretending any longer that an audience wasn't out there to be addressed but having a performer as great as Burl Ives acknowledge their presence at all times and even make eye contact with individuals.[22]

Accordingly, Kazan wrote, "I caused Jo to design our setting as I wished, a large, triangular platform, tipped toward the audience and holding only one piece of furniture, an ornate bed. This brought the play down to its essentials and made it impossible for it to be played any way except as I preferred."[23]

The set was not quite so spare as Kazan remembered it, but the central point of his statement, that the presentational impulse was the dominant aesthetic factor in creating the design, has been fully corroborated by Mielziner. In his memoir, Mielziner described their discussion about the design much as Kazan did. Asked how he thought the "elephant story" should be handled proxemically, Mielziner told Kazan that he thought it should receive as much emphasis as possible: "I suggested that we have an area of the stage on which Big Daddy could come down close to the audience and deliver the lines with dramatic force."[24] Mielziner wrote that Kazan was delighted with his answer, and "from this discussion grew the idea of creating a stage within the stage. It would be steeply raked toward the audience with one corner actually jutting out over the footlights. In its final form it turned out to be a sort of thrust stage."[25]

Mielziner's design was a departure from the subjective realism he had employed in *Menagerie*, *Streetcar*, and *Summer and Smoke*, in that he did not try to suggest through the material elements of the stage language that the events unfolding on stage were filtered through the mind of one of the characters. Instead, the design of the set projected the action out toward the audience, forcing it to become involved as though it were one of the characters. Extremely spare, the set was composed of two platforms, a large diamond-shaped one, a corner of which projected beyond the proscenium, and a smaller rectangle a foot lower at stage right. There were no doors, such actions as opening doors and looking into the mirror being mimed in this production. The only items of furniture Mielziner drew in his sketches were the primary material signifiers: the large bed, which signified both Maggie and Brick's failing marriage and the lingering memory of Straw and Ochello; the entertainment center, which signified both Brick's immediate goal of escape from reality and the vacuous materialism that Williams saw in the fifties; and the daybed, which signified Brick's withdrawal from Maggie, their marriage, and life in general. The actual set, however, also held a wicker night table and a large wicker armchair which could accommodate either Burl Ives or two of the other actors. The overall effect was of a large playing space down front where the actors could address the audience as if from a bare platform (see plate 11).

The lines of the design contributed to this effect. The perspective was such that the corner of the ceiling came down to a point slightly to the left of upstage center, helping to focus the audience's attention on the point of the diamond where the characters addressed the audience. Mielziner took Williams's hints to give lighting a central function in the play, running a scrim from floor to ceiling along two sides of the set with strips of black velour indicating the lines of the columns outside the windows of the room when the light of the moon was projected through them. To signify sunlight, slide projections of blinds were thrown on the scrims, while the gallery and the lawn beyond the windows were blocked out. When characters on the gallery or the lawn were to be seen, the lights behind the scrim were brought up, making the actors visible to the audience, as had been done with *Streetcar*.

Two follow-spots were used in the production. One, on the audience's left, highlighted Maggie throughout Act 1 and picked up Big Mama, Maggie, and Brick in Act 2, as they were in turn nominally being addressed by Big Daddy, who was downstage talking to the audience. In Act 3 the light again shone on Maggie almost without interruption. The follow-spot on the audience's right highlighted the characters Maggie was addressing in Act 1, chiefly Brick, as she had her turn at "recitative." It shone on Big Daddy throughout Act 2 and picked up Brick, Big Mama, Gooper, Mae, and Maggie at various times during Act 3, emphasizing a significant entrance or a significant reaction indexically as it occurred. Contributing to the generally "golden" look of the production's lighting, the follow-spots were amber except when a character went out onto the gallery, when they were changed to blue. The follow-spots not only helped to avoid confusion by focusing the audience's attention where

Kazan wanted it to be, they also contributed to the foregrounding of the theatricality in the production by "framing" specific characters and pieces of action. Kazan stylized the composition of his stage picture in *Cat*, and encoded a great deal of meaning through gesture, movement, and pose in the production. Using the follow-spots to highlight these formal compositions emphasized that what was happening on stage was not real life but theatre.

In designing the furniture, both Kazan and Mielziner took their cue from Williams's earlier description of the set, emphasizing the qualities he had seen in the Robert Louis Stevenson photograph. Kazan had underlined elements of this description in his copy of the script. Listed together, they indicate quite well the direction Mielziner took with the design after their conferences:

Delta's biggest cotton-planter
Far East
The room must evoke some ghosts
Gently . . . poetically haunted by a relationship . . . a tenderness which was uncommon
Samoan Island
tender light on weathered wood
Bamboo . . . wicker
[the entertainment center] monument . . . very complete . . . compact little shrine . . . all the comforts . . . illusions . . . hide [written in the margin, "Brick hides"] such things as the characters in the play are faced with (RV xii–xiv)

From these suggestions came the old wicker headboard with its huge and fantastically shaped design of two cornucopias, the matching wicker furniture, the carpet with its lushly fertile design of oversized flowers and vines, and the one object in the room that competed with the fertility symbol of the bed for the audience's attention, the oversized bar, hi-fi, radio, and television with its sleekly modern fifties lines. This object realized Williams's description of a compact modern shrine to all the comforts and illusions of contemporary life and signified Brick's retreat from human contact.

Kazan has said more than once that Williams did not like the set that Mielziner finally developed for *Cat* because he thought his play should be performed realistically.[26] Kazan has also indicated that the set was a material signifier of his aesthetic vision in opposition to Williams's:

I had the setting I'd asked for; Jo had given me what I wanted. Tennessee had approved of it earlier, when he was ready to approve of damn near anything I asked for, because I was the director he wanted. Now the setting was up on stage, too late to change, and on that setting there was only one way for any human to conduct himself: "out front" it's called. Dear Tennessee was stuck with my vision, like it or not.[27]

The cast

Kazan was equally aggressive about controlling the play's casting. Having long ago won his battle to cast plays without being restricted by a producer, Kazan suffered no interference from the Playwrights Company. Casting with the instincts of the Method director, he has admitted that he "forced" Barbara Bel Geddes on Williams despite the fact that Williams worried about her not having the requisite "melody" in her voice to play his Southern heroine as he imagined her.[28] Kazan apparently never thought of anyone but Burl Ives for the part of Big Daddy. Having directed him in *Sing Out Sweet Land!* and *East of Eden*, Kazan knew he had found what he needed for Big Daddy in Ives's capacity for violence and his "intolerance of parlor-bred manners."[29] Williams was not sure that Ives, whom he knew primarily as a singer, could handle the part, but again he yielded to his trusted director. For Brick, Kazan eventually settled on Ben Gazzara, a talented young actor from Actors Studio who, as Eric Bentley put it, "may not seem Southern, or a football player, or a TV announcer . . . but he is handsome and he can act neurotic intensity."[30] Pat Hingle, another Actors Studio member, was cast as Gooper. Kazan ended up casting the versatile Madeleine Sherwood as Mae, and made the surprising choice of slight, ladylike Mildred Dunnock, who had played Linda Loman in *Death of a Salesman*, for Big Mama.

After an outburst in which Williams interrupted the rehearsal of the first act to tell Bel Geddes that she needed more melody in her voice, Kazan told him not to talk to the actors anymore.[31] Williams said that he understood Kazan's point of view and left the theatre, returning only after several days had passed. And when he returned, he did not talk to the actors. Mildred Dunnock remembered that Kazan had explained to the actors that they shouldn't discuss the play with the playwright because "these characters were not written realistically, and . . . to discuss them as if we were dissecting neighbors would have been untrue to them and to the play."[32] These instructions masked the fact that Kazan knew he and Williams had differing views of *Cat on a Hot Tin Roof*. Williams in fact thought the Pollitts were among the most realistic and likable characters he had created. If he had spoken of them to the actors in that way, he would surely have inhibited the development of the stylized performances Kazan was working toward within the psychological realism of the Method aesthetic. As gently as he could, Kazan was again seizing control of the production and developing the play in accord with his vision rather than what he perceived Williams's to be.

Kazan worked carefully with the actors in rehearsal as he always did, helping them to create their characters "from the inside out" like the dedicated Stanislavskian director that he was. Both Dunnock and Ives have commented that Kazan functioned in the rehearsals of *Cat* like a conductor leading an orchestra. "Ben Gazzara and I were directed by Kazan as if the play were an orchestra piece, a fugue – building, building, building in the confrontation between father and son," said Ives.[33] This effect was not wasted on audiences. As one of the critics at the Philadelphia tryout noticed, "there is a pendulum swing to Williams' writing and this rhythm increases steadily in the direction of Elia Kazan and in the quiet-loud-quiet delivery of the lines, some almost blank verse, by the players."[34] All of the elements of the Kazan signature – deeply felt characterizations, intensity, careful pacing with frequent climaxes, complex pictorial and kinesic effects, and a great deal of environmental activity – were present in this production.

Maggie

Essentially, what Kazan asked of Williams, and what he tried to do in helping his actors to develop the characters, was to emphasize Maggie's difference from the others, the sense that her motivations were higher than the blind greed that characterized the Pollitts. He also tried to get Ben Gazzara to act out Brick's troubled quality by concentrating on what he called the "Southern insides" of the character. Big Daddy he tried to establish as larger than life, both for the other characters and for the audience, and he worked to combine a sense of stature with an underlying sense of the cruelty and violence that had produced it.

As Williams wrote in his "Note of Explanation," Kazan's ideas about Maggie centered mainly on making her more clearly sympathetic to the audience. He wanted her to be less "catty" and more clearly distinguished from Mae. In the margin of his script, for example, he wrote, "Dear T. Please don't bring Margaret down to Mae's level" next to Maggie's catty lines about the show that the children put on for Big Daddy. In Act 3 Kazan wrote "Again!" next to yet another fight between Maggie and Mae, and he wrote "Amen!" next to Big Mama's line, "You children Quit! How dare you!" He crossed out the lines in which Big Mama asked Gooper why he was so determined to see his father dead and Maggie responded that she understood why, writing "Oh, Shit!" in the margin.[35] He also commented that he did not think Maggie should wear pajamas in Act 1.

Kazan's choice of the wholesome Barbara Bel Geddes for the part of Maggie went a long way toward establishing his view of the character. He wanted her to project an image of the healthy, loving young wife whose deprivation of her husband's sexual love was making her own sexual desire unbearable. He did not want the sense of a calculating use of sexuality that was hinted at in Maggie's wearing pajamas "without a thing underneath" because Big Daddy has a "lech" for her. As Kazan developed her, Maggie's sexuality was mostly unconscious, and it was all directed at Brick. Rather than going into the closet to change into pajamas, she took her stained dress off on stage and played the first act in a slip. Kazan had Bel Geddes move about more freely, unconsciously as well as consciously using her body to try to attract Brick. During her long opening monologue, she flopped on her belly on the bed. Kazan had her take a piece of ice and slide it between her breasts as she talked to Brick about Big Daddy's desire for her and drop it on the bar when Brick said that kind of talk was disgusting. He built Maggie's sexual tension to a peak when Brick advised her to take a lover and she said, "I can't see a man but you! Even with my eyes closed, I just see you! Why don't you get ugly, Brick, why don't you please get fat or ugly or something so I could stand it?" (18). She embraced Brick's legs as he stood leaning on his crutch, encoding one of many pictorial statements that conveyed the depths of the need for human connection beneath the words in this play.

Kazan also cut several lines that suggested negative aspects of Maggie's character, such as her answer, "Because I'm a cat" (RV 30), when Mae asks her why she is so catty and her lie about never having seen a cashmere robe before when she takes out Big Daddy's present. He also cut the dialogue between Brick and Big Daddy in which they discuss the fact that Maggie and Mae are both as nervous as cats on a hot tin roof, downplaying the suggestion of similarity between them.

The visual stage language

Big Daddy

The most striking pictorial and kinesic statements Kazan encoded in the performance involved Big Daddy. He brought Big Daddy down front to address the audience four times – three in Act 2 when he talked about his plantation; when he talked about Europe; and when he told the story of the woman sending her little child to solicit him in Barcelona; and one in Act 3, when he told the elephant story. Kazan also used Big Daddy to encode the visual subtext of Act 2 by focusing the audience's attention on Brick's crutch. Big Daddy picked up the crutch when he began talking about Europe and brought it down front with him, then he carried it over to Brick while he talked about the things that money can't buy, and then took it downstage again and leaned on it while he talked about Barcelona, striking the chair with it for emphasis. After his story, Big Daddy tossed the crutch onto the bed with a gesture of strength, and then returned it to Brick so he could go and get a drink. This focus on the crutch, a material signifier of both Brick's weakness and Big Daddy's strength, prepared the audience for the full thematic force of Big Daddy's gesture when he pulled the crutch from Brick's arm, pushing him into a chair and forcing him to listen. With the mounting tension typical of Kazan's direction, Big Daddy pulled the crutch out from under Brick again a few minutes later, sending him sprawling face-down on the floor. The extension from crutch to drink was obvious to the audience a minute later when Big Daddy knocked Brick's drink to the floor as Brick was struggling toward it. And when Brick stumbled, exhausted, into Big Daddy's arms a moment later, the implication that the father was offering to replace his son's artificial supports with his own strength was clear (see plate 12).

As is typical of a Williams play, there was not much physical contact among the members of the Pollitt family indicated in the script. As was typical of a Kazan production, several significant gestures of human contact were added during rehearsal, particularly between Brick and Big Daddy. Big Daddy held Brick after he fell into his arms, and patted his son consolingly as he asked about his need for alcohol. He put his arm on Brick's as he said that they were two people who had never lied to each other, and he touched his son's shoulder as he helped Brick recover from the suggestion that he and Skipper might have loved each other. These gestures of tenderness conveyed the father's love beneath the toughness and even violence of his forcing Brick to face the truth of his self-deceit.

Kazan also prevailed upon Williams to make changes in the dialogue that made Big Daddy on the one hand more colorfully crude and on the other less mean-spirited than he had appeared in earlier drafts. While the coarsest of Big Daddy's language was censored either before or after the play's opening, Williams added his line that Mae would probably "drop a litter" (40) with her next pregnancy, changed the word "sick" to "puke" (41) when Big Daddy complained of the effect that Gooper and Mae's sneaking and spying had on him, and inserted the word "Bull!" when Big Mama told Miss Sally that Big Daddy was dying to see her. Kazan had Ives say "chantecleer" instead of "chandelier," but Williams did not include the malapropism even in the acting version that follows the production script almost word for word. The censored "hump her from hell to breakfast" was changed to the equally colorful "run her from Jackson to Memphis – *non-stop!*" (47).

Brick

The basic posture that Kazan developed for Brick's character was physical helplessness, the material signifier of his weakness of spirit. Brick lay on the couch while Maggie talked to him in Act 1, and he was much less aggressive in his attack on her than Williams had indicated in the earlier scripts, falling down when he swung his crutch at her and lying on the floor while his little niece ran in and emptied her cap gun at him. In Act 2, Brick tried five times to rise from the chair into which Big Daddy had pushed him, and five times Big Daddy forced him back down. A few minutes later, Brick sprawled face down on the gallery when Big Daddy took his crutch, and then tried to crawl toward his drink until Big Daddy knocked it to the floor. Finally he raised himself up, only to stumble into Big Daddy's arms (see plate 13).

Kazan had Brick assert himself more physically as he began to take his father's help and face his trouble. He came downstage and addressed the audience as he told the story of Maggie and Skipper and himself in Act 2, and he reached out to Big Daddy, laying his head against his father's shoulder as he explained why he had told him the truth about his cancer. This prepared the audience for the change Brick showed in Act 3, when he responded warmly to Big Daddy and defended Maggie against Mae. Combined with the growing admiration for Maggie that he showed in Act 3, this slightly steadier, more confident Brick was a more willing partner to Maggie's seduction than the Brick who was conquered in the earlier versions of the play. Kazan also cut some of Brick's lines so the character would fit his views more clearly. He cut Brick's line, "I can hop on one foot, and if I fall, I can crawl" (RV 79) when Big Daddy refuses to get him a drink in Act 2, and he cut a significant part of Brick's speech to Big Daddy when he explains why he has told him the truth about the cancer:

It's hard for me to understand how anybody could care if he lived or died or was dying or cared about anything but whether or not there was liquor left in the bottle and so I said what I said without thinking. In some ways I'm no better than the others, in some ways worse because I'm less alive. (RV 94)

By cutting this revelation of the depth of Brick's despair and leaving the lines about being friends – "and being friends is telling each other the truth" (RV 94) – Kazan kept the character of Brick developing along the lines he saw for it. Brick was changed by his talk with Big Daddy and began to act as though he had some hope for the future and some concern for the people around him. The divergence in their views of how Brick should be developed was the most significant disagreement Kazan and Williams had in their work on the play. Kazan's version of a young man who begins to see that he can change his life after his father helps him to see the truth about the past was a far cry from Williams's portrait of the young man whose chief characteristic is the *"charm of that cool air of detachment that people have who have given up the struggle"* (RV 17).

Big Mama

Kazan's development of Big Mama had three basic origins. The first two are clearly indicated in the script, as Williams defines Big Mama in antipathy to Big Daddy. Like Brick, Big Daddy is very shy of physical contact, and he has a particularly strong aversion to sexual contact with his wife. Also like Brick, he craves privacy. He is constantly annoyed by the intruders who interrupt his conversation with his son. Big Mama, on the other hand, craves physical affection of all kinds, finding it hard to keep her hands off the people she cares for. She also hates "locked doors in a house" (20), and cannot understand why a young married couple should feel the need for privacy.

The other basis for Big Mama's character came from the casting. The allusions in the script to Big Mama's resembling a fat, puffing bulldog or a big game animal simply did not fit Mildred Dunnock, and had to be changed. Big Daddy's line about her "fat old body butting in here and there" (RV 57), for example, was changed to "your damn' busy ole body buttin' in here and there" (38). This notion of general busyness was combined with Big Mama's nosiness about everything that went on in her house, her sense that she can interfere in it, and her need for physical affection to form the basis for the character.

Big Mama's activity while Maggie was talking to Aunt Sally on the telephone in Act 1 gives a good sense of how these three elements were combined in the production. Big Mama came over to the bed in Brick and Maggie's room, saw the whiskey bottle, picked it up, and dropped it suddenly, "*as if it had bitten her*" (22). Picking it up again, she put it on the night stand. Then she picked up Brick's shirt from the bed, crossed the room with it and laid it across the wicker seat. Seeing Brick's pillow on the daybed, she went over and looked at it, unhappily. Then, as Maggie returned unseen from the hall, she picked up the pillow and held it tenderly in her arms. As Maggie watched her, Big Mama went back to the bed, putting Brick's pillow beside his wife's. Big Mama's physical restlessness is as evident in this scene as her concern for Brick and her notion that it is her business to interfere if she perceives that Brick and Maggie's marriage is not going well. Kazan also encoded Big Mama's little intrigues kinesically in Act 2, when he had her pick up the birthday card that Brick had refused to sign and bring it out to him on the gallery while Maggie was showing Big Daddy his cashmere robe, and he had her draw Maggie into a corner to confer about Brick later in the scene.

Big Mama showed her warm and unconscious physical affection for Maggie in Act 1 when she embraced her daughter-in-law and rubbed her back while she told her about the news from the Ochsner Clinic. The extent of Big Mama's unsatisfied craving for affection from Brick and Big Daddy, however, was encoded in Act 2, when she burst into the room shouting for Brick to "Give Big Mama a kiss, you bad boy, you" (32), and he avoided her touch. She went from Brick to Big Daddy, trying to force her way into the big chair where he was sitting as she said, "I want to sit nex' to mah sweetheart, hold hands with him, an' love him up a little!" (32). Big Daddy at first resisted her, refusing to move over, and then, giving up, got up and gave her the chair. Frustrated in both attempts to get affection from her men, Big Mama covered her disappointment with the joke on the preacher, bouncing him on her lap until Big Daddy yelled at her to quit.

Kazan continued the kinesic encoding of Big Mama's physical craving and Big Daddy's refusal to satisfy it later in Act 2, when she came through the room on the way to answer the telephone just as Big Daddy was telling Brick how much he disliked her. Big Mama patted kisses on her husband's mouth on the way to the hall. On her return, she put her arms around him from the back and gave him a hug that made him wince in pain as she said she knew he didn't mean the awful things he had said to her earlier. Big Mama's physical busyness signified a studied denial of the fact that her husband did not love her. Like Maggie, Big Mama embodied the image of a cat on a hot tin roof; and her actions were a physical manifestation of the frustrated love at the center of her life.

The environment

One of the most telling changes Kazan's direction made was in "opening the play out," as if he were thinking about it as a film rather than a stage play. The early drafts of *Cat* suggest a tightly constructed family drama to which the classical unities give the same sense of suspense, inevitability, and deep conflicting passions being fought out in a small enclosed space that the Greek family dramas have. In his direction, Kazan chose to place the family conflict in a larger context by constantly juxtaposing its relentless action against the seemingly casual play of events surrounding it. His direction deliberately juxtaposed the presentational proxemic and kinesic elements mentioned earlier, elements which foregrounded the play's theatricality, with a denser social environment that intensified the play's opposing impulse toward representational realism. This dynamic tension between the subjective and the objective, the presentational and the representational, was the basis for the production's tense energy.

The environment was created in several ways – through greater use of the children and the black plantations workers, through the addition of scenes and kinesic incidents, and through the use of music and sound effects. Once the notion of opening the play out was established, the development of the children was a natural outgrowth of Williams's script. In the pre-production script, Williams has their shrieks from downstairs punctuate Maggie's speeches throughout Act 1, a concrete reminder of her anxiety about not having children. Then he has Dixie burst in on Brick and Maggie and fire her cap pistol at Brick, uttering the truth that Maggie is jealous of Mae because she has no children of her own. The children also appear in Act 2, of course, to sing to Big Daddy. Working on these hints, Kazan developed the children into a constant and annoying presence throughout the first two acts.

During Act 1, Kazan had the children be seen through the scrim running across the lawn several times rather than just heard shrieking downstairs, and he had them sing "Jesus Loves Me" while Maggie was pleading with Brick to sleep with her. At the end of the act, instead of having Dixie run in and fire her cap gun at Brick, he had all of the children run into the room and fire at Brick, and then all run across the room and fire at Maggie. He also made a stronger visual statement of Mae's parading the children before Big Daddy. Before they sang "Happy Birthday," Mae cued them with a pitch pipe, and marched behind them into the room. Then she directed them in the performance of "Skinamar-inka-do" (see plate 14). Later, while Big Daddy was talking to Brick, she tried to get his attention by shepherding the children in a parade, with Buster beating a drum and the others carrying sparklers while they called for Big Daddy to come out. When Brick was telling Big Daddy about Skipper, the audience could see Mae leading the children out onto the lawn to look at the fireworks.

Kazan also developed the children more fully along the lines Williams had suggested when he had Big Daddy say that he hated "that son of a bitch Gooper and his wife Mae and those five same screechers out there like parrots in a jungle" (RV 80). Kazan had the children do things that indicated they were well on the way to becoming little Maes and Goopers. When Mae appeared with Maggie's hunting bow to complain about her leaving it around "nawmal rid-blooded children attracted t'weapons" (16), Kazan had Sonny run after her and ad lib a line about wanting the bow back. Mae shooed him away, but he snuck into the room after her and crouched down behind the bar, listening to the adults' conversation as his parents listened to Brick and Maggie through the wall at night. Maggie discovered him and went over to kneel beside him as she talked about having her hunter's licence, until Mae finally saw him and shooed him away again. During the birthday-party scene, Dixie surreptitiously scraped sugar off the cake. When Maggie brought out the present for Big Daddy, the children shrieked and threw themselves on the gift box, demanding to open it until the adults finally succeeded in getting them out of the room.

Kazan's use of the black workers in *Cat* was similar to that in his films *Baby Doll* and *Wild River*. At one level, this was a naturalistic impulse, shedding light on the forces that shape the Pollitt family by revealing their daily environment, as Kazan had done with the Kowalskis in *Streetcar*. In the new opening to the play that was developed during rehearsals, the family was heard singing the children's song "Boom-Boom" off-stage as the curtain opened on Lacey, the handyman, humming the tune as he crossed the stage with two dust-covered bottles of wine for the celebration. The maid Sookey came in to hurry him up, saying, "Come on, boy – they waitin' for this stuff!" (6). The characters of Lacey and Sookey were woven through the play, appearing for the birthday celebration in Act 2 and during the storm in Act 3. With the other servants and field hands, they sang several songs that provided a commentary on the action. As Maggie and Mae discussed the activities of the no-neck monsters in Act 1, for example, Sookey and Daisy sang "Mighty Lak a Rose," contrasting the popular sentimental conception of children to the more realistic view of Maggie:

> Sweetest l'il feller everybody knows
> Don' know what to call him, but he's mighty lak a rose,
> Lookin' at his mammy, with eyes so shiny blue.
> Makes you think that heaven is comin' close to you.[36]

Of course there was humor in the juxtaposition of the no-neck monsters with this song, but there was also the underlying social comment typical of Kazan in having these black servants sing a song that idealizes a white child. With less humorous but equally strong emphasis, Kazan had the field hands sing "I Just Can't Stay Here By Myself" when the terminally ill Big Daddy re-entered in Act 3 and "Buddy" when Maggie and Brick began to make their rapprochement, a reminder of Skipper and the love that came between them. The last two verses evoked the image of Skipper as Brick and Maggie were preparing to go to bed:

> Well I asked my buddy
> What are you thinkin' of?
> The only thing that's on my mind
> Only thinkin' of my love
>
> They had my buddy on the mountain
> Up the mountain so high
> Last words I heard that poor boy say
> Gimme a cool drink of water 'fore I die.[37]

The more important use of the black workers, however, was to develop the character of Big Daddy and re-emphasize his centrality to the play. In a brief but telling incident, when the singing of "Happy Birthday" began simultaneously by the children and the field hands, Big Daddy went delightedly to the window to wave to the men out on the lawn, ignoring his grandchildren. When the children went into "Skinamarinka" with their salute to Big Daddy, he turned away with a disgusted "Je-sus!" (34). In Act 3, Kazan again emphasized that Big Daddy felt more comfortable with the field hands than with the family, as he stopped to joke with Lacey and Small about the storm before he went into the room with the family. Big Daddy's attitude of easy cameraderie with the black workers contrasted with that of Gooper and Mae during the storm, when Mae chided Sookey about covering up the porch furniture and Gooper ordered Lacey to put the top up on his Cadillac and then put it away, berating him for losing the keys when they were in Gooper's pocket all the time.

All of this action was added during rehearsals, a direct reflection of Kazan's view of how the play should be realized. These bits of realistic detail helped create the tension between the presentational and the representational that Kazan was working for. Kazan's use of the environmental action also helped to establish the central thematic concerns of the play. The first line to be spoken by Big Daddy in the production was the tag line of a joke that was overheard from downstairs while Maggie complained to Brick about Mae's display of her fertility, a joke about two elephants in heat.[38] This of course foreshadowed the "elephant story" as well as giving the audience its first impression of Big Daddy as a crude raconteur and helping to establish the subtext of sexuality. Similarly, Kazan built up the croquet game taking place on the lawn between Dr. Baugh and Reverend Tooker while Maggie was talking to Brick about their sex life, using it as a general metaphor for sex as well as recalling Williams's use of it as the central image in "Three Players of a Summer Game." As Maggie remarked, "Your indifference made you wonderful at lovemaking" (13), Dr. Baugh said, "Yeah, I got you boxed" (14), the *double entendre* signifying both what Brick's sexuality had done to Maggie and what Maggie is trying to do to him. When Maggie said, "later tonight I'm going to tell you I love you an' maybe by that time you'll be drunk enough to believe me" (14), Reverend Tooker was saying "Mmm! You're too slippery for me!" (14) and Dr. Baugh was answering, "Jus' like an eel, boy. Jus' like an eel!" (14). This added aural environment, like the visual environment, helped to create a sense of casual realistic activity as the drama of the Pollitts was played out against it, but it was also plurisignificant – encoding the subtexts that Kazan wanted to emphasize in the play's production.

Despite the aura of casual realism, there was a quality of the obvious in the thematic use of these effects that was not likely to be accidental in the work of a director as sophisticated as Kazan. This quality was also evident in his use of music, as we have seen with the songs, and even more in his use of sound effects. Kazan's employment of visual and sound effects in *Cat* emphasized the play's thematic concerns in a way that the director himself would have characterized as "corny." In place of the sudden blast of Wagner or Beethoven that Williams suggested when Gooper turned on the radio, for example, Kazan substituted a *"loud, unctuous 'political' voice"* saying, "th' disgustin' mendacity which my opponent has shown –" (31), foreshadowing the discussion of mendacity by Brick and Big Daddy which is shortly to ensue with an effect that was too calculated to be realistic. Similarly, when Big Daddy was telling Brick about the sybaritic life he planned to lead now that he had learned he was not dying of cancer, Kazan had the telephone punctuate the speech so that it rang on "cut loose," "ball," and "ball."[39]

An equally heavy-handed effect was produced with the fireworks at the end of Act 2, which punctuated the already extreme tension when Brick talked about Skipper with Big Daddy. Kazan had Mielziner's spectacular lighting effect and the boom which accompanied it go off at "pure" in Brick's speech, "it was a pure an' true thing an' that's not normal!" (57) and at "through" in "it's too late to stop it now, we got to carry it through an' cover ev'ry subject" (57). These bursts of emphasis prepared for the momentous effect at the end of the act when Gooper yelled, "Let'er–go–!" and *"THE FIREWORKS BLAZE[D] FURIOUSLY"* as Big Daddy went out along the gallery shouting "CHRIST – DAMN . . . DAMN ALL – LYIN' SONS OF – LYIN' BITCHES!" (60).

Even more heavy-handed was the encoding of meaning through sound effects from nature. One of these was the hawk cries which Kazan had occur no less than eight times in the course of Acts 1 and 2. When Brick first heard the hawk, he looked up intently, listening to it and watching it circle. His attitude of listening for and to it throughout Act 1 encoded his distraction from what Maggie was saying to him. The hawk also signified Brick's yearning for flight, Big Daddy's coming death, and the family that was gathering to prey upon the old man's remains.

It would be hard to believe that a director as skilled at creating the illusion of reality as Elia Kazan would have produced such heavy-handed effects by accident. They can only be read as part of his overall strategy to "stylize" this play by foregrounding its theatricality against an environment of realistic activity. These effects called attention to themselves as theatre and invited the audience to see them as literary symbols. The effect would be Brechtian if there were any attempt to undermine the audience's sympathy with the characters. As in *Camino Real*, however, Kazan was using his theatricality not to distance the audience from his characters, but to project the characters into the audience and invite the audience to participate in the play. These devices told the audience that it was viewing a play, a play it should feel free to interpret. They did not suggest an ironic attitude toward the characters. On the contrary, the identification of Brick with the symbolic hawk, for example, reminded the audience that he yearned for flight despite the weakness that imprisoned him. The symbolic resonance only increased the audience's sympathy with the characters.

One other element in the stage language Kazan created for *Cat on a Hot Tin Roof* should be noted: the stylization of what he called the "stage picture" in keeping with the production's emphasis of the theatrical. In his review of the production, Eric Bentley suggested that Kazan attempted in its visual style to "conquer that far outpost of the imagination which we call Grandeur."[40] Noting that Kazan had departed further from naturalism in *Cat* than in either *Streetcar* or *Salesman*, Bentley wrote:

Just as there is less furniture and less scenery, so there is a less natural handling of actors, a more conscious concern with stagecraft, with pattern, with form. Attention is constantly called to the tableau, to what, in movies, is called the individual "frame." You feel that Burl Ives has been *placed* center stage, not merely that he *is* there; in the absence of furniture, a man's body is furnishing the room. When the man lifts his crippled son off the floor, the position is held a long moment as for a time-exposure. My wife nudges me at this point, and whispers, "Why, it's a Michaelangelo."[41]

Bentley noted that "all the groupings are formalized," suggesting that his review should have been accompanied by diagrams showing "where Mr. Kazan put everybody, by twos, by threes, this one over here moon-gazing though the imaginary window, this one over there ego-gazing at the imaginary mirror, all fixed to the spot until the director's signal is given to move."[42]

The unusual number of photoessays on *Cat on a Hot Tin Roof* in the magazines of 1955 cannot be attributed solely to the then sensational subject of Barbara Bel Geddes clad in a slip. Appearing over and over in these articles are the compositions created by Elia Kazan and his actors to provide a visual code for the audience that was as arresting and as eloquent as Williams's verbal text. Again and again the powerful signification of the carefully composed stage pictures was recognized and reproduced: Maggie crouching on her knees in front of Brick as she clutched his legs and looked desperately off to the right while Brick kept his hand on her head and looked past her; Big Daddy knocking Brick's crutch out from under him with a sweeping gesture and sending him face-first to the floor; Big Daddy cradling his son's head against his huge chest as he helped him off the floor; Maggie leaning her body back against Big Daddy and her head on his shoulder as he ran his hands down the front of her body, feeling for life; Mae lining her children up in front of Big Daddy like prize livestock on display; Maggie with her hands cupped around her breasts, trying to interest her husband in her body again; Maggie curled on the huge bed like a cat, pointing an accusatory finger toward Brick; Brick sitting on the bed and stretching his hand out toward Maggie; Maggie on her knees before the massive figure of Big Daddy (see plate 15).

As Kazan staged it, the play was both a series of eloquent speeches delivered straight to the audience and a series of eloquent pictorial compositions encoding some of its deepest meaning, both surrounded by constant noise and activity that was at the same time realistically detailed and overtly theatrical. As Bentley noted, the production's effectiveness resulted "from the interaction between formality in the setting, lighting, and grouping and an opposite quality – informality is hardly the word – in the individual performances. The externals of the physical production belong, as it were, to the old theatre, but the acting is internal, 'Stanislav-skyite.'"[43] The tension that Kazan created between the realism of deeply felt and projected psychological characterizations set in a detailed milieu and the conscious theatricality of the stage language made for a brilliant production. It was not, however, the tight, claustrophobic, classically structured family drama that Williams had first imagined the play to be. The process of collaboration had produced a far denser, more complex and very different play.

The aftermath

In his review of the production, Eric Bentley reiterated his charge that Williams was allowing Kazan to tamper with his plays, asserting that the "uncoordinated double vision" of the performance process had resulted in a failed production:

In the last act, while the script is resolutely non-committal, the production strains for commitment to some sort of edifying conclusion. While nothing is actually concluded, images of edification are offered to our eyes. Barbara Bel Geddes is given an Annuciation scene (made of more golden light and a kneeling posture). At the very end . . . comes the outward form of that *Tea and Sympathy* scene without its content. And, in many places throughout, a kind of mutually frustrating activity has the effect of muffling the emotions that are supposed to sound out loud and clear.[44]

As he had with *Streetcar* and with *Salesman*, Bentley was in one sense simply repeating his notion that a strong director can violate the integrity of the playwright's aesthetic vision by intruding his own on the play. There was a slight difference here, however, in that while the effect of

Kazan's collaboration had clearly been positive in the two earlier instances, Bentley was suggesting that here it was negative, that Kazan's artistic vision opposed and undermined Williams's. It was a serious charge, and it was not without effect on the already anxious playwright.

William Becker, writing a review essay on three new plays for the *Hudson Review*, took precisely the opposite point of view from Bentley's. Noting that the team of Williams, Kazan, and Mielziner was "as potent an artistic force as Broadway can boast today," he argued that "the *kind* of theatre produced by this particular team is . . . *the* singular dramatic achievement of the postwar decade on Broadway,"[45] and that it had made a significant aesthetic advancement as yet unrealized in Europe:

The technique of it is based on a curious dialectic of intense realism and rather eloquent fantasy, a dialectic which is present in every part of the final creation – it is there in the writing, in the open half-abstracted settings, in the play of the lights, in the postures and delivery of the actors. It is an intensification of life posed against abstractions from it, artifice breaking down into nature, nature building up into artifice. Specifically, it is real speech with unnatural inflections, solid furniture in rooms with no walls, naturalistic acting that assembles itself into highly posed and static images, normal realistic light that gives way to follow-spots and chiaroscuro, talk that develops special rhythms and elevates itself into speech.[46]

The dialectic of realism and fantasy was at the center of *Camino Real* as well as *Cat*, and, as Becker recognized, could only have been created through a collaborative process "in which the individual contributions are so harmoniously blended as to create a fully synthetic piece of theatre."[47]

In this brief statement, Becker had defined precisely the achievement of artistic collaboration that Williams, Kazan, and Mielziner had reached in their first plays together. Although Kazan had run somewhat roughshod over Williams's opinions in his insistence on emphasizing the presentational side of the dialectic rather than the representational side in the production of *Cat*, his and Mielziner's development of the play had proceeded from that junction of opposites he saw at the heart of Williams's work. Becker was recognizing an artistic collaboration that had been developing for nearly ten years before the work on *Cat* and was now at its peak, or perhaps just past it. The tensions inherent in the dynamics of collaboration, urged on by attitudes like Bentley's, began to come to the surface after the artistic and commercial success of *Cat on a Hot Tin Roof*.

Despite his protestations that his relationship with Kazan was in every way helpful rather than "dangerous" to his art, Williams conveyed the impression in his "Note of Explanation" for including the earlier third act with the published play that Kazan had coerced him into making major changes he did not agree with and that the chief consideration in this action was the play's commercial success. Although he knew Williams well enough to understand some of the motivation for the unusual publication of the earlier version of the third act and this note, Kazan was surprised and hurt by its implications about his collaborative role:

I thought his book made me out to be something of a villain corrupting a "pure artist." I especially resented Tennessee's calling "my" third act – which I didn't write, plan, or edit – the "commercial" third act. I'd had no such purpose in mind. It was Williams who wanted the commercial success, and he wanted it passionately. All he'd had to say was: "Put it back the way I had it first," and I would have. Apart from friendship and devotion, I'd have had to restore his original by the mandate of the Dramatists Guild. His complaining about me in print hurt me, even though I appreciated the anxiety he felt . . . But I decided to swallow the indignity; it was his play and his reputation and his life. Besides, I truly loved the man and always would.[48]

On the face of it, Williams's action is inexplicable. Kazan may have been more domineering in the collaborative process with *Cat* than he had been in the earlier plays, but his role in helping Williams to develop the script was not substantially different from what it had been with *Camino Real*, or with *The Rose Tattoo*. Bentley's charges that Williams allowed the director to interfere with his artistic vision were more fully articulated this time, but they were not substantially different from those about *Streetcar*, which Williams had angrily rejected. Williams, however, felt deeply that his artistic integrity *had* been violated during the production of *Cat*. Although he stoutly maintained ever after that Kazan had been good for this play, as he had been for the others, some comments that he made almost twenty years after the incident shed some light on what he was actually experiencing:

You know, on the surface, I didn't resent his making me change it so much, but it was like a deep psychic violation, I was very disturbed after that experience with *Cat*. In fact, I couldn't write for several months after that. I went to Rome and simply could not write.[49]

Three years later, he said in *Memoirs* that he had disagreed even with the re-writing of Maggie's character, which he had said he "embraced wholeheartedly" (RV 125) at the time, as well as feeling that he "had to violate [his] own intuition"[50] by bringing Big Daddy back in Act 3.

Of greatest importance in studying the artistic collaboration between playwright and director is that, despite the facts of their interaction, Williams felt that something in his innermost artistic imagination had been denied or interfered with during the process of collaboration on *Cat on a Hot Tin Roof*. That the source of his feeling was not logically demonstrable did not make it less real to him, and it affected his future work with Kazan and with other directors in a fundamental way. In November of 1955, eight months after *Cat*'s opening, Williams wrote to Audrey Wood about the upcoming production of *Orpheus Descending* that he was determined to express himself alone, not a director or actors. He said that there was a sense of falsity about the ending of *Cat*, and that he did not want that ever to happen again, even if it meant giving up the "top-rank names" as co-workers.[51] But no matter how violated he might have felt by his sense that Kazan had compelled him to make changes that he did not believe in, and no matter how determined he was to maintain artistic control over his work in the future, the fact is that Williams continued to work with Kazan, to solicit his advice, and to rely on his judgement in the writing and production of his plays for another five years. Williams's artistic and emotional dependence on his collaborator was more profound than his feelings of violation, but the combination of these feelings produced a deep ambivalence in his attitude toward Kazan that contributed to the disintegration of their creative relationship.

It cannot be denied that Kazan's suggestions had precipitated a fundamental change in the meaning of *Cat on a Hot Tin Roof*. Williams had written a play about death and life, strength and weakness. Death would conquer the raging power of a strong man determined to live, he was saying, but new life could also spring from the death of the spirit. Big Daddy might be defeated, but Maggie would triumph, and thus the next generation would be made possible. By bringing Big Daddy back into Act 3 to accept the death he rages against in Act 2, and by having him participate in the making of the new generation through his laying of hands on Maggie, Williams took away his raging defiance and replaced it with wisdom and acceptance. By exchanging Maggie's triumph over Brick for a hopeful truce, Williams replaced his homage to Maggie's amoral life spirit and indomitable will with a hopeful affirmation of the possibility for regeneration in the human soul.

Nonetheless, it should not be forgotten that Tennessee Williams wrote both of these plays. Kazan's advice to bring Big Daddy back did not mean that he had to come back to hear Maggie's announcement that she had life in her body and to confirm it, nor did the suggestion that Brick go through some change as a result of his truth-telling with Big Daddy necessarily mean that he would cooperate with Maggie's desire to bring new life into the world. In rewriting the play to please Kazan, Williams ended up with a play that he liked less than the one he had first conceived, but it was he who made the changes in the script. Once the concept was there, Kazan's direction emphasized the victory of life over death that occurred in the third act. The collaboration on this play was perhaps most disturbing to

Williams because Kazan's ideas had altered his fundamental conception of the play early in its writings. In this play, for the first time, his and Kazan's readings of the play's meaning had differed significantly. Seeing the play through Kazan's eyes had altered his conception of it, and he felt the deep involvement of his collaborator in his part of the creative process as a violation. His publication of the earlier third act was an act of protection by an author who felt that he somehow no longer "owned" his play, an attempt to preserve his original vision. Over the next few years, Williams was to be preoccupied with his relationship with Kazan, and he tried several times to understand it by trying to articulate it more clearly.

5   Realism and Metatheatre: *Sweet Bird of Youth*

Baby Doll and the interim

With the public display of his complaints in the published version of *Cat*, Williams had put a strain on his relationship with Kazan that was evident in the next two projects they collaborated on, the film *Baby Doll* and the play *Sweet Bird of Youth*. The idea for *Baby Doll* had begun to take shape back in 1951 when the two had decided to drop the original plans for producing *Ten Blocks on the Camino Real* as a one-act play on a bill with *27 Wagons Full of Cotton*. Instead of producing the second play, Williams and Kazan decided to combine it with another early one-act, *The Unsatisfactory Supper*, and make it into a movie. The work resulted in the controversial *Baby Doll*, but not before the collaborators had weathered some serious aesthetic disagreements. Since Williams was rather apathetic toward the writing at first, Kazan went ahead and put a script together from the two plays.[1] Williams felt that the script was a misreading of his plays – a melodrama instead of the "grotesque folk-comedy" he had written originally.[2] Putting Kazan in his artistic place, Williams wrote him a letter noting that, although he considered Kazan the greatest living director, he was not impressed with his talent as a script doctor.[3] Three months later, Williams wrote to Audrey Wood that he had received a long-distance call from Jack Warner praising the script to the skies. Somewhat embittered, the playwright remarked that Kazan probably wrote better than it read.[4]

Kazan remembered that Williams had first become enthusiastic about the film after he'd seen Carroll Baker play Baby Doll Meighan in a scene at Actors Studio. When Williams embraced Baker and sang out "She's it!," Kazan "seized on this flare of enthusiasm to wring a promise from [Williams] that he'd come south with [Kazan] and work seriously on the script" (L 562).[5] Kazan has remembered subsequent events in slightly different ways at different times. It is clear, however, that Williams came down to Benoit, Mississippi, but left after a few days, giving the explanations that it was too cold to swim in the town's outdoor swimming pool and that he felt people in the town were hostile to him because of his homosexuality.[6] Williams went on to Coral Gables, Florida, where *Sweet Bird of Youth* was to have its first production in the spring, sending Kazan a new ending for the film from there.

Despite Williams's seemingly reluctant involvement in *Baby Doll*, he did a substantial amount of work on the script.[7] Nonetheless, Williams dissociated himself from the film early on, portraying it as largely Kazan's creation. In a 1957 interview, he said, "I hope people don't associate me with *Baby Doll* alone ... I am not ashamed of it, but a movie is the creation of the director. It is a very different medium from the stage."[8] He went on to say that Elia Kazan "is a fine director. I think he did a fine job. But the movie has many things in it that I did not write. It has at least one scene that I objected to when it was being filmed. It was symbolic in a way that I considered bad taste."[9] Williams declined to identify the scene, but his public remarks on the subject could only have aggravated the friction his "Note of Explanation" in the reading version of *Cat* had introduced into his relationship with Kazan. In later years, however, Williams changed in his attitude toward *Baby Doll*, expressing his pride in both his work and Kazan's. When asked in 1965 which of the films made from his work he liked, he replied, "every film which Kazan made of my work – he made two. *Baby Doll* pleased me very much – that was an original film script."[10]

In the four years between the work on *Baby Doll* and the production of *Sweet Bird of Youth*, Williams and Kazan remained in close touch. Kazan came to Florida along with Cheryl Crawford and Audrey Wood to see the early production of *Sweet Bird* at Coral Gables in April of 1956, and the two men began working toward a Broadway production. Meanwhile, Kazan made his film *A Face in the Crowd* with Budd Schulberg and directed William Inge's *The Dark at the Top of the Stairs* and Archibald MacLeish's *J. B.* on Broadway. The "Kazan magic" was very obviously still at work in these productions, both resounding commercial and critical successes. Perhaps in an attempt to answer critics who accused him of violating the integrity of playwrights, Kazan allowed his correspondence with MacLeish and parts of his notebooks on *J. B.* to be published in *Esquire*.[11] The attacks on his directorial "tampering" did not stop, however, some critics using the *Esquire* piece as evidence for what they saw as unwarranted interference with the author's "original intention."[12] Williams, whose relationship with Kazan had been complicated by the experiences with *Cat* and *Baby Doll*, had to watch him direct a play by Williams's admitted rival William Inge with great success while Williams gave the rejected *Orpheus Descending* to Harold Clurman – a director he had never felt comfortable with and whose work he did not particularly admire. *Orpheus* ran just eight weeks after being savaged by the critics.

In 1957 Williams wrote an article for *Playbill* which was meant to clarify his views on the author–director relationship, but which ended up expressing his ambivalence much as the note in *Cat* had. One thing he was certain about was the collaborative nature of drama. "Whether he likes it or not," he wrote, "a writer for the stage must face the fact that the making of a play is, finally, a collaborative venture, and plays have rarely achieved a full-scale success without being in some manner raised above their manuscript level by the brilliant gifts of actors, directors, designers, and frequently even the seasoned theatrical instincts of their producers."[13]

In the essay, Williams outlined three stages of the playwright's relationship with his collaborators. The first was that of the terrified neophyte who would agree to almost anything to get his play on the stage, the second that of the "Name" playwright who, having had one notable success, now became a "great, uncompromising Purist, feeling that all ideas but his own are threats to the integrity of his work" (A & D 94). According to Williams this stage might remain as a kind of arrested development, or it might give way after a failure or two to a third stage in which the playwright came to understand that his own view of his work could be fallible and came to believe in "the existence of vitally creative minds in other departments of theater than the writing department." He continued, "even if, sometimes, they wish him to express, or let him help them express, certain ideas and feelings of their own, he has now recognized that there are elements of the incomplete in his nature and in the work it produces" (A & D 95).

This statement could certainly be seen as a conciliatory gesture toward the director he had offended with his earlier remarks about *Cat*, but he went on to say that there was danger in this third stage: "There is the danger that the playwright may be as abruptly divested of confidence in his own convictions as that confidence was first born in him. He may suddenly become a sort of ventriloquist's dummy for ideas which are not his own at all" (A & D 95). Having said this, Williams immediately distanced himself from any anxiety on this score, adding, "but that is a danger to which only the hack writer is exposed, and so it doesn't much matter. A serious playwright can only profit from passage into the third phase, for what he will now do is this: he will listen; he will consider; he will give a receptive attention to any creative mind that he has the good fortune to work with" (A & D 95–96). Williams then went on to describe the peculiar situation of the playwright whose "work is so highly individual that no one but the playwright is capable of discovering the right key for it." "When this rare instance occurs," he wrote, "the playwright has just two alternatives. Either he must stage his play himself or he must find one particular director who has the very unusual combination of a truly creative imagination plus a true longing, or even just a true willingness, to devote his own gifts to the faithful projection of someone else's vision. This is a thing of rarity" (A & D 96–97).

Williams was of course describing his own relationship with Elia Kazan, the Elia Kazan who had directed *A Streetcar Named Desire*. Kazan had been handed a finished script for *Streetcar*, and by his own account had only been interested in creating the fullest theatrical representation of what he saw as Williams's vision in the play. Again by his own account, Kazan had been less and less satisfied with the limitations of his creative role and had, with *The Rose Tattoo*, *Camino Real*, *Cat on a Hot Tin Roof*, and *Baby Doll* become increasingly more involved in the shaping and even writing of the work, encouraged by the attitude of a not only receptive but creatively and emotionally dependent playwright. Both Williams's resentment of Kazan's role in this complex relationship and his keen perception of its elements was evident in his description of the inevitably ensuing conflict:

> There are very few directors who are imaginative and yet also willing to forego the willful imposition of their own ideas on a play. How can you blame them? It is all but impossibly hard for any artist to devote his gifts to the mere interpretation of the gifts of another. He wants to leave his own special signature on whatever he works on.
>
> Here we encounter the sadly familiar conflict between playwright and director. And just as a playwright must recognize the value of conceptions outside his own, a director of serious plays must learn to accept the fact that nobody knows a play better than the man who wrote it. The director must know that the playwright has already produced this play on the stage of his imagination, and just as it is important for a playwright to forget certain vanities in the interest of the total creation of the stage, so must the director. (A & D 97)

Williams was describing a struggle for creative hegemony over the play. Whose vision was the production, and the published scripts that were prepared from it, to express? His answer was ambivalent. The playwright's first, but the playwright's enriched by the creative minds of his collaborators. The question was, where did collaboration begin and end. When did a director, designer, actor, or producer step over the line that violated the playwright's creative hegemony? Williams chose not to answer to this question.

Preparing for the production

Williams remarked in an interview that *Sweet Bird* was "in the works too long,"[14] making it difficult for him to maintain its structural integrity during its various stages of revision. It was definitely longer in the making than his earlier plays had been. During the forties and early fifties, Williams typically completed a play in eighteen months to two years, often working on two or more manuscripts at the same time. As we have seen, he usually showed the first complete draft of a play to Audrey Wood and to Kazan for their comments, using the detailed response he received from the director in his revisions of the manuscript. With *Sweet Bird* he began a new practice of trying out a "work in progress" in a regional or off-Broadway theatre, revising it heavily both during rehearsals and after he had had the benefit of a full production, before he took the play to Broadway. Like *Cat*, *Sweet Bird* originated in two separate story-lines and sets of characters that Williams brought together to make the full-length play. One was about a young gigolo who uses his older patron, originally a middle-aged man, to help him return to his home town in order to win back "his girl." The other, which went back to a play called "The Pink Bedroom," was about a corrupt political boss and his disenchanted mistress. In reworking the script, Williams soon saw that his aging homosexual would have to be made into a woman, and he created the aging movie queen who became Alexandra del Lago, the Princess Kosmonopolis. He moved the focus on the Boss and his mistress into the background as he reworked the story of Chance Wayne and the Finleys, putting the young lovers at the center, but once his imagination caught fire with the Princess, he was never able to subordinate the story of Chance and her to the story of Chance and Heavenly. Williams remained unhappy with the script throughout its productions in Coral Gables, Florida in 1956, on Broadway in 1959, and in Los Angeles in 1961, for each of which he reworked the script substantially.

Williams wrote a program note for the Coral Gables production which betrayed his nervousness in putting his work before the public so hastily:

This is an experimental work in more ways than one or two or three! It has never taken me less than a year to write a play. This one has been written in a few weeks. After barely two weeks' writing, it was put in rehearsal, and all during the rehearsal period I have been working on it, constantly submitting new scenes and "bits" to the directors and actors. I'm not quite sure what possessed me to undertake such a reckless adventure.[15]

The playwright went on to say that he was not asking for any special consideration by referring to the play as a work in progress, but asked the audience to treat it as a finished play. "In this way," he wrote, "even if your reaction is totally or partially negative, you will be more helpful than if you made concessions. This is a raw work, but it has enough in it of what I want to say about human relationships, to make me continue with it, despite any immediate reaction."[16] The production was a way of assessing audience response without having to rely on his own instincts, or those of others, for what would succeed in the theatre. He was to make use of this test frequently in the future.

The Broadway production of *Sweet Bird of Youth* actually began at the end of April, 1956 when Kazan, Wood and producer Cheryl Crawford came to Florida to see the production directed by George Keathley at the Studio M Playhouse. In May, Crawford sent Williams her "notes" on the play, suggesting that he make the unfulfilled yearnings of Chance Wayne, then called Phil Beam, clearer to the audience. She also commented that "the marijuana smoking scene in Act One made [her] feel a little giggly, seemed like *piling* on too much and an overfamiliar way of showing vice, particularly after the extraordinary original and brilliant image of the oxygen mask."[17] Crawford suggested that the beginning of Act 2, at that time set in a church and a hospital, be moved to the Finleys' house, that Miss Lucy seemed to have no function in the bar scene because she and Phil did not interact, and that Phil's monologue was too direct and explicit. Williams took her advice to heart. He eventually did move the beginning of Act 2 to the Finleys' house, and he united Chance and Miss Lucy in opposition to the Boss in the bar scene.

Meanwhile Audrey Wood was working on a deal for the film rights to *Sweet Bird*. In July Williams sent her a scenario which he admitted was a poor synopsis, commenting that he never could reduce his plays to summaries.[18] In the scenario he wrote that *Sweet Bird* was about the betrayal of people's hearts by personal and social corruption, identifying the sources of corruption as the individual will-to-power and the fierce competition in capitalist society.[19] Despite the rather confused scenario, Wood succeeded in selling the film rights to MGM long before the play was produced on Broadway, a personal triumph for Williams over the studio that had fired him after a few weeks as a studio writer in 1943 and had rejected his original scenario for *The Glass Menagerie* before it had been produced as a play.

Cheryl Crawford has written in her autobiography that she put in a bid to produce *Sweet Bird* as soon as she had seen the Coral Gables production in 1956. She wrote to Audrey Wood, "I must put in the strongest appeal I can make to be in on *Sweet Bird of Youth*," reminding Wood of the hard work she had done to keep *The Rose Tattoo* going for two seasons and to raise the money for *Camino Real*, a very poor risk in the commercial theatre of 1953. Crawford closed the letter with no doubt of her interest in producing the play: "I want desperately to be involved with *Sweet Bird*, and I believe I can bring something of value to a production."[20] The question of the producer was left up in the air for two years, however, as Williams, Kazan, and Wood went on with their plans for the play. By March of 1958, Crawford's letters to Wood had reached a note of what she described as quiet desperation,[21] but the agreement to have Crawford produce the play was not finally concluded until July. At that time Williams wrote to Crawford, telling her how delighted he was that she was going to work with them and apologizing for the delay in making the final decisions. He explained that he had had to work out a financial set-up with Wood and Kazan before a final commitment could be made to a producer.[22] This negotiation was far from the old Broadway model in which the producer essentially bought a play and hired a director for it. Here the fundamental financial control of the production as well as the artistic control was in the hands of Kazan and Williams, through his agent Audrey Wood. Kazan also invested $37,500 in *Sweet Bird*, for 10 percent of the capitalization.

Crawford seemed to have learned her lesson about paying top dollar for the best designer after *Camino Real*. Although his contract was not signed until November 19, 1958, there seemed to be no question of Jo Mielziner's involvement in the production from its beginning. As early as August, he was at work on the script, doing preliminary breakdowns of lighting and prop needs and preliminary sketches early in the month.[23] The first idea for costume designer had been Lucinda Ballard, but Kazan, who had had trouble with her volatile temperament when they worked together on *J. B.*, suggested Anna Hill Johnstone, the costumer for most of his films. She was hired, and Williams's old friend Paul Bowles was commissioned to compose the "Lament," which was to be the only original music in the production.

As the production team was being assembled, Williams was hard at work on revisions. The writing of *Sweet Bird* was done during one of his worst periods psychologically. On September 7, 1956, he wrote to Maria St. Just that he was "a total wreck, nervously."[24] On January 3, 1957, he apologized for not having written recently: "These last few months in my life are the worst that I can remember, and that's why I haven't kept in touch with you. I was too preoccupied with the necessary business of trying not to crack up, and I am far from sure that I have succeeded" (St. Just 139). The failure of *Orpheus Descending* in the spring did not help his condition. On June 17, he wrote that he was supposed to leave the next day "for the plush-lined loony-bin at Stockbridge, Massachusetts and the start of analysis" (St. Just 148). He underwent intense psychoanalysis throughout the following year. In April he wrote: "The old doctor says that I am passing through 'purgatory.' I thought I had been going through that all my life, but he seems to think it has to get worse before it can get any better. Well, it ain't better yet!" (St. Just 151).

Beginning work on *Sweet Bird* revisions in the same month, Williams piled up page after page of manuscript.[25] In August he wrote to Crawford from Rome that he was cutting down on the play's potential for sensationalism.[26] This potential and the lack of cohesion between the Chance–

Princess story and the Boss Finley story were the two major problems he saw in the script at that time, but he thought they could be solved before rehearsals began.[27] He hoped to do this by beginning Act 2, scene 1 in Boss Finley's house with a sharp focus on Chance's return to St. Cloud, as opposed to the two short scenes dramatizing Heavenly's "miracle" in the church on Easter Sunday and her trip to the hospital to prove with X-rays that her uterus had been restored. At this stage, Williams reduced the "miracle" incident to exposition, having Tom Jr., Scudder, and Heavenly tell the story of the "miracle" to the Boss at the Finleys' house. Williams also thought the telephone call between Chance and Heavenly, which at that time made up Act 2, scene 2, should be cut so there would be no conversation between the boy and girl in the play. He thought Chance should not show the nude photos of Heavenly as a young girl to Scudder, as he did in the current version, but to the Princess, in order to motivate her mixed feelings of jealousy and compassion.[28]

Williams did not manage to complete the script revisions as quickly as he had hoped to. The pre-production script, from which the play was set up in galleys for *Esquire* in December, 1958, retained the phone-call scene and the discussion of Heavenly's "miracle," but it included the change in Act 1, scene 2, in which Chance showed the photographs of Heavenly to the Princess. Williams continued to do substantial work on the script during the rehearsal and tryout periods, even submitting a revised third act for the *Esquire* version, which appeared in the April, 1959 issue. The phone-call scene and the "miracle" scene were cut only in the last stages of rehearsal.

While he worked on a script which continued to frustrate him, Williams faced the possible loss of his director. In mid September he wrote to Crawford from London that Audrey Wood had called to tell him Kazan was making outrageous financial demands. Williams said he had just received a cable telling him he had to make up his mind whether to keep Kazan as director by noon that day. Obviously frantic, Williams wrote to Crawford that Wood thought Kazan was making impossible demands because he had had a change of heart about the play and wanted out. Finding it hard to believe that a friend would treat him in this way, Williams asked Crawford to intervene, adding that he was willing to give the best possible terms to Kazan at his own expense, because he felt this play needed the director more than any of the others. The artistic quality of the production came first, he said, and the money far second.[29] Crawford sent the letter to Kazan, and the problem was resolved, but Williams's nervous state and his lack of belief in the play persisted.

The other aspects of the production went more smoothly. Crawford wrote exuberantly to Williams that she was "running Broadway now – 'count of you."[30] People were "begging" her to take their checks for *Sweet Bird* – a pleasant contrast to her experience with *Camino Real*. Crawford was also pleased with the result of her negotiations with Warner Brothers to get long-time Actors Studio member, now Hollywood star, Paul Newman released from his movie contract in order to do the play. Newman's contract for the play, signed on September 22, specified that he would receive "first star billing" and that he would be paid 10 percent of the box office receipts. It also specified that the contract was entered into with the understanding that Kazan was to direct the play. Newman was given the right of approval should another director be chosen for any reason.

Everyone breathed easier once Newman had been engaged, but although he gave an excellent performance as Chance Wayne, it was the casting of Geraldine Page as the Princess that proved to be the making of the production. Williams had originally written the part for Anna Magnani, an actress whose flare for the theatrical is central to the Princess's character. Kazan, however, chose Geraldine Page, then a young member of Actors Studio who had made a name for herself in José Quintero's off-Broadway production of *Summer and Smoke*. Crawford disagreed with the choice, thinking that Page was just too young for the part.[31] Kazan stuck by his choice, however, and, as he had in the past, Williams trusted Kazan's instincts about the play's casting. Time was to prove him right, but not before some difficult moments had been endured by all concerned. After some reluctance on Crawford's part, Sidney Blackmer was cast as Boss Finley. Madeleine Sherwood, who had played Mae in *Cat*, was given the role of Lucy, and three young actors from the Studio, Diana Hyland, Rip Torn, and Bruce Dern, were cast as Heavenly, Tom Jr., and Stuff.

By October Mielziner had completed his set design, working closely with Kazan as always. Because the design relied heavily on lighting, however, Mielziner was very concerned about the choice of stage manager. In early December, he prompted Kazan to write to Crawford, reminding her that the stage manager would have to have great expertise in lighting.[32] Crawford wrote to Mielziner the next day to reassure him that Dave Pardoll, the chosen stage manager, had the necessary experience to handle the complicated lighting.

The other technical difficulty in the staging was the huge television screen that was to be set up in the bar scene for the projection of Boss Finley's speech. Kazan has written that the television screen was introduced to help carry off the weak second act. The audience would see the projected image of the Boss at the same time as it saw the man himself speaking from the forestage, he explained, in order to indicate the pervasiveness of his power in the community and the reality of his threats of violence against Chance Wayne. Kazan maintains that, although the device "made Tennessee nervous," it "worked effectively and made its point" in front of an audience (L 544). In creating the effect, the advice of experts from MGM was sought early in December, and Mielziner eventually produced the projection, but he was never happy with it. As he recalled the difficulties involved in combining live actors with filmed images, Mielziner noted that the problem was primarily one of scale. The filmed image lost authenticity in the third dimension when it was scaled down to the size of a living actor, and the combination of the actor's voice, heard unamplified, and the electronic-sounding voice heard on the film created a serious production problem. Unlike Kazan, Mielziner thought the device caused "a lack of cohesion in what was otherwise a stunning performance and a colorful production."[33]

As Kazan and Mielziner continued their work on the staging, Kazan became increasingly worried about Williams's lack of progress on the promised revisions. At the end of December, he wrote to the playwright, expressing his fear that Williams was working on other things – specifically some screenplays and the new play *Period of Adjustment*, which was about to open at Coral Gables – rather than making the revisions of *Sweet Bird* that had to be ready for rehearsals in a few weeks. Reminding Kazan that he had directed *J. B.* while *Sweet Bird* was in preparation, Williams protested that the distractions afforded by the *Period* production were good for *Sweet Bird*, and that he had been working on his revisions daily. He added that he was leaving for Havana the next day to prepare himself for the trials of production and asked Kazan to arrange for his swimming privileges at the New York Athletic Club during rehearsals.[34]

Despite these preparations, the production nearly met its end after the first reading early in January. Williams and Kazan have both described the scene at the first reading and its aftermath, with different emphases. Williams's description in *Memoirs* is the more striking:

The reading begins.

About halfway through it I leap from my chair and cry out, "Stop it, stop it! It can't go on, it's too awful!"

A total hush descends upon the rehearsal hall as I stride deliriously out into Times Square. I go home and knock myself out with booze and a pill . . . Evening comes in due course. Then there is a strong knock at the door: the sort of knock that says, Open up in the name of the law!

I open up and there stand Molly and Gadg [Elia] Kazan sweetly and genially smiling as if nothing has happened of an unusual nature . . . I am now dreadfully ashamed of my conduct before the company but not yet swerved from my conviction that the play should not go on.

Gadg and Molly talk to me as you do to a wounded animal or a sick child. Gradually my desperate resolve crumbles: I love them. I decide to trust them.[35]

Kazan's description of the event was less histrionic, but no less cognizant of the near disaster of the first reading. "At the first reading of the play by its cast," he wrote, "everything fell apart. Tennessee left before it was over. Gerry Page quickly returned to her dressing room" (L 545). At this point, Kazan reported, Page was certain that she could not play the part of the Princess. After reassuring her and confirming his belief in her talent, Kazan went to see Williams. He found that Page's "fearful and hesitant reading that first day [had] convinced Tennessee that she didn't have the bravura for the role ... more seriously, he doubted his own play; he wanted it withdrawn. I believe that only the rather mystical faith he had in me persuaded him to go ahead. I had never seen him so timorous after the first reading" (L 545).

The degree to which Williams's deep insecurity and his dependence on Kazan continued to plague both him and the production, however, is evident from an incident he recounted in *Memoirs*, when a young writer from Actors Studio was seated directly beside Kazan, in Williams's accustomed place, during one of the rehearsals. Williams wrote that he "paranoiacally" suspected the young man had been brought in to rewrite his work and was only reassured when he was again sitting in his "rightful place next to our great white father Kazan."[36]

Aside from keeping his author steady, Kazan's biggest challenge was getting the performance out of Page that he knew was in her to realize the character of the Princess. He recalled that he had had to use "some extreme measures – like making her 'camp' the part for a few rehearsals, to break down the inhibitions that the truth-seeking of the Method often causes in our actors" (L 545). In an interview, Page described his technique as "very strong and forceful." Detecting Page's fear and shyness when she was told to go downstage and address the audience, Kazan told her, "Every time you go down there and you get scared, get louder and nastier." Although Page remembered that she had frightened herself in performance, "every time [she] did what he said, the audience loved it."[37]

Throughout the rehearsal period, the problems with the second act continued to plague both playwright and director. To Kazan, *Sweet Bird* "seemed to be two one-act plays, one about the Princess and one about Chance Wayne and his girl."[38] In an interview he stated bluntly that "*Sweet Bird* was a script with a fault, a serious fault: its interest was split between two characters . . . I thought that play needed some sort of directorial 'holding up.' . . . I did some stunts with that play, because I thought it needed it."[39]

Williams had a particularly hard time with the revision of the second act. It was not until the rehearsal period that he was able to make the changes he had envisioned the previous August, and even then he found it difficult. Two weeks after the opening, Williams wrote to Brooks Atkinson that the rehearsal period had been the most gruelling work-out of his career, all centered on Act 2. He added that there were at least ten versions of the act, and he still wasn't sure whether they had ended up with the right one.[40] In an interview shortly after the opening, Williams explained that the second act was particularly hard for him because he wasn't interested in Boss Finley or Heavenly as characters. He also complained that he was "inundated with notes suggesting changes – from somebody other than the director" and that he "felt castrated," adding that "any other point of view except the director's and author's together should be left alone. Otherwise it creates chaos. They demoralise the writer, sap what is left of his confidence."[41] The interfering point of view was probably that of producer Crawford. It was she who had suggested moving the beginning of Act 2 to Boss Finley's house, thus making the boss a major character in the play, and had encouraged the deletion of the phone call between Chance and Heavenly in which Heavenly explained what had happened to her in Los Angeles. On the other hand, Williams referred in a later interview to line changes suggested by Geraldine Page as "enormously valuable," noting that he often made line changes suggested by actors "if they're intelligent and care about the play."[42]

Williams gave a deeper reason for his failure to produce a satisfactory second act a year after the production had opened: "The truth is, the second act of that play is just not well written. I was in a terrible state of depression at the time, and couldn't function, except on just a craftsmanship level. Kazan wanted a great second act, and I couldn't give it to him."[43] At the time, Williams was rewriting the script for the acting version published by Dramatists Play Service in 1962. In revising the second act, Williams cut the scene at the Boss's house that had been urged on him by Crawford and began Act 2 with the bar scene that makes up Act 2, scene 2 in the reading version published by New Directions in 1959. In the acting version, Act 2, scene 2 consists of face-to-face confrontation between Heavenly and Chance which retains much of the material from the telephone conversation that makes up Act 2, scene 2 in the earliest version published by *Esquire*. In other words, Williams took out the changes that Crawford had suggested to him when she had seen the production in 1956 and essentially restored the play to its earlier form.

In later interviews, Williams ascribed the faults of *Sweet Bird* to his inability to develop the characters of Boss Finley and Chance Wayne to his satisfaction. Of the Boss he wrote:

I have to understand the characters in my play in order to write about them because if I just hate them I can't write about them. That's why Boss Finley wasn't right in *Sweet Bird of Youth*, because I just didn't like the guy, and I just had to make a *tour de force* of his part in the play . . . The one thing I cannot – I can understand maybe – but, no I don't even understand that kind of self-infatuated, self-blindness and cruelty, you know, such as he . . . Finley . . . personified.[44]

Chance, he said, is not an effective character because he "is used in a symbolic manner. It is a ritualistic death, a metaphor. He had to be real to be important. You cannot use a character as a dramatic symbol if he is important. You cannot use a character as a dramatic symbol if he is not first real for you. I didn't discover his real value until the end."[45]

Williams left no doubt of his continued admiration of and affection for his director throughout the rehearsal process. In an interview a week before the Philadelphia opening, Williams tried to define the essence of his relationship with Kazan:

He has been good for my work. Often. But beneath that recognition from me there is a deeper current not so easily put. There is a kind of subterranean communication between a playwright and a director. No matter what, it is there. Between an inept writer and a blazing director or between a blazing writer and a fool of a director. It has to be. But there is also a limit to this subterranean reading of each other. The limit comes at the moment of change. Some directors feel compulsion to change, even rewrite, a playwright during rehearsal. This is castration of a writer and I cannot stand for that. We never reach that moment.[46]

Despite Williams's descriptions of his inability to function as a writer, Kazan had only good to say of Williams's work and conduct during the rehearsals for *Sweet Bird*:

He was always very fair to me during rehearsals . . . whatever his personal complaints. He was as fine to work with as he had been on the other plays. He was never difficult, never falsely critical, always generous. He worked every day, he brought in new material for rehearsals every afternoon. He was really an adorable man to work with, and I loved and respected him enormously.[47]

In his autobiography, Kazan has confessed a conviction that he "took over" the production of *Sweet Bird of Youth* as he had the production of *Cat on a Hot Tin Roof*. As he had with *Cat*, Kazan felt that he pushed Williams into a less realistic treatment of the play than Williams would have preferred, perhaps abusing the playwright's belief in his magical directorial powers in order to gain artistic control. "Again I had the feeling that I was violating the author," he wrote, "and that there was a gap between us, on one side of which I was satisfied, while he, on the other, was not. I was again determined, however, to go my own way and produce the play as I saw it" (L 545).

The designer's language

In conceiving the production of *Sweet Bird of Youth*, Kazan went through the same process he had with *Cat*, essentially taking a script grounded in the objective realism of representational theatre and increasing its subjectivity by imposing a presentational theatricality upon the representational base. Many critics commented on the play's similarity to *Cat*, which was evident not only in the resemblance of Boss Finley to Big Daddy and Chance Wayne to Brick Pollitt but in the production's presentational focus on the intersubjectivity of actor and audience and the general plan of the set. Like his design for *Cat*, Mielziner's design for *Sweet Bird* was basically a unit set whose centerpiece was a large, raked bed. Because *Sweet Bird* was not confined to the bedroom, however, the play also called for scenes on the Finleys' front porch and in the bar of the hotel. Mielziner met this demand with a staging technique he had discovered when he was designing *Death of a Salesman*, a play that needed to maintain continuity of action while it shifted to the various locations of the scenes in Willy Loman's mind. By taking selective realism to its furthest point of abstraction, Mielziner was able to produce a convincing scene change using projections, an expressive lighting code, and the very minimum of furniture. In *Salesman* a single desk and chair became first the office of Willy's employer and then that of his friend Charlie. A corner of the stage became a Boston hotel room with a change of lighting and the projection of a wallpaper pattern.

Employing this principle in the design for *Sweet Bird*, Mielziner created a set with three levels. At the rear of the stage was a four-foot high "gallery" with ramps at the left and right, and portable steps that could be added or removed for various scenes. This triangular platform came to a point at about the center of the stage. At stage right of the point was the second platform, eighteen inches high, on which the huge bed was placed in Acts 1 and 3. In Act 2, scene 1, this platform became the Finleys' porch through the replacement of the bed with two rattan chairs and a table. The table and chairs remained for the bar scene in Act 2, scene 2, when the platform became the terrace of the bar. The area at stage left of the point was at stage level. It contained a trunk, a chair, a tabouret with the telephone, a chaise longue, several pieces of the Princess's pink alligator luggage, and Chance's metal suitcase in Acts 1 and 3. These objects were removed for the scene at the Finleys' house and replaced during the bar scene with a small bar unit and a table with four chairs (see plate 16).

Aside from these minimal pieces of furniture, the play's three settings were all created with light and projections. As in *Cat*, the set contained no doors or windows. The actors mimed the opening of a door or looking out of a window when it was called for. A cyclorama at the rear of the stage covered by a permanent gauze scrim allowed for the projection of shutters in the first scene and of palms, sea, and sky when the "shutters" were "opened," much as the blinds and the sky had been projected in *Cat*. A new feature of the staging in *Sweet Bird* was the use of two sets of transparent travelers – light curtains that could easily be pulled open and closed by the actors – one at the front and one at the rear of the stage. These travelers represented window curtains in the hotel room. When the play began, the front traveler was lighted from the front, leaving the set in darkness. As Chance came on and lit his cigarette, the onstage lights built up behind the traveler, revealing the dim scene in the hotel room to the audience. Then Chance parted the traveler, looking out to see what kind of a day it was, as an amber spotlight of "sunshine" hit him. Then Chance pulled the traveler open, revealing the set fully to the audience. As Chance and the Princess prepared to have sex at the end of Act 1, scene 1, Chance closed the front traveler, hiding them from the audience. To signify the sex act, a cloud effect was projected onto the traveler along with the musical accompaniment of the "Lament," as "corny" a moment as Elia Kazan ever produced in the theatre, but one that he introduced during rehearsals to replace the simple dimming of the lights that Williams had called for in the pre-production script. At the end of the play, Chance went to the traveler after he said his final lines, held it a moment while he shook his head, and slowly pulled it closed.

The intrusiveness of this material framing device is a good indication of the attitude Kazan and Mielziner took to the production of *Sweet Bird of Youth*. Believing they had a weak script, they seemed determined to shift as much of the play's signification as they could to the material elements of the stage language. More than any of their earlier collaborative efforts, *Sweet Bird* was a play whose story-line was propelled by the codes of lighting, space, movement, and gesture.

The traveler at the rear of the stage was used much as the front traveler was. In the opening scene, shutters were projected on it. The waiter Fly "opened them" when he entered the room, letting in more light, much to Chance's irritation. When the Princess looked out of the window to see where she was, Kazan had Page look straight into the audience, out of the "front" window, where she saw the palm garden and the highway, and then at the rear projection, where she saw the beach and the water. The use of mime in the opening scene, very similar to that in *Cat*, also signalled the play's combination of representational realism and subjectivity to the audience. When Fly entered, carrying a very real tray with a coffee service for one, a vase with a rose in it and two glasses – one containing a Bromo – he knocked on the imaginary door. Chance looked into an imaginary mirror, just as Maggie had, arranging his thinning hair before he mimed opening the door.

The pre-production script had specified a white platform for Boss Finley's house, with a door frame and a single white column against a backdrop of sea and sky. Williams noted that the effect should be all blue and white, as strict as a canvas by Georgia O'Keefe. As such, the set would have been a typical example of the established Mielziner style of combining abstract frameworks with lighting effects. Mielziner and Kazan decided to go one step further with this set, however, and do without the framework. The stage contained only the table and chairs and a small bench. At the beginning of Act 2, the servant Charles opened the rear traveler to reveal a sea-and-sky drop with projections of the Boss's house and porch, the palms, and an urn filled with dying foliage on it. The scene was thus created almost completely with light, realizing successfully Mielziner's notion of abstract realism. For the second scene, the furniture remained, and the sea-and-sky drop was replaced with a drop with stylized projections of blue palms, a subjective representation of the characters' environment. The platform, which had now become the terrace of the bar, also was surrounded by numerous tiny bulbs representing stars. The rear platform became the gallery leading to the hotel ballroom with the hanging of a large, ornate red chandelier above it and the addition of a staircase with an ornate handrail, painted red and hung with tassles. These two details signified the decadent milieu of the grand hotel in which Chance is now most comfortable. The bar unit and a table with chairs made the area at stage left into the hotel bar. Again the major design principle was selection, using minimal furniture and letting the lighting effects carry the main burden of both signification and mood.

The set for Act 3 was identical to that for Act 1, except for certain details signifying flight. The bed was made, with the Princess's satin sheets folded on top of it. The focal point of the scene was not the bed, as it had been in Act 1, but the Princess's pink alligator luggage, piled at the center of the stage to signify flight and impermanence. The Princess and Chance sat on these pieces of luggage as they discussed the future at the end of the play. The rear traveler was open, the effect on the scrim and backdrop changed to an evening sky and sea, which became increasingly stormy as Act 3 progressed, an omen of Chance's impending doom, just as the storm in *Cat* had been used. Again the design was spare and efficient, with the burden of mood and environment placed on the lighting.

Aside from the scrim and the projections, Mielziner's basic lighting scheme was simple in concept, although technically complicated. General lighting was determined by having the travelers serve as "window curtains." When the travelers were opened, the general lighting of the stage was brought up; when they were closed, or it was dark outside, the stage remained dim. Most of the play was lit by two follow-spots, which were used in three major ways. The first was to single out one character, typically framing the actor as he or she came downstage for a long speech, as with the Princess's story of her "comeback" in Act 1, scene 1; Chance's story of his life in Act 1, scene 2; and the Princess's telephone conversation with Sally Powers in Act 3. During these speeches, the rest of the stage was often dimmed out, so that the audience's complete attention was focused on the character who was speaking. The second method was to open the follow-spot out to include two characters, or shine both follow-spots on a whole group, as in the bar scene. This allowed for the emphasis of an interaction between two characters, as when the spot shone on Chance and the Princess in bed and on Chance and Lucy in the bar. It could also serve to focus the audience's attention on one element in a scene, as it did on the group surrounding the bragging Chance in the bar (see plate 17). The third method was to iris the secondary light down to a small pin-head spot that would barely pick out the face of a character in the background. This was used to show Chance's reaction to the Princess's speeches and to remind the audience of the menace facing Chance as the secondary spot just barely picked up Tom Jr. and his henchmen while Chance spoke his final lines after the Princess had left in Act 3.

Most of the play was dimly lit except for the spots, and Mielziner's emphasis of the spotlight served two fundamental aesthetic purposes. The obvious effect was to foreground the play's theatricality. The lighting in this play was clearly not an attempt to reproduce the lighting of objective reality, but an overt statement to the audience of where its attention was being directed. Williams's script invited this interpretation with the Princess's speech as she waited for Chance to complete the call to Sally Powers:

I seem to be standing in light with everything else dimmed out. He's in the dimmed-out background as if he'd never left the obscurity he was born in. I've taken the light again as a crown on my head to which I am suited by something in the cells of my blood and body from the time of my birth.[48]

Taking his cue from this statement, Mielziner made the contrast between the spotlight and the dimness the central element in the visual code. The lighting scheme re-emphasized the role-playing that Kazan used as the basis for both the Princess's characterization and Chance's. The fundamental concept for the production was in fact metatheatre – in the platforms that served as stages on which characters performed for each other; in the spotlights that emphasized their performances; in the placement of the figures on stage; in the movement and gestures of the roles the characters slipped on and off during the play. Both Kazan and Mielziner used all the eloquence of the stage language that was available to them to emphasize the performances within the performances of Paul Newman and Geraldine Page.

The other important function Mielziner's lighting scheme served was a narrative one. Several critics compared the use of spotlights in the production to the use of the "close-up" shot in film, suggesting that Kazan's experience as a film director was being reflected in his work for the stage. There may have been something to this, but Mielziner's lighting plan was more complex and more comprehensive than this. He used the lighting not only to isolate characters for close-ups, but, as a skilled film director employs the camera, for the basic function of narration as well. It was the combination of lighting effects that was important to Mielziner's plan, a combination that directed the audience's attention to the significant action in the scene as it happened, providing an additional thread of narrativity to a script that was perceived to have a weak structure. To do this, Mielziner combined the close-up spots with wider spots that might be seen as the equivalent of "medium shots" in film. In the bar scene, for example, the follow-spot was opened up on Chance and Lucy as they talked and danced a few steps, foregrounding Chance's long-awaited moment in the limelight in his home town. The other figures in the bar remained in dimness as this interaction took place. When Chance came downstage to deliver his speech about "sex envy," both follow-spots irised down, one barely picking out Chance's face while the other showed the facial reactions of the group at the bar. When Chance joined the group at the table, laughing and talking too loud, both follow-spots were opened up on the group, isolating it from the rest of the bar and exposing Chance in a harsher light than had been thrown on him before.

Although this use of light served the same functions of directing the audience's attention, carrying the narrative thread, and framing specific attitudes and reactions that are served by the camera in film, it did not have the camera's sequential limitations. While the most skilful director and film editor can only show one shot after another, conveying action, reaction, and context only through montage, Mielziner was able to achieve these functions simultaneously. He could show the close-up of the speaker alone. He could throw equal light, and therefore equal emphasis, on the speaker and the reactor, dimming out all distractions. He could flood the speaker with light and show the reactor as a dim and therefore insignificant figure in the background. He could light the full stage, therefore emphasizing the speaker's environment and the context in which he or she spoke. All of this he could and did do with the lighting in *Sweet Bird of Youth*. The result was a lighting plan that carried a great deal of the stage language's expressive burden.

The playwright's language

Heavenly

As can be seen from his later comments, the most controversial elements of *Sweet Bird*'s production for Williams were the changes in the script that he felt he was required to make but was never satisfied with. The most important of these took place during rehearsals, under great pressure, and changed the meaning of the play significantly. Most significant was the deletion of the telephone call between Chance and Heavenly that had originally made up Act 2, scene 2 of the play. In this conversation, punctuated by Chance's plaintive refrain, "Heavenly, what happened," Heavenly told the story of her having come out to Los Angeles to see Chance two years before. "Mr. Stars of Tomorrow," who had met her at the airport because Chance was in the county jail on a drug charge, had brought her to a party where she had been drugged and gang-raped. Too humiliated to reveal this to her local doctor, she had allowed the venereal disease contracted from the rape to go untreated until it was decided she must have a hysterectomy to cure her. This telephone call appears in the April, 1959 *Esquire* version of the play, and the substance of the conversation appears in the 1962 Dramatists Play Service version.

In the New York production, this scene was replaced by the scene at Boss Finley's in which the Boss and Tom Jr. plan their vengeance on Chance, a scene that Williams said was difficult for him to write because he had no sympathy with Boss Finley as a character. More significantly for the meaning of the play, however, the responsibility for Heavenly's venereal disease was ascribed more directly to Chance in the production. In the New York version, the explanation was shifted from Heavenly to Tom Jr., who accused Chance in the bar of having given the disease to Heavenly on his last visit to St. Cloud. Tom Jr. implies that Chance had contracted the disease by servicing "this rich bitch, Minnie . . . that slept with any goddam gigolo bastard she could pick up on Bourbon Street or the docks" (ND 102), making Chance's transmission of it to Heavenly all the more reprehensible. Challenged by Tom to explain why he didn't look after Heavenly when he found out he had the disease, Chance says only that he had already left town, and he thought Heavenly would call or write him if anything was wrong. Tom Jr. reminds Chance he has had no address for some time. Obviously this version made Chance a less sympathetic character, diminishing the tragic overtones of his impending fate. In the New York version, rather than having been helplessly unknowing when Heavenly was diseased, Chance was actively responsible for it. This made for a grisly sense of poetic justice in the castrating of Chance, shifting the play's mood from tragic to melodramatic.

In another move apparently made to diminish the play's emphasis of Heavenly, and therefore its reliance on the ingenue role, all mention of Heavenly's "miracle" was cut from the play. As mentioned earlier, the 1956 Coral Gables production had used two scenes, in the church and the hospital, to establish Heavenly's delusion that her fertility had been restored. In the pre-production script, as in the *Esquire* version, these scenes were reduced to a short scene at the Finleys' house in which Tom Jr. provides the exposition:

Tom, Jr.: Papa she thought a miracle happened to her this mawning in the Catholic church, she had a sensation, she said, like a miracle had given her back the organs that Scudder had to cut out of her body. She run out of church to the Thomas J. Finley Hospital, she called Gawge away from a patient that was in shock recovery room, to take some X-ray pitchers to show, to prove, that this miracle had happened.[49]

After learning that the X-rays show no restoration of her uterus, Heavenly tears them up, and the Boss devotes his thoughts to making sure no one knows of the incident so it won't damage his political career. Cutting this scene not only diminished Heavenly's importance, it also diminished the Easter symbolism that had played a constant ironic subtext beneath Chance's, Heavenly's, and the Princess's protestations of their hopes for a new life in the play's earlier versions.

Chance

Chance's character was made more negative in other ways as well. Earlier versions had contained suggestions that he was a victim of the corruption surrounding him, both in Boss Finley's St. Cloud and in the decadent world on "the coast" where he has been seduced by money, drugs, and alcohol, and has learned his current trade of gigolo. Significant lines were cut from Chance's "life story," in which he described Boss Finley as a politician who rides "the racial hate-horse" and objects to Chance because he wants Heavenly to marry "some V. I. P. that he wanted to get something out of."[50] This speech made it clear that the Boss's political corruption and bigotry had affected Chance Wayne directly. Cutting it took away one motivation for Chance's behavior that would make an audience sympathize with him.

Another significant cut was the part of Chance's speech in the bar when he described the women he had become involved with "on the coast" –

middle-aged "top stars" in danger of slipping who "don't want to feel involved or responsible, they don't want to feel anything that might touch them a little if anything still could." As he ruefully removes the fallen hairs from his comb, Chance elaborates on a refrain of the "shallowness and the callousness of the system" that has corrupted him (E 138). Although hardly a positive reflection on Chance, this speech brought out the pathos in his situation, allowing the audience to feel some sympathy for him. These two cuts together took away the partial excuse of "the system" for Chance's behavior. Each element of complexity that was removed from the play's morality moved it away from the tragic and toward the less ambiguous melodrama that Kazan developed in the production.

Cuts in Chance's conversation with Aunt Nonnie at the beginning of the bar scene took away another element of his history and his relationship with Heavenly. In keeping with the original explanation for Heavenly's disease, Chance had explained to Aunt Nonnie that he didn't know what had happened to Heavenly on the coast because he had been in jail. Aunt Nonnie reminisced sentimentally about the close relationship that had existed between her and Chance when he was a boy, saying that she felt closer to him that even to Heavenly. Chance responded in kind, remembering that she had given him pocket money and called him "son," and asking her to do so again (E 133).

Like the speech about the coast, this dialogue made Chance more human, more vulnerable, if not more admirable. The relationship between Chance and Nonnie that was developed in this scene also shed some light on Chance's early sexual experiences with the fifteen-year-old Heavenly. Several lines in the earlier scripts point to Nonnie's living out some vicarious relationship with Chance through Heavenly. As Chance told the story of his first making love to Heavenly in the Pullman car, Williams's stage direction said that Nonnie answered with "(a flurry of feeling that may have several components) . . . I know, I – I –" (E 134). When Chance told Nonnie that he had cried in Heavenly's arms that night, and had not known that what he was crying for was "youth that would go" (ND 82), Nonnie had originally answered, "I think I knew what happened, when I wasn't able to find you, that she was comforting you for the loss of the contest. Wasn't it partly, the loss of the contest that you cried for? Not just youth that would go?" (E 134). Nonnie not only interjected a note of commonplace reality into Chance's romantic posturing with this line, she also projected her own feelings, those of a protective older woman, onto the young Heavenly. These suggestions that the lonely old aunt was living vicariously through Heavenly and Chance were cut from the play during rehearsals, along with Boss Finley's line, referring to

Nonnie and Chance: "Old maids are famous for finding virtues in men in which no one else can see anything else but vice" (E 125).

Boss Finley

While the character of Chance Wayne was being made less sympathetic during rehearsals, the character of Boss Finley was being smoothed over somewhat, made less offensive and less crass. The two major instances of this were his discussion of Chance's castration and his description of his sex life with his wife. In the production the Boss had Tom Jr. take care of the details of Chance's removal from St. Cloud, saying, "Don't ask me, don't tell me nothin' . . . I don't want to know how, just go about it" (ND 59). In the pre-production version, it had been the Boss who had planned Chance's castration, in detail, with great relish. The Boss gave specific directions to Tom and Scudder: "If he stays on here tonight, I want him removed discreetly to my boat, *The Starfish*, and on *The Starfish*, Scudder, I want you to operate on him the way you done on my daughter; a clean, professional job I want done on him, making him safe to live in a world that still has clean people in it" (E 125). After a startled but pleased reaction from Tom Jr., the Boss went on to say that the patient should be discreetly deposited across the state line and removed to a private hospital "to recuperate discreetly from this surgery" in a room with a bowl of Easter lilies to remind him to lead "a lily-pure life from now on" (E 125). The detail of this speech not only made Chance's impending fate more real, it concretized the coldly calculating hatred that impelled the Boss's activities.

The Boss's lack of humanity and the grotesque forms his love took were evident in the dialogue that was cut from his scene with Heavenly in which he explained to his daughter why her mother had occasionally screamed at night: "Sometimes I had to use violence with her because she . . . wasn't *warm*-blooded like I was. She had a way of always drawing away until I had to use force" (E 127). The Boss's explanation of why he valued his wife's fair skin was also cut during rehearsals; "I value such fair skin: highly! – I value it as highly as the hills that it comes from! – and the pure blood it comes from which I am bound and determined to protect from pollution!" (E 127). Taking these passages out reduced the sense of perverted evil in Boss Finley's character considerably. His crasser mannerisms, such as hawking and spitting, were also taken out, making him a more plausible if less colorful character. In general a process similar to the revision of Big Daddy's character went on with the Boss. The extremes of his character were modified; the roughest edges were smoothed out. While the Boss Finley of the New York version was far from the monumental character that was Big Daddy, he was also far from the grotesque embodiment of hatred, bigotry, and revenge that Williams had first envisioned. He became simply a corrupt, bigoted Southern politician.

The Princess

While Williams rewrote some of the Princess's lines, sometimes, as noted earlier, at Geraldine Page's request, he made few changes affecting the character of the Princess during rehearsals. Act 1, in which she is the central figure, remained almost untouched throughout the several revisions the script received during and after rehearsals. Williams did change her name from Ariadne del Lago, the Princess Pasmezoglu, to Alexandra del Lago, the Princess Kosmonopolis, but the reason for giving up the obvious symbolic resonance of the name Ariadne was legal rather than aesthetic.[51] The incident in Act 2 when the Princess meets Miss Lucy in the bar was cut considerably, making both characters slightly less sympathetic. In the pre-production script, Miss Lucy had come up to the Princess when she tottered into the bar, disheveled, with her dress unzipped, looking for Chance. After trying to fix the Princess's zipper for her, Miss Lucy had offered to take her upstairs, explaining that she had been president of her local fan club. After the Princess snapped back rudely to let her alone, Miss Lucy responded that none of the star's pictures was as sad as what had happened to her in real life. In the production script, this dialogue was reduced to a few lines which not only shortened the scene, but deleted the dramatization of some important traits in the two characters. Miss Lucy's native good-heartedness and her quickness to strike back when she is injured had both been present in miniature here, foreshadowing her kindness to the Heckler and her abetting his attack on the Boss to help her get revenge on him. The dramatization of the faded star and her fan also concretized the state to which Alexandra del Lago had fallen and the humiliation she faces in living out each day.

Lucy's relationship with the Heckler was developed further during rehearsals, however, making their cooperation against the Boss more affecting. Rather than have the Heckler's initial exchange on entering the bar be with Stuff, Kazan and Williams gave Stuff's lines to Miss Lucy, having her take an interest in the Heckler from the first. She actively helped him to get a jacket and tie so he could get into the ballroom and hid him until it was time to make his appearance.

Minor changes in dialogue were also made for the same reasons that operated in the revision of earlier plays. Heavenly's line that she had been "spayed like a dog" and Tom Jr.'s line that Heavenly was lying on the beach "like a dead body washed up on it" were cut, presumably for reasons of taste. A number of repetitive lines were cut, and Kazan used his characteristic technique of overlapping dialogue to increase the pace and the tension during the Boss's televised speech. In general, however, the changes in dialogue tended to make the characters less extreme – less decadent, less evil, less on the edge of human experience – and to replace the sense of tragedy in Chance Wayne's fate with a sense of melodramatic poetic justice. The effect may have been to make the play more acceptable to audiences, but it also made the play less complex. It replaced a general sense of evil and corruption in humanity with the more comfortable concept of good and bad characters.

The director's language

As Mielziner had with the play's lighting, Kazan worked carefully to encode the play's meaning kinesically, using movement and gesture in conjunction with the lighting code to carry the storyline as well as to foreground the play's theatricality. Kazan brought the actors to the edge of the stage when they had big speeches to make, achieving an even more overt theatricality than he had in *Cat* by freezing the action on the rest of the dim stage while the speaker stood in Mielziner's spotlight and addressed the audience. This technique achieved an intersubjective moment on the stage, when the audience reacted directly to what the character thought and felt rather than passively watching an objective representation of the action he or she was involved in. It also intensified the metatheatrical emphasis of the production by foregrounding the role-playing that Kazan saw as central to the characters of the Princess and Chance. Again, the method of staging was presentational, but its aim was a deeper sympathy between audience and character rather than the alienation of a Brechtian production. Not only the lighting, but every principle of the play's staging was built around the foregrounding of the characters' metatheatrical role-playing. As Kazan noted, Mielziner's diamond-shaped projecting platforms brought the eye's attention auto-matically to center stage. The absence of detail in the set kept the audience's attention on the actors, who became not only characters, but the most conspicuous objects on the set as well.

By the time he directed *Sweet Bird*, Kazan had become a master at composing eloquent stage pictures, using the plastic qualities of the actors' bodies to their greatest aesthetic and semiotic effects. As he had in *Cat*, he worked with each actor to develop stylized gestures, movements, and attitudes that together encoded an iconic representation of the character's psychology and that worked in combination to encode the relationships between characters.

Chance and the Princess

Chance and the Princess each had several characteristic attitudes and gestures that encoded particular aspects of their characters. As Chance, Paul Newman often crouched or knelt on the floor, expressing the powerlessness to which Chance has been reduced by people or events that are stronger than he is. In Act 1 he crouched on the floor in a tiny spot of light next to the telephone, trying to get through to Heavenly after Scudder had warned him to stay away from her. Later he crouched in the corner rolling a joint as the Princess stood in the spotlight telling the story of her comeback, and he hunched on the floor next to the bed as the Princess stretched out on it, languidly smoking her hashish. In Act 3 he sat hunched over on his suitcase, waiting for his fate to strike, while the Princess tried unsuccessfully to convince him to leave St. Cloud with her (see plate 18).

Encoding the metatheatrical subtext, Newman had a completely different bodily attitude, and a set of gestures to go with it, when he was "on stage," when he was in the spotlight playing the role of Chance Wayne for the public. His mannerism of constantly combing or rearranging his thinning hair was suggested by Williams in the pre-production script. This became the central one of a set of gestures that expressed Chance Wayne's attempt to preserve his image of young Hollywood playboy. He treated his clothes with great care, constantly adjusting his tie or his cuffs, and he made a great flourish of lighting a cigarette. Chance's gestures and positions in the bar were broad, relaxed, and open. He leaned back in his chair, rocking back and forth until he fell to the floor because he was too drugged to keep his balance when he talked to his boyhood friends. When he talked to Aunt Nonnie about his dream for the future, he straddled the bench he sat on, talking progressively louder and more excitedly until she had to quiet him. As opposed to the crouching, fearful animal of Act 1, the Chance Wayne of Act 2 was a grade B actor playing the consummate playboy, just at the edge of losing his grip on the role.

Newman's third attitude was Chance Wayne in those intersubjective moments when Chance was alone, communicating directly with the audience. For a moment after Scudder left him in Act 1, he stood stricken, looking straight out front and communicating his honest grief to the audience. During his life story, he came downstage and again communicated directly with the audience, without a pose, and with the sparest of gestures. At the end of the play, after the Princess had left, and Chance waited fatalistically for Tom Jr. and his henchmen, he stood straight, looking directly at the audience as he spoke the play's controversial closing lines: "I don't ask for your pity, but just for your understanding. Not even that – no. Just for your recognition of me in you, and the enemy, time, in us all" (ND 124). The appeal was made directly to the audience, a final bid for its sympathy and its identification with Chance.

Geraldine Page had essentially two attitudes in the production, the metatheatrical role of Alexandra del Lago – in which she came into the spotlight wherever she was, exuding power and self-confidence – and the reality of the Princess – dependent, unsteady, sometimes even cowering – which came through in moments of weakness. In Act 1 Page came center stage and played Alexandra to the hilt. She stood in the spotlight, completely ignoring Chance as she posed and executed broadly eloquent gestures. She looked like a great pink butterfly as she grandly spread her arms in her voluminous chiffon negligée (see plate 19). In Act 3, Kazan had Page foreground the role-playing that was the basic concept of the production by having her unconsciously "prepare." She took a string of pearls out of her jewel box and put it on, making herself into Alexandra del Lago before she took the telephone to talk to gossip communist Sally Powers. This effect was repeated at the end of the play when, as the Princess left Chance, she picked up her props of purse and jewel box and draped herself in her mink stole before she went back out into the world to become Alexandra del Lago once more. When she momentarily lost the security of the role and became just the Princess, Page would take similar attitudes to those that Newman took as Chance. When her fear took hold of her in Act 1, she too crouched on the floor, and she crumbled in the bar scene, falling into Chance's arms.

The progress of the relationship between Chance and the Princess could be read kinesically in the narrative of their relative attitudes and gestures. In Act 1, scene 1, the Princess's position generally signified superior power (see plate 20). She lounged on the bed or postured at center stage while Chance hovered in the background, rolled joints for her, or sat on the floor next to the bed. During the Princess's moment of despair, they crouched together on the floor as Chance took her in his arms, both temporarily at the same level of impotence. Kazan created a madonna image in scene 2, as arresting in its way as the *pièta* image in *Camino Real* and *Cat* had been. While Chance knelt on the floor confessing his past to the Princess, she sat on the bed draped in a taffeta *peignoir*. At one point Chance put his head in her lap, establishing a relationship of dependence on his side and nurturing on hers. As the scene continued, the Princess sat with stately dignity on the bed while Chance knelt before her, an image of supplication. The Princess stood while

Chance continued to kneel before her, the powerful and the powerless. These attitudes were reversed in Act 2, during the scene on the terrace of the bar, when the Princess has humiliated herself by coming to look for Chance. She fell to her knees, kissing Chance's hand as she begged him to come back to the room. With a princely dignity equivalent to her royal pose in Act 1, he lifted her up, urging her to get hold of herself.

In Act 3, the Princess hovered about Chance, touching and clinging to him as she tried to convince him to leave St. Cloud with her, while he sat on his suitcase still as a stone, looking straight off to the audience. As the Princess gradually regained her sense of self and of her power during the call to Sally Powers, she again launched into the role of Alexandra del Lago in full force, standing in the spotlight at center stage in her glittering sequined gown while Chance watched anxiously from the dim background. When he pleaded with her to talk to Sally Powers about him and Heavenly, the Princess kicked and hit at him, getting him out of her way as if he were a troublesome puppy. Chance crouched on the floor with the telephone as he desperately tried to make another call to Sally Powers, repeating the image of Act 1, scene 1. He fell to his knees before the Princess when he said that she had castrated him by ordering him to have sex with her. Finally, Chance slumped onto his suitcase, a foot or so lower than the Princess, who perched on the trunk in her mink stole, offering with all the security of her role as Alexandra del Lago to extricate him from the fearful situation he now faced. As the Princess made her exit, a star reborn, the defeated Chance remained slumped on the suitcase at center stage, incapable even of the flight the suitcase signified.

Boss Finley and Heavenly

With the Boss, Kazan used much the same visual and kinesic code he had developed for Big Daddy in *Cat*. Although Sidney Blackmer did not have the sheer bulk that made Burl Ives such a prodigious figure to begin with, he achieved a sense of power through quiescence. Clad as Ives had been in a luxurious dressing gown, Blackmer stood straight and still while Rip Torn jumped about excitedly in the scene at the Finleys'. Blackmer's gestures were extremely spare, his hands most often at his sides or clasped behind him. Williams's original notion for the Boss – that of a rural primitive thinly covered with the veneer of civilized behavior – was discarded for a visual icon of power fueled by carefully controlled hatred. As in Act 1, Kazan composed the groupings of actors carefully in Act 2, keeping the Boss slightly apart and aloof from the anxious and deferent Scudder and the overactive Tom Jr. When Heavenly entered the Scene, Kazan fulfilled the artistic impulse behind Williams's original direction that the scene should become overtly stylized during the conversation between the Boss and Heavenly: "*the two players' movements may suggest the stately, formal movements of a court dance*" (ND 67). Although he did not follow Williams's suggestions exactly, Kazan did stylize the scene. Gestures were spare; groupings were carefully composed; and the actors held their positions for a long time. For the most part, the Boss was still, with his hands at his side, but in several significant gestures, he touched Heavenly's neck threateningly, held her hands in his, and cupped her face in his hands (see plate 21).

Heavenly too was very still; her few gestures and positions were dance-like. Dressed in a black knit bathing suit and a dark purple wrap-around skirt, Diana Hyland looked like a dancer. Her face, neck, and bare arms showed white in the spotlight against her dark clothes and the darkness of the stage, making for a dramatic image when her arms were raised in a gesture of despair or her hands were clasped helplessly in front of her, as they often were during the scene with the Boss. At the end of the scene, a trace of the phone call between Chance and Heavenly was retained in the production, with Heavenly hanging up on Chance as soon as he identified himself. Kazan had Hyland play this scene almost as dance, with the phone call mimed and her anguish encoded in carefully choreographed gestures.

Expanding the kinesic narrative

In his attempt to provide support for the play's narrative structure, Kazan also used kinesics and scenic composition to supply a new narrative thread that would provide additional suspense to the weak second act. He brought three new characters into the bar scene, called simply the first, second, and third men. Boss Finley's anonymous henchmen, their function was to serve as a visual representation of the menace facing Chance throughout the scene so the audience could not forget during the distractions of the Boss Finley story that Chance was moving toward an ominous end. The men started out on the fringes of the scene in the bar, moving about in the shadows. Two of them entered and stood at the bar while Chance was talking with Aunt Nonnie. The men quickly crossed the stage and exited when they spotted Chance. Shortly afterward, the third man came in and stood in the shadows, watching Chance while he sang with the piano. Then the third man walked across the stage and sat at the table on the terrace, where the second man quickly joined him. The sense that the whole town was joined in its hostility to Chance was encoded visually when the two men moved in on the center table where Chance was grouped with Scotty and Bud and the women. When Scotty and Bud had gotten rid of Violet and Edna, they joined the three men on the terrace, waiting in the shadows for their moment. Then they ran off to meet Finley's car, making it clear whose henchmen they were.

The sense of menace encoded in these movements climaxed in a typically Kazanian scene of entrapment and violence. After disrupting the Boss's speech, the Heckler appeared for a moment to have escaped when he arrived on the steps leading into the bar, looking back to see whether he was being followed from the ballroom. As the Heckler came down the steps, he took off his borrowed tie and jacket, handing them to Miss Lucy, who tried to hustle him off to the right. As he got to the doorway, however, the pageboy appeared, blocking his way, and the Heckler backed away toward the center of the stage. When he tried to go out through the terrace, he saw Stuff coming toward him, and turned and started off downstage right. There the third man appeared, blocking his way, and the Heckler backed up on the terrace. At this point, Tom Jr. came down from the ballroom, followed by Bud, Scotty, and the second man, and crossed to the center of the gallery. As the Heckler realized that he was surrounded, Miss Lucy screamed. The Heckler made a break for it on the terrace; Tom Jr. tripped him; and Stuff and another one of the men ran over and kicked him repeatedly in the face and head. As the men quickly dispersed, Miss Lucy came up to comfort the motionless Heckler. Meanwhile Chance had stood at the side in a pinhead spotlight watching aghast while his own future was enacted.

This scene left no doubt that both Chance and the audience would be aware of the danger facing him if he remained in St. Cloud. It made the moments when he was deciding whether to leave with the Princess in Act 3 more suspenseful, and it made the ending, as he asked for the audience's understanding before he went off to meet the violence promised by the menacing background figures of Tom Jr. and his henchmen, more powerful. A master at manipulating the visual and kinesic elements of the stage language, Kazan pulled out all the stops in this production to secure the audience's emotional engagement.

Kazan also made visual statements that replaced the most racist lines, which were cut from the dialogue. In his television speech, the Boss had originally said: "we must maintain separation of these two races in our places of learning and must not permit a colored majority in any state or county to select our leaders for us! and to *legislate* faw us!" (E 148). Williams had also suggested that an "Uncle Tom" on the platform appear on the screen when the Boss referred to his great love for "the colored people." Kazan encoded the Boss's racial bigotry and the black characters' awareness of just exactly what he stood for in a less overt way. In Act 2, scene 2, as the Boss talked about preserving "the pure white blood of the South" (ND 73), he and the servant Charles simply looked at each other. During the television speech, the black waiter Fly came out onto the terrace and stood watching, a silent reminder of the other side of the story. Interestingly, these visual statements were much less overt than the verbal statements Williams had planned originally, a reversal of the attitudes about social comment usually ascribed to Williams and Kazan.

Neither music nor sound played a big role in *Sweet Bird*. Williams told Crawford early on that he did not want a great deal of music.[52] The only music Kazan used in the production was the "Lament" for lost youth composed by Paul Bowles, which was used to intensify the poignance of emotional moments, and Chance's theme song, "Big, Wide, Wonderful World," which he sings in the bar as an ironic counterpoint to his true state of mind. The only important sound effect was the cry of the gulls, which the Princess calls "pigeons with laryngitis," serving along with the stylized palm projections to create the subjective sense of the Gulf environment with the same minimalist selectivity used in the rest of the staging.

After Sweet Bird

Although it was a commercial success, running for 375 performances before it closed, none of those involved with producing *Sweet Bird* were very pleased with it finally, except for the performances of Geraldine Page and Paul Newman. As with *Cat*, the most damaging criticisms for Williams and Kazan that it received were those that repeated the old charges that Kazan was an overbearing director who interfered with the playwright's vision and that Williams was a weak-willed writer who allowed his work to be adulterated in order to achieve commercial success. One critic declared:

> The Broadway production of *Sweet Bird of Youth* has made it incontrovertibly clear that the Williams–Kazan collaboration has reached the point of diminishing returns. The play, a hodgepodge of familiar Williams' [*sic*] themes, sensationalism, and pseudo-poetically stated truisms, might have been an interesting one-acter. Certainly its content and scope do not justify the two-and-a-half hour ordeal it now demands. Again, most of the unnecessary padding can be traced to Mr. Kazan's influence on Mr. Williams.[53]

Williams made not the slightest implication this time that Kazan had tried to influence him to change the script. His only comment was the remark mentioned earlier that he had been bombarded with notes from "someone other than the director." Nonetheless, Kazan remembers that he took constant criticism for tampering with Williams's play: "I kept reading and hearing that I was in some way displacing the author's unique intentions and drowning his more sensitive gifts under my crude effects" (L 546).

This criticism was to have an important effect, not only on the relationship of the two artists, but on Kazan's subsequent career. He has written that he was resentful and defensive about the criticism at the time, but that he came to realize "there was some truth in what was being written and said about my impact: A sort of distortion was going on." In the late fifties, Kazan was realizing that he needed to speak for himself. Out of the process of producing *Sweet Bird* was born "the resolve to stop forcing myself into another person's skin but rather to look for my own subjects and find, however inferior it must be to Tennessee's, my own voice" (L 546). *Sweet Bird of Youth* was to be Elia Kazan's last Broadway play.

Kazan's growing need for self-expression and Williams's complicated feelings of dependence and resentment about the director's role in the creation of his plays, both intensified by the critical attacks on their collaboration, were bound to lead to some ending of their professional relationship. When it came, it was no great explosion of pent-up resentment, although some reporters tried to portray it that way, but an inevitable parting of the ways. After the production of *Sweet Bird*, it was a general assumption that Williams, Kazan, Mielziner, and Cheryl Crawford would be working together on *Period of Adjustment*, Williams's self-styled "serious comedy" about marital relationships which had been tried out under his direction at Coral Gables just before the rehearsals for *Sweet Bird* had begun. Casting had already started when, in September of 1960, Kazan decided that he would not be able to direct the play because he would not be finished with the film he was working on, *Splendor in the Grass*, written by William Inge. As noted earlier, Kazan had turned down other Williams plays, even after he had been involved in developing the scripts, notably *The Rose Tattoo* and *Orpheus Descending*. Williams had been extremely upset each time, expressing his resentment that Kazan chose to work with Arthur Miller and Budd Schulberg over him to Audrey Wood and others. Perhaps more upset this time, when the writer involved was William Inge, Williams expressed his feelings to a critic, who was only too happy to convey them to Kazan, forcing what he called Kazan's "big walk-out" to become a public issue.

In an article for the *New York Times*, Arthur Gelb reported that "Mr. Williams professes to regard the withdrawal as the termination of what had been a fabulously successful dramatist–director alliance, which began in 1947 with the production of 'A Streetcar Named Desire.'"[54] Writing the article in the form of statements by Williams and rebuttals by Kazan, Gelb quoted Williams as saying that Kazan "has suddenly gotten the crazy idea that he is not good for my work," and Kazan as answering, "I offered to do the play when I was through with my movie, but Tennessee was not willing to wait till then. I consider him the greatest living playwright and would certainly like to work with him again, if he will ask me."[55] Noting that "Mr. Williams believes that a public airing of his interpretation of the facts is in order," Gelb continued:

"I think," Mr. Williams said, "that Kazan has been upset by people who accuse him of looking for popular success – people who snipe at his so-called melodramatic interpretation of my plays . . . The charge that Kazan has forced me to rewrite my plays is ridiculous. Nobody can budge me an inch. Kazan simply tried to interpret, honestly, what I have to say. He has helped me reach my audience, which is my aim in life – the bigger the audience, the better . . . "There are people" he said, "who have put the blame on Kazan for the ending, which they didn't like, of 'Cat on a Hot Tin Roof'." ("Read the preface Tennessee wrote to 'Cat,'" suggested Mr. Kazan, somewhat ominously. "The sniping all started then.")[56]

Kazan remembered the events surrounding his decision not to do the play, which should have been "an incident of no great moment," as a decisive moment in Williams's view of their relationship:

The event, which should have been routine, took place when Williams was feeling competition with William Inge, who'd had four hits in a row, and at a time when I was about to do a film based on something Inge had written. Tennessee saw the incident as a rejection, a signal that I preferred working with Inge. He made me aware of his feeling that he couldn't trust anyone, not even a director to whom he'd given several great hits. (L 595)

For his part, Kazan admitted that "it took a struggle for [him] to say no to Williams," that he had felt he was in some sense betraying his friend (L 595). At the same time he was exhilarated by the sense that he would no longer be "serving" the vision of another, but working out his own vision in his work:

How good it felt, despite the cold wind of Tennessee's disappointment, to be free. I'd felt the same way about other authors, but now I was admitting it. I no longer had to pretend to be the concerned champion of their view of life. I no longer wanted to handle the phalanx of backers and agents protecting each new play, deal with their anxieties and their hysteria, find the right actors, scenery, and costumes, and, while keeping everyone reassured, push the whole through to commercial success . . . So I resigned – my announcement to myself – from the elite club of sought-after Broadway directors, walked away at the peak of my success. By refusing the Williams play, I was, in effect, refusing all other plays by authors of similar stature. I was abdicating from the successful career I'd made. I vowed not to look back. (L 596)

After *Splendor in the Grass*, Kazan went on to become, with Robert Whitehead, a founding director of the Lincoln Center Repertory Company, resigning after two controversial seasons. After that his work became increasingly more personal, and increasingly expressive of his single creative vision. He wrote his own screenplay for *America, America* (1963), which was based on his family's experience in emigrating from Greece. From this he turned to the solitary creative process of writing novels, succeeding immediately with the best-seller, *The Arrangement* (1966), his semi-autobiographical story of an advertising executive who drops out of the fast track at the peak of his success, rediscovers his own values through a rather extreme mid-life crisis, and begins to live a new life in the Connecticut countryside.

Williams repented very soon of his public announcement that his working relationship with Kazan was over. In 1962 he told an interviewer: "one of the most regrettable things in my life is that I don't think that Kazan and I will ever work again together, and it wasn't my choice. It was his. I think that he is the most brilliant director we have."[57] Asked if there had been a complete break between the two, Williams replied, "Well, there was certainly – on my part at least – there was certainly no change in my friendship for him, and I think probably he still likes me, but our liking is ambivalent, you know."[58] In the years following, neither artist mentioned the other except in terms of affection and admiration, Williams saying several times that he still hoped to work with Kazan again and maintaining to the end that Kazan was the most brilliant director working in the American theatre. In fact, for a brief time in 1974, there was a possibility that Kazan might direct a David Merrick production of *Red Devil Battery Sign*. When Kazan decided to pursue his writing and film projects instead, Williams, by his own account, "accepted his defection with impeccable grace – and a sly bit of pleasure," noting that "a couple of sexagenerians are at least one too many for a new play" (St. Just 306). Their friendship remained close, cemented by a special understanding that Kazan had for the complicated being that was Tennessee Williams. When Williams returned to his apartment after Frank Merlo's funeral in 1963, unable to go to the cemetery to watch the interment of his long-time friend and lover, it was Elia and Molly Kazan who went with him. In *Memoirs* Williams expressed the depth of their unspoken understanding in his description of this incident: "I kept up a good front but I noticed them exchanging looks. They knew I had lost what had sustained my life."[59]

In losing Kazan, it might be said that Williams had lost a good deal of what had sustained his work and an important catalyst for his creativity. The long decline in Williams's creative powers that had begun during the writing of *Sweet Bird of Youth* certainly was attributable to his increasing dependency on drugs and alcohol and his inability to adjust to the loss of

Merlo, but he had also lost an important perspective on his work. In 1981 he remarked, "You know, I always used to write for (Elia) Kazan, although he no longer works as a director. What made him a great director was that he had an infinite understanding of people on an incredible level."[60] One of those people was Tennessee Williams.

Kazan's own drive to control the aesthetic process and its final product was ultimately as destructive to this finely tuned creative collaboration as were Williams's contradictory dependence on and resistance to his director, both emotional and artistic. But together they created four significant plays and, with Jo Mielziner, left their signature on a stage language that became recognizable throughout the world. These three artists in collaboration had found a way to represent subjectivity on the stage simultaneously with objective reality and to use the disjunction between the two creatively: to suggest the inevitable failure of understanding among human beings whose perception of reality is always ultimately subjective, to secure the emotional engagement of the audience in a play whose meaning is fundamentally intellectual and symbolic, to challenge the spectators' natural passivity and draw them into an inter-subjective relationship with characters from whom they would otherwise remain detached.

The theatre that developed from this collaboration juxtaposed realism and expressionism, presentational techniques and representational frameworks, Stanislavskian psychological realism and Meyerholdian theatricality. These artists used techniques developed in the Brechtian theatre of alienation to serve the antithetical goal of empathy between actors and audience. They developed and refined the codes of meaning in the stage language so that it could not only emphasize particular thematic statements, but convey fine nuances of characterization and atmosphere and even carry the main burden of narrativity as well. After synthesizing their eclectic aesthetics into a recognizable stage language with consistent and resonant codes of meaning, they manipulated the basic paradigm in creative ways for each production. And the paradigm remains in active use among theatre artists. There is no doubt that their creative collaboration was among the most important of the twentieth-century theatre.

Notes

1 TENNESEE WILLIAMS AND ELIA KAZAN: THE AESTHETIC MATRIX

1 "Writing for the Group," *New York Times*, November 19, 1939: section 2, 3.
2 *Elia Kazan: A Life* (New York: Knopf, 1988) 362. Subsequently referred to in the text as "L."
3 Henry Hewes, "The Boundaries of Tennessee," *Saturday Review*, 39 (December 29, 1956): 23.
4 Nancy Tischler, *Tennessee Williams: Rebellious Puritan* (1961; repr. New York: Citadel, 1965) 112.
5 Robert Anderson, quoted in Jeanine Basinger, John Frazer, and Joseph W. Reed, Jr., *Working with Kazan* (Middletown, CT: Wesleyan Film Program, 1973) n.p.
6 Quoted in Michel Ciment, *Kazan on Kazan* (New York: Viking, 1974) 37–38.
7 Tennessee Williams, *Memoirs* (Garden City, NY: Doubleday, 1975) 134–35.
8 *Memoirs* 102.
9 Tennessee Williams, *The Glass Menagerie* (New York: Dramatists Play Service, 1948) 7. Unless otherwise noted, subsequent references are to this, the "acting version," of the play and appear in the text.
10 June Bennett Larsen, "Tennessee Williams: Optimistic Symbolist," in *Tennessee Williams: A Tribute*, ed. Jac Tharpe (Jackson: University Press of Mississippi, 1977) 416.
11 "Tennessee Williams," *The American Theater Today*, ed. Alan Downer, 79. See also Esther Jackson, *The Broken World of Tennessee Williams* (Madison: University of Wisconsin Press, 1965) 103–04.
12 "Tennesse Williams" 79.
13 Ibid.
14 See, for example, Donald Spoto, *The Kindness of Strangers: The Life of Tennessee Williams* (New York: Ballantine, 1986) and Tischler, *Tennessee Williams* 102.
15 *The Dramatic Imagination* (New York: Theatre Arts Books, 1941) 18–19.
16 *What is Theatre?* (New York: Atheneum, 1968) 153.
17 Ciment, *Kazan on Kazan* 21.
18 For a full discussion of Dean's theories, see Alexander Dean, *Fundamentals of Play Directing* (New York: Holt, Rinehart, and Winston, 1960).

19 Michel Delahaye, "A Natural Phenomenon: Interview with Elia Kazan," *Cahiers du Cinema in English*, 9 (March 1967): 14.
20 Ciment, *Kazan on Kazan* 40–41.
21 Ibid. 16.
22 Lyubov Vendrovskaya and Galina Kaptereva (eds.), *Evgeny Vakhtangov* (Moscow: Progress, 1982) 151.
23 Ciment, *Kazan on Kazan* 32.
24 Ibid. 95. See also, Frederic Morton, "gadg!," *Esquire*, 47 (February 1957): 122.

2   SUBJECT AND OBJECT: "A STREETCAR NAMED DESIRE"

1 Quoted in Audrey Wood, with Max Wilk, *Represented by Audrey Wood* (Garden City, NY: Doubleday, 1981) 152.
2 *Memoirs* (Garden City, NY: Doubleday, 1975) 111. Subsequently referred to in the text as "M."
3 Wood remembered that the wire read "BLANCHE HAS COME TO LIVE WITH US" (Wood, *Represented* 153), a slight difference but a telling one in relation to the play.
4 Williams wrote to Margo Jones that he had told Selznick he wanted Kazan, John Huston, or her to direct *Streetcar*, and that Selznick had refused to work with a woman director. (Undated, unpublished letter, Harry Ransom Humanities Research Center, University of Texas at Austin.)
5 *Elia Kazan: A Life* (New York: Knopf, 1988) 328. Subsequently referred to in the text as "L."
6 See also Wood, *Represented* 153–54.
7 Irene Mayer Selznick, *A Private View: Irene Mayer Selznick* (New York: Knopf, 1983) 299.
8 Unpublished letter to Margo Jones, May 23, 1947, Harry Ransom Humanities Research Center, University of Texas at Austin.
9 Unpublished letter from Audrey Wood to Tennessee Williams, April 18, 1947, Harry Ransom Humanities Research Center, University of Texas at Austin.
10 Kazan, *Elia Kazan* 342–43. Audrey Wood remembered that it was her husband and partner William Liebling who had first thought of Brando and mentioned him to Kazan, and that Kazan was not enthusiastic about the idea at first. She also said that it was Liebling who lent Brando the fare to Cape Cod (Wood, *Represented* 89–91).
11 Letter from Tennessee Williams to Audrey Wood, August 29, 1947, Harry Ransom Humanities Research Center, University of Texas at Austin, quoted in Deborah G. Burks, "'Treatment Is Everything': The Creation and Casting of Blanche and Stanley in Tennessee Williams' 'Streetcar,'" *The Library Chronicle of the University of Texas at Austin*, n.s. 41 (1987): 32.
12 Quoted in *Conversations with Tennessee Williams*, ed. Albert J. Devlin (Jackson: University Press of Mississippi, 1986) 330–31.
13 Unpublished letter from Tennessee Williams to Audrey Wood, 23 March,

1945. Harry Ransom Humanities Research Center, University of Texas at Austin.

14 Quoted in Wood, *Represented* 150 and Burks "Treatment" 22.

15 See especially Vivienne Dickson, *"A Streetcar Named Desire*: Its Development through the Manuscripts," *Tennessee Williams: A Tribute*, ed. Jac Tharpe (Jackson: University Press of Mississippi, 1977) 154–71; Sarah Boyd Johns, "Williams' Journey to 'Streetcar': An Analysis of Pre-Production Manuscripts and Drafts of 'A Streetcar Named Desire.'" Dissertation, University of South Carolina, 1980; and Burks, "Treatment."

16 Unpublished manuscript fragment, Harry Ransom Humanities Research Center, University of Texas at Austin.

17 "The Primary Colors," manuscript fragment, Harry Ransom Humanities Research Center, University of Texas at Austin, quoted in Burks, "Treatment" 20.

18 "The Passion of a Moth (A Play in Ten Scenes)," unpublished manuscript fragment, Harry Ransom Humanities Research Center, University of Texas at Austin.

19 Tennessee Williams, *A Streetcar Named Desire*, 2nd rev. edn. (New York: Dramatists Play Service, 1953) 96. Subsequent page references to *Streetcar* are to this version unless they are designated "ND," in which case they refer to the revised "reading version" (New York: New Directions, 1951[?]). Essentially a transcription of the stage manager's script for the Kazan production, with about one hundred variants, the Dramatists Play Service version is the closest published script to that used in the production, and is therefore the one usually referred to in the text. The New Directions version, prepared from the pre-production script, often records Tennessee Williams's earlier ideas before the play entered the collaborative process, and is used here mainly to record these earlier ideas.

20 "A Streetcar Named Desire," revised version for Rehearsals.

21 Ibid.

22 Two of the best treatments are Esther M. Jackson, *The Broken World of Tennessee Williams* (Madison: University of Wisconsin Press, 1966) 104–07 and C. W. E. Bigsby, *A Critical Introduction to Twentieth-Century American Drama* (Cambridge: Cambridge University Press, 1983), vol. II, 63–66.

23 Jackson, *Broken World* 107.

24 According to Harold Clurman, "all Group productions were 'stylized' . . . The Group's basic style consisted in forming a conception of the material at hand and so presenting it that it would appear consistent with the quality of reality mirrored in the play's text . . . Even plays as close to traditional realism as *The House of Connelly* and *Awake and Sing* were, in the Group's view, poetic plays and stylized as such, though accepted as 'realism' by the majority of the audience and theatre commentators" (*The Fervent Years*, 2nd edn. New York: Hill and Wang, 1957, 234–35).

25 "Notebook for *A Streetcar Named Desire*," *Directors on Directing*, ed. Toby Cole and Helen Krich Chinoy, 2nd edn. (Indianapolis: Bobbs-Merrill, 1963) 364–5. Subsequently referred to in the text as "N."

26 "A Streetcar Named Desire," unpublished manuscript marked "Tenn's own

copy," Harry Ransom Humanities Research Center, University of Texas at Austin.

27 *Designing for the Theatre* (New York: Bramhall House, 1965) 141.

28 "Notes on *Streetcar*," dated July 26, 1947 and August 6, 1947, Jo Mielziner Collection, Billy Rose Theatre Collection, New York Public Library at Lincoln Center.

29 "Notes on *Streetcar*," August 6, 1947.

30 "Inside Stuff – Legit," *Variety*, December 1947.

31 "Streetcar Conductor: Some Notes from Backstage," *Theatre Annual*, 8 (1950): 29.

32 "'A Streetcar' Runs on Electricity," New York *World-Telegram*, October 16, 1947.

33 The "Leko follow-spot" was developed by the Century Lighting company under Mielziner's close friend and collaborator Edward Kook to achieve more subtle and precise effects than the carbon arc-spot that was commonly used in musicals during the forties. Mielziner used the Leko for his sets because its incandescent tungsten lamp "can be gently and smoothly dimmed from a good, strong, warm beam to a pale shadow of light. It has all the subtlety of control of the best stage lights. It can have a soft edge. It can be shaped to cover an actor's head and, by coming up on an individual dimmer, it can pick up an actor imperceptibly and, with reverse technique, lose him at the end of a scene" (Mielziner, *Designing* 41–42).

34 Downing, "Streetcar Conductor" 30.

35 Ibid. 28–29.

36 "Music and Sound Cues," in script marked "Final Version," and dated December 3, 1947, Harry Ransom Humanities Research Center, University of Texas at Austin.

37 Henry Schvey has suggested that the white and red represent the two sides of Blanche's nature, "innocence and promiscuity," and that the "change of costume from red satin to blue, at the end of the play, obliges us to see Blanche as casting off her sensual side in favour of a new innocence, with strong implications of spiritual rebirth." ("Madonna at the Poker Night: Pictorial Elements in Tennessee Williams' *A Streetcar Named Desire*," *From Cooper to Philip Roth: Essays on American Literature*, ed. J. Bakker and D. R. M. Wilkinson [Amsterdam: Rodopi, 1980] 74.) See also Mary Ann Corrigan, "Realism and Theatricalism in *Streetcar*," *Modern Drama*, 19 (1976): 386–87.

38 Mimeo State Manager's Script, quoted in Burks, "Treatment" 35.

39 Prop chart for *A Streetcar Named Desire*, Harry Ransom Humanities Research Center, University of Texas at Austin.

40 Quoted in Frederic Morton, "gadg!," *Esquire*, 47 (February 1957): 118–19.

41 *Streetcar* Final Version. The Raggedy Andy doll is indicated in the script, and pictures from the production show Karl Malden holding one, but the prop chart lists a kewpie doll instead. Whichever was used, the effect was the opposite of what would have been conveyed with the Mae West doll.

42 Quoted in Virginia Stevens, "Elia Kazan: Actor and Director of Stage and Screen," *Theatre Arts*, 31 (December 1947): 22.

43 R. C. Lewis, "A Playwright Named Tennessee," *New York Times Magazine*, December 7, 1947: 19.

44 See also Ciment, *Kazan on Kazan* 71.

3   REALISM AND FANTASY: "CAMINO REAL"

1   Quoted in Vernon Rice, "The Talking Tennessee Williams," New York *Post*, March 18, 1953: 66.
2   Quoted in ibid. 66.
3   *Memoirs* (Garden City, NY: Doubleday, 1975) 101.
4   Unpublished letters from Tennessee Williams to Audrey Wood, February 27, 1946 and March 12, 1946, Harry Ransom Humanities Research Center, University of Texas at Austin. In her autobiography, Wood wrote that although she had told Williams she didn't think *Ten Blocks* was ready for the theatre when he first showed it to her, and had urged him not to show it to anyone else until it was, she had always admired the play, and was fully supportive of the 1953 production. (*Represented by Audrey Wood* [Garden City, NY: Doubleday, 1981] 162).
5   Unpublished letter from Eli Wallach to Dan Isaac, May 7, 1966, Billy Rose Theatre Collection, New York Public Library at Lincoln Center. See also Williams, *Memoirs* 165.
6   Unpublished letter from Tennessee Williams to Audrey Wood, August 28, 1951, Harry Ransom Humanities Research Center, University of Texas at Austin.
7   *Five O'Clock Angel: Letters of Tennessee Williams to Maria St. Just 1948–1982* (New York: Knopf, 1990) 40. Subsequently referred to in the text as "St. Just."
8   Tennessee Williams to Audrey Wood, August 28, 1951.
9   Unpublished letter from Tennessee Williams to Audrey Wood, June 21, 1950, Harry Ransom Humanities Research Center, University of Texas at Austin.
10 See unpublished letter from Tennessee Williams to Audrey Wood, February 15, 1949, Harry Ransom Humanities Research Center, University of Texas at Austin, and St. Just 18.
11 Unpublished letter from Audrey Wood to Tennessee Williams, October 11, 1951, Harry Ransom Humanities Research Center, University of Texas at Austin.
12 Tennessee Williams to Audrey Wood, October 27, 1951.
13 *New York Times*, December 21 1951. Williams's version of the story was typical of his attitude toward his chosen director; "Suddenly Kazan accepted an assignment to direct some other play; I was upset and retreated to Key West. But I wouldn't relinquish the idea of *Ten Blocks on the Camino Real* so I continued to work on it and expanded it into *Camino Real*. Meanwhile, the play that Kazan had decided to do in preference to *Ten Blocks* was a failure. *There's* poetic justice. And then he was ready to take on the revised play of *Camino Real*. Well, it was a big thing to take on at that time, but Kazan has never been lacking in courage and he went ahead" (*Memoirs* 165–66).
14 Williams's attitude toward Kazan's political difficulties was sympathetic but tinged with pragmatism. He wrote to Maria Britneva that he was considering José Quintero and Peter Brook as possible directors in case Kazan was no longer able to work on Broadway: "I take no attitude about it, one way or another, as I am not a political person and human venality is something I always expect and forgive. But I am not yet sure that Gadg will not disappoint

me, personally, as he did with *Tattoo*. That remains to be seen" (St. Just 56).

15 Unpublished letter, Tennessee Williams to Cheryl Crawford, February 10, 1952, Billy Rose Theatre Collection, New York Public Library at Lincoln Center.

16 Unpublished letter, Tennessee Williams to Cheryl Crawford, June 29, 1952, Billy Rose Theatre Collection, New York Public Library at Lincoln Center.

17 Williams wrote to Maria Britneva that, when the mostly negative first-night reviews came out, "Mother Crawford took us off royalties and we've never gotten back on, so practically everybody, author, director, composer, choreographer and designer, worked mostly for nothing. The actors have taken big cuts. She is hoping, as usual, to scrape along by such economies as lighting the stage by fire-flies and a smokey old kerosene lamp, substituting a bit of percussion on an old washtub for a five-piece band, etc., but even so the prospects for an extended run are but dim" (St. Just 75).

18 *Designing for the Theatre* (New York: Bramhall House, 1965) 153.

19 Jo Mielziner to Tennessee Williams, August 26, 1952, Harry Ransom Humanities Research Center, University of Texas at Austin. Published in *Dictionary of Literary Biography: Documentary Series*, vol. IV, ed. Margaret A. Van Antwerp and Sally Johns (Detroit: Gale, 1984) 136.

20 Jo Mielziner to Tennessee Williams, August 26, 1952.

21 Unpublished letter, Tennessee Williams to Elia Kazan, 2 [October? 1952], Harry Ransom Humanities Research Center, University of Texas at Austin.

22 *One Naked Individual: My Fifty Years in the Theatre* (Indianapolis: Bobbs-Merrill, 1977) 191.

23 *Elia Kazan: A Life* (New York: Knopf, 1988) 497.

24 Ibid.

25 Ibid. 498.

26 Unpublished letter, Tennessee Williams to Elia Kazan (summer 1952), Harry Ransom Humanities Research Center, University of Texas at Austin.

27 Unpublished letter, Tennessee Williams to Elia Kazan (fall 1952), Harry Ransom Humanities Research Center, University of Texas at Austin.

28 Unpublished letter, Elia Kazan to Tennessee Williams, November 17, 1952, Harry Ransom Humanities Research Center, University of Texas at Austin.

29 *Camino Real* (New York: Dramatists Play Service, 1965) 90–91. Subsequent page references to the play are to this, the acting version, and appear in the text. The Dramatists Play Service text, and the New Directions reading version, were prepared from Williams's substantially revised scripts well after the Broadway production opened and contain added scenes as well as major changes from the production script.

30 *American Blues: Five Short Plays* (New York: Dramatists Play Service, 1948) 58. Subsequent page references to *Ten Blocks on the Camino Real* are to this version and appear in the text.

31 Unpublished letter, Tennessee Williams to Brooks Atkinson, April 3, 1953, Billy Rose Theatre Collection, New York Public Library at Lincoln Center.

32 Eli Wallach to Dan Isaac, May 7, 1966.

33 The reference is to Kilroy's speech: "Y'know what it is you miss most? When you're separated. From someone. You lived. With. And loved? It's waking up in the night! With that – warmness beside you! . . . Once you get used to that.

Warmness! It's a hell of a lonely feeling to wake up without it! Specially in some dollar-a-night hotel room on Skid! A hot-water bottle won't do. And a stranger. Won't do. It has to be some one you're used to. And that you. *KNOW LOVES* you!" (85). The lines originally appeared in Kilroy's long opening monologue (see *Ten Blocks* 47).

34 Unpublished letter, Elia Kazan to Tennessee Williams, December 10, 1952, Harry Ransom Humanities Research Center, University of Texas at Austin.

35 Molly Day Thacher Kazan to Tennessee Williams, December 9, 1952, Harry Ransom Humanities Research Center, University of Texas at Austin, published in Thomas H. Pauly, *An American Odyssey: Elia Kazan and American Culture* (Philadelphia: Temple University Press, 1983) 168.

36 Elia Kazan to Tennessee Williams, December 10, 1952. While cordial relations between Williams and Kazan were quickly restored, Williams evinced a growing resentment toward Molly Kazan and her attempts to interfere in the play's development. He wrote the following week to Maria Britneva: "I had a terrible fight with Molly Kazan after the first reading. She is my bête-noir[*sic*]!. . . She then sent out 'circulars' to everybody saying that I must cut 45 minutes out of the play and that if 'we kept her with it we would have a play.' I'm so glad you don't like her" (St. Just 69).

37 Quoted in John Gruen, "Tennessee Williams," *Close-Up* (New York: Viking, 1968); repr. in *Conversations with Tennessee Williams*, ed. Albert J. Devlin (Jackson: University Press of Mississippi, 1986) 118.

38 Seymour Milbert, unpublished notes on rehearsals, January 30, 1953, Billy Rose Theatre Collection, New York Public Library at Lincoln Center. Subsequently referred to in the text as "Milbert."

39 "Sixteen Blocks on the Camino Real," duplicated manuscript with notes, additions, and cuts, n.d., Harry Ransom Humanities Research Center, University of Texas at Austin.

40 Quoted in Henry Hewes, "Tennessee Williams – Last of Our Solid Gold Bohemians," *Saturday Review*, March 28, 1953; repr. Devlin, *Conversations* 33.

41 Hewes, "The Last" 33.

42 *Camino Real* rehearsal script, Harry Ransom Humanities Research Center, University of Texas at Austin.

43 "Red is the sun! Red is the sun of blood! White is the moon! White is the moon of fear."

44 John McClain, "Williams' Play Baffling to Some," New York *Journal American*, March 20, 1953.

45 Director's Notes for *Camino Real*, March 12, 1953, Billy Rose Theatre Collection, New York Public Library at Lincoln Center. Subsequently referred to in the text as "Notes".

46 Michel Ciment, *Kazan on Kazan* (New York: Viking, 1974) 81–82.

47 Kazan, *A Life* 498.

48 *The Dramatic Event* (New York: Horizon, 1954) 108.

49 See Tennessee Williams, "Playwright Seeks Creation of a World Whose Existence Is Out of Time," *New York Times*, March 15, 1953 (repr. as "Foreword" to *Camino Real*); Elia Kazan, "Playwright's Letter to the World," New York *Herald Tribune*, March 15, 1953: section 4, 2; Hewes,

"The Last" and Rice, "The Talking."

50 See especially the draft of a letter from Tennessee Williams to Walter Kerr, Billy Rose Theatre Collection, New York Public Library at Lincoln Center, and Kerr's reply, April 13, 1953, published in Van Antwerp and Johns (ed.), *Dictionary* 139.

51 Unpublished letter from Tennessee Williams to Cheryl Crawford, March 31, 1953, Billy Rose Theatre Collection, New York Public Library at Lincoln Center.

52 Unpublished letter from Tennessee Williams to Brooks Atkinson, June (7 or 8) 1953.

53 Bentley, *Dramatic Event* 108.

54 Ibid. 274.

55 Unpublished undated letter from Tennessee Williams to unidentified recipient, Harry Ransom Humanities Research Center, University of Texas at Austin.

56 Bentley, *Dramatic Event* 274–75.

4   PRESENTATION AND REPRESENTATION: "CAT ON A HOT TIN ROOF"

1 Letter from Elia Kazan to Tennessee Williams, n.d., Harry Ransom Humanities Research Center, University of Texas at Austin; Published in Thomas H. Pauly, *An American Odyssey: Elia Kazan and American Culture* (Philadelphia: Temple University Press, 1983) 202.

2 Unidentified newspaper clipping, Harry Ransom Humanities Research Center, University of Texas at Austin.

3 *Cat on a Hot Tin Roof* (New York: New American Library, 1958) 141. This "reading version," which contains both versions of the third act that Williams published in 1955, will subsequently be referred to in the text as "RV" and is the source used for most quotations. The Dramatists Play Service version, revised by Williams and published in 1958, is used when it contains material used in the production that did not appear in the 1955 reading version. It is subsequently referred to in the text by page number. The New Directions version currently in print contains the script as revised by Williams for the 1974 American Shakespeare Theatre production, and so is not referred to here.

4 Nancy M. Tischler, *Tennessee Williams: Rebellious Puritan*, 2nd edn. (New York: Citadel, 1965) 208–09.

5 Unpublished letter, Tennessee Williams to Audrey Wood, (May?) 23, 1954, Harry Ransom Humanities Research Center, University of Texas at Austin.

6 *Five O'Clock Angel: Letters of Tennessee Williams to Maria St. Just 1948–1982* (New York: Knopf, 1990) 103. Subsequently referred to in the text as "St. Just."

7 *Memoirs* (Garden City, NY: Doubleday, 1975) 169.

8 *Elia Kazan: A Life* (New York: Knopf, 1988) 543.

9 Hobe [Morrison], "'Cat' Censored, But by Whom?," *Variety*, 13 April, 1955: 73.

10 *Cat on a Hot Tin Roof*, mimeo rehearsal script, Harry Ransom Humanities Research Center, University of Texas at Austin.

11 *Cat on a Hot Tin Roof*, mimeo script from which pre-production script was prepared, Harry Ransom Humanities Research Center, University of Texas at Austin.

12 "To a Friend whose Work has come to Nothing," *Variorum Edition of the Poems of W. B. Yeats*, ed. Peter Alt and Russell K. Alspach (New York: Macmillan, 1971) 291.

13 *Cat on a Hot Tin Roof*, typed copy of manuscript with Elia Kazan's notes in ink, n.d., Harry Ransom Humanities Research Center, University of Texas at Austin.

14 "Do not go gentle into that good night," *The Collected Poems of Dylan Thomas* (New York: New Directions, 1953) 128.

15 *Memoirs* 168.

16 Michel Ciment, *Kazan on Kazan* (New York: Viking, 1974) 47.

17 Quoted in Richard Schechner and Theodore Hoffman, "'Look, There's the American Theatre': An Interview with Elia Kazan," *Tulane Drama Review*, 9 (Winter, 1964): 71.

18 *A Life* 541–42

19 "Notes for the Designer," included with mimeo script of *Cat on a Hot Tin Roof*, n.d., Harry Ransom Humanities Research Center, University of Texas at Austin; published in reading version, xiii.

20 "Rewrite of Scene Description," November 24, 1954, Harry Ransom Humanities Research Center, University of Texas at Austin.

21 Ibid.

22 *A Life* 542–43.

23 *A Life* 543.

24 *Designing for the Theatre: A Memoir and a Portfolio* (New York: Bramhall House, 1965) 183.

25 Ibid. 183.

26 See Schechner and Hoffman, "Look, There's the American Theatre" 71 and *A Life* 542.

27 *A Life* 543.

28 Ibid. 540.

29 Ibid. 543.

30 "Theatre," *New Republic*, 132 (April 11, 1955): 28.

31 *A Life* 541.

32 Quoted in Donald Spoto, *The Kindness of Strangers: The Life of Tennessee Williams* (New York: Ballantine, 1986) 221.

33 Quoted in Spoto, *Kindness* 220.

34 Henry T. Murdock, "Williams' Play at the Forrest," *Philadelphia Inquirer*, March 8, 1955. As Dan Isaac's analysis has shown, this basically sexual rhythm derives directly from the speeches Williams wrote for Big Daddy. His "speeches imitate the very mood and rhythm of [his] sexual intercourse, and they become for [him] the dance of death." ("Big Daddy's Dramatic Word Strings," *American Speech*, 40 [Dec. 1965]: 278).

35 *Cat* manuscript, Kazan's copy.

36 "Mighty Lak a Rose," words by Frank L. Stanton, music by Ethelbert Nevin (Philadelphia: John Church, 1901).

37 "My Buddy," words by Gus Kahn, music by Walter Donaldson, Columbia sound recording, 1952.

38 *Cat on a Hot Tin Roof* mimeo stage manager's copy, Harry Ransom Humanities Research Center, University of Texas at Austin.
39 The sound cues are in the stage manager's script.
40 "Theatre" *New Republic*, 132 (April 4, 1955): 22.
41 Ibid. (April 4): 22.
42 Ibid. April 4: 22.
43 Ibid.
44 Ibid. April 11: 28.
45 "Reflections on Three New Plays," *The Hudson Review*, 8 (Summer 1955): 268.
46 Ibid. 268.
47 Ibid. 268.
48 *A Life* 544.
49 Jim Gainers, "A Talk about Life and Style with Tennessee Williams," *Saturday Review*, April 29, 1972; repr. Devlin, *Conversations* 217.
50 *Memoirs* 169.
51 Unpublished letter, Tennessee Williams to Audrey Wood, November 18, 1955, Harry Ransom Humanities Research Center, University of Texas at Austin.

5 REALISM AND METATHEATRE: "SWEET BIRD OF YOUTH"

1 *Elia Kazan: A Life* (New York: Knopf, 1988) 562. Subsequently referred to in the text as "L."
2 Unpublished letter, Tennessee Williams to Elia Kazan, July 23, 1955, Harry Ransom Humanities Research Center, University of Texas in Austin.
3 Tennessee Williams to Elia Kazan, July 23, 1955.
4 Tennessee Williams to Audrey Wood, September 19, 1955, Harry Ransom Humanities Research Center, University of Texas at Austin.
5 Carroll Baker wrote in her autobiography that Williams had originally wanted Marilyn Monroe, then an Actors Studio member, for the part, and that he thought Baker far too thin, but that Williams had changed his mind after Kazan had persuaded him to come and watch her perform (*Baby Doll: An Autobiography*, New York: Arbor House, 1983).
6 See *A Life* 562 and Michel Ciment, *Kazan on Kazan* (New York: Viking, 1974) 75.
7 Anthony C. Hilfer and R. Vance Ramsey maintain that their exhaustive study of the *Baby Doll* manuscripts at the University of Texas "points inescapably to two conclusions: a staggering effort was required to change the early material into the very different final script, and effort of this kind is typical of Williams' process of composition . . . Williams' effort did not end until the filming of the last scene was completed" ("*Baby Doll*: A Study in Comedy and Critical Awareness," *The Ohio University Review*, 11 (1969): 76).
8 Louise Davis, "That Baby Doll Man: Part I," *The Tennessean Magazine* (March 3, 1957); repr. Albert J. Devlin, *Conversations with Tennessee Williams* (Jackson: University Press of Mississippi, 1986) 44.
9 Devlin, *Conversations* 44.

10 John Gruen, *Close-Up* (New York: Viking, 1968); repr. Devlin, *Conversations* 119.

11 "The Staging of a Play," *Esquire*, 51 (May 1959): 144–57.

12 See, for example, John J. O'Connor, "The Great God Gadg," *Audience*, 7 (winter 1960): 28–31.

13 "Author and Director: A Delicate Situation," *Playbill* (September 30, 1957); repr. in *Where I Live: Selected Essays by Tennessee Williams*, ed. Christine R. Day and Bob Woods (New York: New Directions, 1978) 93. Subsequently referred to in the text as "A & D."

14 Quoted in W. J. Weatherby, "Lonely in Uptown New York," *Manchester Guardian Weekly*, 23 July 1959; repr. Devlin, *Conversations* 60.

15 "A Program Note from the Author," Harry Ransom Humanities Research Center, University of Texas at Austin.

16 Ibid.

17 Cheryl Crawford to Tennessee Williams, reproduced in Cheryl Crawford, *One Naked Individual* (Indianapolis: Bobbs-Merrill, 1977) 194.

18 *Sweet Bird* scenario, Tennessee Williams to Audrey Wood, July 23, 1956, Harry Ransom Humanities Research Center, University of Texas at Austin.

19 *Sweet Bird* scenario.

20 Quoted in Crawford, *One Naked Individual* 193.

21 Unpublished letter, Cheryl Crawford to Audrey Wood, March 4, 1958, Billy Rose Theatre Collection, New York Public Library at Lincoln Center.

22 Unpublished letter, Tennessee Williams to Cheryl Crawford, July 23, 1958, Billy Rose Theatre Collection, New York Public Library at Lincoln Center.

23 Mielziner's breakdowns for lighting, August 8, 1958, and props and scenery, August 10, 1958, are in the Billy Rose Theatre Collection, New York Public Library at Lincoln Center.

24 *Five O'Clock Angel: Letters of Tennessee Williams to Maria St. Just 1948–1982* (New York: Knopf, 1990) 138. Subsequently referred to in the text as "St. Just."

25 For an analysis of the changes made during this period, see Drewey Wayne Gunn, "The Troubled Flight of Tennessee Williams's *Sweet Bird of Youth*: From Manuscript through Published Texts," *Modern Drama* 24 (1981): 31–32 and Gilbert Debusscher, "And the Sailor Turned Into a Princess: New Light on the Genesis of *Sweet Bird of Youth*," *Studies in American Drama, 1945–Present* 1 (1986): 25–31.

26 Unpublished letter, Tennessee Williams to Cheryl Crawford, August 13, 1958, Billy Rose Theatre Collection, New York Public Library at Lincoln Center.

27 Tennessee Williams to Cheryl Crawford, August 13, 1958.

28 Tennessee Williams to Cheryl Crawford, August 13, 1958.

29 Unpublished letter, Tennessee Williams to Cheryl Crawford, September 14, 1958, Billy Rose Theatre Collection, New York Public Library at Lincoln Center.

30 Cheryl Crawford to Tennessee Williams, August 5, 1958, quoted in Crawford, *One Naked Individual* 195.

31 Ibid. 195.

32 Unpublished letter, Elia Kazan to Cheryl Crawford, December 8, 1958, Billy

Rose Theatre Collection, New York Public Library at Lincoln Center.
33 Jo Mielziner, *Designing for the Theatre: A Memoir and a Portfolio* (New York: Bramhall House, 1965) 202.
34 Unpublished letter, Tennessee Williams to Elia Kazan, December 29, 1958, Harry Ransom Humanities Research Center, University of Texas at Austin.
35 *Memoirs* (Garden City, NY: Doubleday, 1975) 173–74.
36 Ibid. 174.
37 "The Bottomless Cup: An Interview with Geraldine Page," *Tulane Drama Review*, 9 (1964): 115.
38 Quoted in Gene D. Phillips, *The Films of Tennessee Williams* (Philadelphia: Art Alliance, 1980) 155.
39 Ciment, *Kazan on Kazan* 81.
40 Unpublished letter, Tennessee Williams to Brooks Atkinson, March 27, 1959, Billy Rose Theatre Collection, New York Public Library at Lincoln Center.
41 Devlin, *Conversations* 60.
42 Quoted in Dotson Rader, "The Art of the Theatre V: Tennessee Williams," *The Paris Review*, 81 (fall 1981); repr. Devlin, *Conversations* 336–37.
43 Arthur Gelb, "Williams and Kazan and the Big Walk-Out," *New York Times*, May 1, 1960: section 2, 3.
44 Lewis Funke and John E. Booth, "Williams on Williams," *Theatre Arts*, (January 1962); repr. Devlin, *Conversations* 103.
45 Jeanne Fayard, "Meeting with Tennessee Williams," *Tennessee Williams* (Paris: Editions Seghers, 1972); repr. Devlin, *Conversations* 211.
46 Quoted in Whitney Bolton, "Williams Talks on Violence," *Philadelphia Inquirer*, February 1, 1959.
47 Quoted in Donald Spoto, *The Kindness of Strangers: The Life of Tennessee Williams* (New York: Ballantine, 1986) 115–16.
48 *Sweet Bird of Youth* (New York: New Directions, 1959) 116. The script that was used in the New York production, a copy of which is in Billy Rose Theatre Collection, New York Public Library at Lincoln Center, essentially combined what is now Act 1 of the acting version (New York: Dramatists Play Service, 1962) with Acts 2 and 3 of the New Directions Version. Subsequent references to the script will appear in the text designated "ND" for New Directions or "DPS" for Dramatists Play Service.
49 *Sweet Bird of Youth*, Esquire, 51 (April 1959): 127. Subsequently referred to in the text as "E."
50 *Sweet Bird of Youth* pre-production mimeo script, Harry Ransom Humanities Research Center, University of Texas at Austin; also *Esquire* 123. Where the pre-production script is identical to the *Esquire* version, page references to the *Esquire* version will be given in the text for subsequent quotations.
51 A week after the play opened in New York, Audrey Wood was contacted by the lawyers of a childhood playmate of Williams's, named Ariadne Pasmezoglu and sometimes called "Princess," who objected to the use of her name for this rather disreputable character. Williams apologized for his indiscretion, explaining through Wood that he had forgotten the origin of the character's name, and agreeing to change it, which he did, both in production and in the published versions of the play (Audrey Wood with Max Wilk, *Represented by Audrey Wood* [Garden City, NY: Doubleday, 1981] 178).

52 Unpublished letter, Cheryl Crawford to Audrey Wood, November 20, 1958, Billy Rose Theatre Collection, New York Public Library at Lincoln Center.

53 John J. O'Connor, "The Great God Gadg," *Audience*, 7 (Winter 1960): 27–28.

54 "Williams and Kazan and the Big Walk-Out" 1.

55 Ibid. 1.

56 Ibid. 1, 3.

57 Funke and Booth, *Williams* 99–100.

58 Ibid. 100.

59 *Memoirs* 195.

60 Devlin, *Conversations* 335.

Select bibliography

The bibliography is divided into the following sections: books; articles on Kazan and Mielziner; articles on Williams; selected reviews and newspaper stories, classified under the title of the play to whch they refer: *Camino Real*, *Cat on a Hot Tin Roof*, *The Glass Menagerie*, *A Streetcar Named Desire*, and *Sweet Bird of Youth*.

BOOKS

Adler, Thomas P. *Mirror on the Stage*, Lafayette, IN: Purdue University Press, 1987.
A Streetcar Named Desire: *The Moth and the Lantern*. Boston: Twayne, 1990.
Alpert, Hollis. *The Dreams and the Dreamers*. New York: Macmillan, 1962.
Arnott, Catherine. *Tennessee Williams on File*. London: Methuen, 1985.
Baker, Carroll. *Baby Doll: An Autobiography*. New York: Arbor Houses, 1983.
Bakker, J. and D. R. M. Wilkinson. *From Cooper to Philip Roth: Essays on American Literature*. Amsterdam: Rodopi, 1980.
Basinger, Jeanine, John Frazer and Joseph W. Reed, Jr. *Working with Kazan*. Middletown, CT: Wesleyan Film Program, 1973.
Bentley, Eric. *In Search of Theatre*. New York: Knopf, 1953.
The Dramatic Event: An American Chronicle. New York: Horizon, 1954.
What is Theatre?. New York: Atheneum, 1968.
(ed.). *Thirty Years of Treason: Excerpts from Hearings before the House Committee on Un-American Activities 1938–68*. New York: Viking, 1971.
Bigsby, C. W. E. *A Critical Introduction to Twentieth-Century American Drama*. 3 vols. Cambridge: Cambridge University Press, 1983.
Bloom, Harold (ed.). *Tennessee Williams*. New York: Chelsea House, 1987.
Bock, Hedwig and Albert Wertheim (eds.). *Essays on Contemporary American Drama*. Munich: Hueber, 1981.
Carlson, Marvin. *Theories of the Theatre*. Ithaca: Cornell University Press, 1984.
Carnovsky, Morris. *The Actor's Eye*. New York: Performing Arts Journal, 1984.
Carpenter, Charles A. *Modern Drama Scholarship and Criticism 1966–1980*. Toronto: University of Toronto Press, 1986.
Ciment, Michel. *Kazan on Kazan*. New York: Viking, 1974.
Clay, James H. and Daniel Krumpel. *The Theatrical Image*. New York: McGraw Hill, 1967.
Clurman, Harold. *The Fervent Years: The Story of the Group Theatre and the Thirties*. 2nd edn. New York: Hill and Wang, 1957.

Lies Like Truth. New York: Macmillan, 1958.

On Directing. New York: Collier, 1972.

All People are Famous. New York: Harcourt Brace, 1974.

Cohn, Ruby. *Dialogue in American Drama.* Bloomington: Indiana University Press, 1971.

Cole, Toby (ed.). *Acting, A Handbook of the Stanislavski Method.* 2nd edn. New York: Crown, 1955.

Cole, Toby and Helen Krich Chinoy. *Directors on Directing: A Source Book of the Modern Theater.* 2nd edn. Indianapolis: Bobbs-Merrill, 1963.

Crawford, Cheryl. *One Naked Individual: My Fifty Years in the Theatre.* Indianapolis: Bobbs-Merrill, 1977.

Dean, Alexander. *Fundamentals of Play Directing.* New York: Holt, Rinehart, and Winston, 1960.

Demastes, William W. *Beyond Naturalism: A New Realism in American Theatre.* Westport, CT: Greenwood, 1988.

Devlin, Albert J. (ed.). *Conversations with Tennessee Williams.* Jackson: University Press of Mississippi, 1986.

Donahue, Francis. *The Dramatic World of Tennessee Williams.* New York: Ungar, 1964.

Downer, Alan S. *The American Theater Today.* New York: Basic Books, 1967.

Elam, Keir, *The Semiotics of Theatre and Drama.* London and New York: Methuen, 1980.

Falk, Signi, *Tennessee Williams.* 2nd edn. Boston: Twayne, 1978.

Fayard, Jeanne. *Tennessee Williams.* Paris: Editions Seghers, 1972.

French, Warren. *The Forties: Fiction, Poetry, Drama.* De Land, FL: Everett/Edwards, 1969.

The Fifties: Fiction, Poetry, Drama. De Land, FL: Everett/Edwards, 1970.

Ganz, Arthur. *Realms of the Self: Variations on a Theme in Modern Drama.* New York: New York University Press, 1980.

Garfield, David. *A Player's Place: The Story of the Actors Studio.* New York: Macmillan, 1980.

Gascoigne, Bamber. *Twentieth-Century Drama.* London: Hutchinson Library, 1962.

Gassner, John. *The Theatre in Our Times.* New York: Crown, 1954.

Dramatic Soundings: Evaluations and Retractions Culled from Thirty Years of Dramatic Criticism. New York: Crown, 1968.

Golden, Joseph. *The Death of Tinker Bell: The American Theatre in the 20th Century.* Syracuse: Syracuse University Press, 1967.

Goldstein, Malcolm. *The Political Stage: American Drama and Theatre of the Great Depression.* New York: Oxford University Press, 1974.

Goncharov, N. M. *The Directorial Lessons of Vakhtangov.* Moscow: Iskusstvo, 1957.

Goodman, Randolph. *Drama on Stage.* New York: Holt, Rinehart, and Winston, 1961.

Gruen, John. *Close-Up.* New York: Viking, 1968.

Gunn, Drewey Wayne. *Tennessee Williams: A Bibliography.* Metuchen, NJ: Scarecrow, 1980.

Hartigan, Karelisa. *Within the Dramatic Spectrum.* Lanham: University of America, 1986.

Heilman, Robert B. *The Iceman, The Arsonist, and The Troubled Agent: Tragedy and Melodrama on the Modern Stage.* Seattle: University of Washington Press, 1973.

Himmelstein, Morgan Yale. *Drama Was a Weapon: The Left-Wing Theatre in New York, 1929–41.* New Brunswick: Rutgers University Press, 1963.

Hirsch, Foster. *A Portrait of the Artist: The Plays of Tennessee Williams.* Port Washington, NY: Kennikat, 1979.

A Method to Their Madness: The History of the Actors Studio. New York: Norton, 1984.

Hobson, Harold. *The Theatre Now.* London: Longmans Green, 1953.

Hornby, Richard. *Script Into Performance: A Structuralist View of Play Production.* Austin: University of Texas Press, 1977.

Drama, Metadrama, and Perception. Lewisburg, PA: Bucknell, 1986.

Hurrell, John D. *Two Modern American Tragedies: Reviews and Criticism of* Death of a Salesman *and* A Streetcar Named Desire. New York: Scribner, 1961.

Jackson, Esther Merle. *The Broken World of Tennessee Williams.* Madison: University of Wisconsin Press, 1966.

Jauslin, Christian. *Tennessee Williams.* Hanover: Fredrich, 1969.

Johns, Sarah Boyd. "Williams' Journey to 'Streetcar': An Analysis of Pre-Production Manuscripts and Drafts of 'A Streetcar Named Desire'." PhD dissertation, University of South Carolina, 1980.

Jones, David Arthur. *Great Directors at Work: Stanislavsky, Brecht, Kazan, Brook.* Berkeley: University of California Press, 1986.

Jones, Robert Edmond. *The Dramatic Imagination.* 1941; repr. New York: Theatre Arts Books, 1970.

Kantor, Bernard R., Irwin R. Blacker, and Anne Kranch. *Directors at Work.* New York: Funk and Wagnalls, 1970.

Kazan, Elia. *Elia Kazan: A Life.* New York: Knopf, 1988.

Kernan, Alvin B. (ed.). *The Modern American Theatre: A Collection of Critical Essays.* Engelwood Cliffs, NJ: Prentice-Hall, 1967.

Kerr, Walter. *Pieces at Eight.* New York: Simon and Schuster, 1957.

Knauf, David. *Papers in Dramatic Theory and Criticism.* Iowa City: University Press of Iowa, 1969.

Krutch, Joseph Wood. *The American Drama Since 1918.* New York: George Braziller, 1957.

Leavitt, Richard F. (ed.). *The World of Tennessee Williams.* New York: Putnam, 1978.

Lewis, Alan. *The Contemporary Theatre.* New York: Crown, 1962.

American Plays and Playwrights of the Contemporary Theatre. 2nd edn. New York: Crown, 1970.

Lewis, Robert. *Slings and Arrows: Theatre in My Life.* New York: Stein and Day, 1984.

Londré, Felicia Hardison. *Tennessee Williams.* New York: Ungar, 1979.

Lumley, Frederick. *New Trends in 20th-Century Drama.* 4th edn. New York: Oxford, 1972.

McCann, John S. *The Critical Reputation of Tennessee Williams.* Boston: G. K. Hall, 1983.

Marranca, Bonnie (ed.). *The Theatre of Images*. New York: Drama Book Specialists, 1977.

Maxwell, Gilbert. *Tennessee Williams and Friends*. Cleveland: World, 1965.

Michaels, Lloyd. *Elia Kazan: A Guide to References and Resources*. Boston: Hall, 1985.

Mielziner, Jo. *Designing for the Theatre: A Memoir and a Portfolio*. New York: Bramhall House, 1965.

Miller, Arthur. *Timebends: A Life*. New York: Grove, 1987.

Miller, Jordan. *Twentieth-Century Interpretations of* A Streetcar Named Desire: *A Collection of Critical Essays*. Engelwood Cliffs. NJ: Prentice-Hall, 1971.

Miller, J. William. *Modern Playwrights at Work*. New York: French, 1968.

Nathan, George Jean. *Theatre in the Fifties*. New York: Knopf, 1953.

Navasky, Victor. *Naming Names*. New York: Viking, 1980.

Nelson, Benjamin. *Tennessee Williams: The Man and His Work*. New York: Obolensky, 1961.

Parker, R. B. The Glass Menagerie: *A Collection of Critical Essays*. Engelwood Cliffs, NJ: Prentice-Hall, 1983.

Pauly, Thomas H. *An American Odyssey: Elia Kazan and American Culture*. Philadelphia: Temple University Press, 1983.

Phillips, Gene D. *The Films of Tennessee Williams*. Philadelphia: Art Alliance, 1980.

Rasky, Harry. *Tennessee Williams: A Portrait in Laughter and Lamentation*. New York: Dodd, Mead, 1986.

Rogers, Ingrid. *Tennessee Williams, a Moralist's Answer to the Perils of Life*. Frankfurt: P. Lang, 1976.

Ruas, Charles. *Conversations with American Writers*. New York, Knopf, 1985.

Scanlon, Tom. *Family, Drama, and American Dreams*. Westport, CT: Greenwood, 1978.

Schechner, Richard. *Essays on Performance Theory*. New York: Drama Book Specialists, 1977.

Selznick, Irene Mayer. *A Private View*. New York: Knopf, 1983.

Simonson, Lee. *The Art of Scenic Design*. New York: Harper, 1950.

Smith, Bruce. *Costly Performances: Tennessee Williams: The Last Stage, a Personal Memoir*. New York: Paragon House, 1990.

Smith, Harry W., Jr. "Mielziner and Williams: A Concept of Style." PhD dissertation, Tulane University, 1965.

Sontag, Susan. *Against Interpretation, and Other Essays*. New York: Farrar, Straus & Giroux, 1966.

Spoto, Donald. *The Kindness of Strangers: The Life of Tennessee Williams*. Boston: Little Brown, 1985, repr. Ballantine, 1986.

Stanton, Stephen S. (ed.). *Tennessee Williams: A Collection of Critical Essays*. Engelwood Cliffs, NJ: Prentice-Hall, 1977.

Steen, Mike. *A Look at Tennessee Williams*. New York: Hawthorn, 1969.

Steinbeck, Elaine and Robert Wallsten. *Steinbeck: A Life in Letters*. New York: Viking, 1975.

Styan, John. *The Dark Comedy: The Development of Modern Comic Tragedy*. 2nd edn. Cambridge: Cambridge University Press, 1968.

Tharpe, Jac. *Tennessee Williams: A Tribute*. Jackson: University Press of Mississippi, 1977.

Tischler, Nancy M. *Tennessee Williams: Rebellious Puritan*. 2nd edn. New York: Citadel, 1965.

Tobias, Arthur. "The Liberal Paradox: Clifford Odets, Elia Kazan, and Arthur Miller." PhD dissertation, Indiana University, 1980.

Van Antwerp, Margaret A. and Sally Johns (eds.). *Dictionary of Literary Biography: Documentary Series*. Vol.IV: *Tennessee Williams*. Detroit: Gale, 1984.

Vendrovskaya, Lyubov and Galina Kaptereva (eds.). *Evgeny Vakhtangov*. Moscow: Progress, 1982.

von Szeliski, John. *Tragedy and Fear: Why Modern Tragic Drama Fails*. Chapel Hill: University of North Carolina Press, 1971.

Weales, Gerald. *American Drama Since World War II*. New York: Harcourt, Brace, 1962.

Tennessee Williams. Minneapolis: University of Minnesota Press, 1965.

Williams, Edwina Dakin, as told to Lucy Freeman. *Remember Me to Tom*. New York: Putnam, 1963.

Williams, Jay. *Stage Left*. New York: Scribners, 1974.

Williams, Tennessee. (entries listed in alphabetical order)

American Blues: Five Short Plays (includes *Mooney's Kid Don't Cry, The Dark Room, The Case of the Crushed Petunias, The Long Stay Cut Short; or, The Unsatisfactory Supper, Ten Blocks on the Camino Real*). New York: Dramatists Play Service, 1948.

Baby Doll. New York: New Directions, 1956.

Camino Real. Norfolk, CT: New Directions, 1953; repr. Dramatists Play Service, 1965; repr. vol.II, *The Theatre of Tennessee Williams*. New York: New Directions, 1971.

Cat on a Hot Tin Roof. New York: New Directions, 1955; repr. New American Library, 1958; repr. vol.III, *The Theatre of Tennessee Williams*. New York: New Directions, 1971; revised version Dramatists Play Service, 1958; 2nd revised version, New Directions, 1975.

Five O'Clock Angel: Letters of Tennessee Williams to Maria St. Just 1948–1982. With Commentary by Maria St. Just. New York: Knopf, 1990.

The Glass Menagerie. New York: Random House, 1945; repr. vol.I, *The Theatre of Tennessee Williams*. New York: New Directions, 1971; revised version, Dramatists Play Service, 1948.

Memoirs. Garden City, NY: Doubleday, 1975; repr. Bantam, 1976.

A Streetcar Named Desire. New York: New Directions, 1947; revised version, 1951 [?]; repr. vol.I, *The Theatre of Tennessee Williams*. New York: New Directions, 1971; 2nd revised version, Dramatists Play Service, 1953.

The Rose Tattoo. New York: New Directions, 1951; repr. vol.II, *The Theatre of Tennessee Williams*. New York: New Directions, 1971.

Sweet Bird of Youth, Esquire (April 1959): 115–55; revised version, New York: New Directions, 1959; repr. vol.IV, *The Theatre of Tennessee Williams*. New York: New Directions, 1972; 2nd revised version, Dramatists Play Service, 1962.

Tennessee Williams's Letters to Donald Windham 1940–1965. New York: Holt, Reinhart, 1977.

Where I Live: Selected Essays. Ed. Christine R. Day and Bob Woods. New York: New Directions, 1978.

Wood, Audrey, with Max Wilk. *Represented by Audrey Wood.* Garden City, NY: Doubleday, 1981.

Yacowan, Maurice. *Tennessee Williams and Film.* New York: Ungar, 1977.

Zuber-Skerrit, Ortrun (ed.). *Page to Stage: Theatre as Translation.* Amsterdam: Rodopi, 1984.

ARTICLES ON KAZAN AND MIELZINER

Anderson, Robert. "Walk a Ways with Me." *Theatre Arts,* 38 (January 1954): 30–31.

Archer, Eugene. "Elia Kazan: The Genesis of a Style." *Film Culture,* 2, 2 (1956): 5–7, 21–24.

Ardrey, Robert. "Writing for the Group." *New York Times,* November 19, 1939: section 10, 3.

Brustein, Robert. "American's New Culture Hero: Feelings Without Words." *Commentary,* 25 (Fall 1958): 123–29.

Byron, Stuart and Rubin Martin. "Elia Kazan." *Movie,* 19 (Winter 1971–72): 1–13.

Chinoy, Helen. "The Way We Were: 1931–1941." *Educational Theatre Journal,* 28 (December 1976): 532–37.

Ciment, Michel. "Pour en finir avec les mises au point." *Positif,* 192 (April 1977): 23.

Clurman, Harold. "In a Different Language." *Theatre Arts,* 34 (January 1950): 18–20.

Collins, Gary. "Kazan in the Fifties." *The Velvet Light Trap,* 11 (Winter 1974): 41–45.

Delahaye, Michael. "A Natural Phenomenon: Interview with Elia Kazan." *Cahiers du Cinema in English,* 9 (March 1967): 8–40.

The Drama Review, Special Issue on The Group Theatre, 28 (Winter 1984).

Dundy, Elaine. "How to Succeed in the Theatre without Really Being Successful." *Esquire,* 13 (May 1965): 88–91, 153–58.

Goyen, William. "After the Fall of a Dream: A Behind-the-Curtain Report on What Went Wrong with Lincoln Center Repertory." *Show,* 4, 8 (September 1964): 44–47, 86–89.

Gray, Paul. "Stanislavsky and America: A Critical Chronology." *Tulane Drama Review,* 9, 2 (Winter 1964): 57.

Hey, Kenneth. "Ambivalence as a Theme in *On the Waterfront* (1954): An Interdisciplinary Approach to Film Study." *American Quarterly,* 31, 5 (1979): 666–96.

Hillier, Jim. "Kazan and Williams." *Movie,* 19 (Winter 1971): 17–18.

Isaacs, Hermine Rich. "First Rehearsals: Elia Kazan Directs a Modern Legend." *Theatre Arts,* 28 (March 1944): 143–50.

Johnston, Alva. "Aider and Abettor – I." *The New Yorker*, 24 (October 23, 1948): 37–46 (Profile of Jo Mielziner).

"Aider and Abettor – II." *The New Yorker*, 24 (October 30, 1948): 28–38.

Jones, Christopher John. "Image and Ideology in Kazan's *Pinky*." *Literature/Film Quarterly*, 9, 2 (1981): 110–20.

Kazan, Elia "The Director's Playbill." New York *Herald Tribune*, September 12, 1943: 1, 3, 5–6.

"Audience Tomorrow: Preview in New Guinea." *Theatre Arts*, 20 (October 1945): 568–77.

"Entr'acte." *Theatre Arts*, 31 (June 6, 1947): 10–11.

"About Broadway and the Herring Catch." *New York Times*, October 16, 1949: section 3, 1, 3.

"Long, Long Ago." *Theatre Arts*, 34 (September 1950): 39.

"Letter." *Saturday Review*, 35 (April 5, 1952): 22.

"A Statement." *New York Times*, April 12, 1952: 7.

"Where I Stand." *Reader's Digest*, 61 (July 1952): 45–46.

"The Movie That Had to Be Made." New York *Herald-Tribune*, May 31, 1953: section 4, 1, 3.

"Writers and Motion Pictures." *Atlantic Monthly*, 199 (April 1957): 67–70.

"Paean of Praise for a Face Above the Crowd." *New York Times*, May 26, 1957: section 2, 5.

"An Interview: Elia Kazan." *Equity*, 42 (December 1957): 10–13.

"Ten Best for a Repertory Theatre." *New York Times Magazine*, November 9, 1958: 74–75.

"The Staging of a Play." *Esquire*, 51 (May 1959): 144–57.

"Candid Conversation with Elia Kazan." *Show Business Illustrated*, 2, 2 (February 1962): 26–27.

"Theater: New Stages, New Play, New Actors," *New York Times Magazine*, September 23, 1962: 18, 26, 28–29.

"Notebook for *Streetcar*." *Directors on Directing*, ed. Toby Cole and Helen Chinoy. Indianapolis: Bobbs-Merrill, 1963: 364–79.

"In Quest of the Dream." *New York Times*, December 15, 1963: section 2, 9.

"Process Development of Repertory, or a Team Needs Patience and Years." *World Theatre*, 14 (January 1965): 85.

"Elia Kazan Ad-Libs on 'The Changeling' and Its Critics." *Show*, 5, 1 (January 1965): 38–41.

"All you Need to Know, Kids." *Action*, 9, 1 (January–February 1974): 4–11.

Kazan, Elia and Harold Clurman. "To the Theatre Going Public." New York *Herald Tribune*, March 1, 1947: 17.

Kazan, Elia and Art Smith, "Dimitroff." *New Theatre*, 1 (July/August 1934): 20–24.

"Kazan Talks." *Time*, 59 (April 21, 1952): 106.

Kitses, Jim. "Elia Kazan: A Structural Analysis." *Cinema*, 7, 3 (winter 1972–73): 25–36.

Knight, Arthur and Henry Hewes. "The Williams–Kazan Axis." *Saturday Review*, 39 (December 29, 1956): 22–24.

Michaels, I. Lloyd. "Auteurism, Creativity, and Entropy in *The Last Tycoon*." *Literature/Film Quarterly*, 10, 2 (1982): 110–19.

Mielziner, Jo. "Scene Designs for *The Glass Menagerie*." *Theatre Arts*, 29 (April 1945): 211.

"Death of a Painter." *American Artist*, 13 (November 1949): 32–37, 61–62.

"Jo Mielziner Designs for the Theatre." *Theatre Design and Technology*, 17 (May 1969): 25.

Miller, Arthur. "Arthur Miller Ad-Libs on Elia Kazan." *Show*, 4 (January 1964): 55–56, 97–98.

Morehouse, Ward. "Keeping Up with Kazan." *Theatre Arts*, 41 (June 1957): 20–22, 90–91.

Morgan, Thomas B. "Elia Kazan's Great Expectations." *Harper's*, 225 (September 1962): 66–75.

Morton, Frederic. "gadg!" *Esquire*, 47 (February 1957): 49, 118–23.

Movie, Special Issue on Elia Kazan. 19 (Winter 1971–72).

Navasky, Victor. "Naming Names." *New West*, (November 3, 1980): 31.

O'Connor, John J. "The Great God Gadg." *Audience* 7 (Winter 1960): 25–31.

Poling, James. "Handy 'Gadget'." *Collier's*, 129 (May 31, 1952): 56–61.

Postlewait, Thomas. "Simultaneity in Modern Stage Design and Drama." *Journal of Dramatic Theory and Criticism*, 3 (1988): 5–31.

"A Quiz for Kazan." *Theatre Arts*, 40 (November 1956): 30–32, 89.

Schechner, Richard. "New York: Sentimentalist Kazan." *Tulane Drama Review*, 9 (Spring 1965): 194–98.

Schnathmeier, Susanne. "The Unity of Place in Elia Kazan's Film Version of 'A Streetcar Named Desire' by Tennessee Williams: A Traditional Dramatic Category Seen from a Semiotic Point of View," *Kodikas/Code/Ars Semeiotica*, 10 (1987): 83–93.

Schumach, Murray. "A Director Named 'Gadge'." *New York Times Magazine*, November 9, 1947: 18, 54–56.

"The Shape of Things." *The Nation*, 174 (April 26, 1952): 394.

Silver, Charles and Joel Zucher. "Visiting Kazan: An Interview." *Film Comment*, 8 (Summer 1972): 15–19.

Smith, Harry W. "Tennessee Williams and Jo Mielziner: The Memory Plays." *Theatre Survey*, 23 (1982): 223–35.

Stevens, Virginia. "Elia Kazan: Actor and Director of Stage and Screen." *Theatre Arts*, 31 (December 1947): 18–22.

Sweeney, Louise. "Director and Writer Elia Kazan." *Christian Science Monitor*, November 30, 1983: 24.

Tailleur, Roger. "Kazan and the HUAC." *Film Comment*, 4, 1 (Fall 1967): 43–58.

Tiller, de Teel Patterson. "The New Stagecraft: An American Legacy in Renderings in the Museum Collection." *Arts in Virginia*, 15 (Spring 1975): 22–31.

Zolotow, Maurice. "Viewing the Kinetic Mr. Kazan." *New York Times*, March 9, 1952: 1, 3.

"In the Script: A Streetcar Named Desire." *Sight and Sound*, 21 (April–June 1952): 173–75.

ARTICLES ON WILLIAMS

Adler, Jacob H. "Tennessee Williams's South: The Culture and the Power." *Tennessee Williams: A Tribute*, ed. Jac Tharpe. Jackson: University Press of Mississippi, 1977: 30–52.

Adler, Thomas P. "The (Un)reliability of the Narrator in *The Glass Menagerie* and *Vieux Carré*." *Tennessee Williams Review*, 3 (1981): 6–9.

Adler, Thomas P., Judith, H. Clark, and Lyle Taylor. "Tennessee Williams in the Seventies: A Checklist." *Tennessee Williams Newsletter*, 2 (1980): 24–29.

Ashton, Roger. "Correspondence." *New Republic*, 132 (April 25, 1955): 23.

Atkinson, Brooks. "Theatre: Tennessee Williams's 'Cat'." *New York Times*, March 26, 1955.

Balch, Jack. "Kazan Rehearses Williams' *Sweet Bird of Youth*." *Theatre*, 1 (March 1959): 22–23.

Barksdale, Richard K. "Social Background in the Plays of Miller and Williams." *CLA Journal*, 6 (March 1963): 161–69.

Beaufort, John. "Tennessee Williams's 'Cat'." *Christian Science Monitor*, April 2, 1955.

Beaurline, Lester A. "*The Glass Menagerie*: From Story to Play." *Modern Drama*, 8 (September 1965): 145–49.

"The Director, the Script, and the Author's Revisions: A Critical Problem," *Papers in Dramatic Theory and Criticism*, ed. David M. Knauf. Iowa City: University Press of Iowa, 1969: 78–91.

Becker, William. "Reflections on Three New Plays." *Hudson Review*, 8 (1955): 268–72.

Bentley, Eric. "Broadway Today." *Sewanee Review*, 54 (January–March 1946): 314–16.

Berkman, Leonard. "The Tragic Downfall of Blanche DuBois." *Modern Drama*, 10 (December 1967): 249–57.

Berkowitz, Gerald M. "The 'Other World' of *The Glass Menagerie*." *Players* 48 (April–May 1973): 150–53.

"Williams' 'Other Places' – A Theatrical Metaphor in the Plays." *Tennessee Williams: A Tribute*, ed. Jac Tharpe. Jackson: University Press of Mississippi, 1977: 712–19.

Berlin, Normand. "Complementarity in *A Streetcar Named Desire*." *Tennessee Williams: A Tribute*, ed. Jac Tharpe. Jackson: University Press of Mississippi, 1977: 97–103.

Bernard, Kenneth. "The Mercantile Mr. Kowalski." *Discourse*, 7 (Summer 1964): 337–40.

Bluefarb, Sam. "*The Glass Menagerie*: Three Visions of Time." *College English*, 24 (April 1963): 513–18.

Borny, Geoffry. "The Two Glass Menageries: An Examination of the Effects on Meaning that Result from Directing the Reading Edition as Opposed to the Acting Edition of the Play." *Page to Stage: Theatre as Translation*, ed. Ortrun Zuber-Skerritt. Amsterdam: Rodopi, 1984: 117–36.

"Williams and Kazan: The Creative Synthesis." *Australasian Drama Studies*, 8 (1986): 33–47.

Brandon, Henry. "The State of the Theatre: A Conversation with Arthur Miller". *Harper's*, 221 (November 1960): 63–69.

Brandt, George. "Cinematic Structure in the Work of Tennessee Williams." *American Theatre*, ed. John R. Brown and Bernard Harris. London: Arnold, 1967: 163–87.

Brooking, Jack. "Directing *Summer and Smoke*: An Existentialist Approach." *Modern Drama*, 2 (1960): 377–85.

Brooks, Charles B. "The Multiple Set in American Drama." *Tulane Drama Review*, 3 (December 1958): 35–37.

Brown, Ray C. B. "Tennessee Williams: The Poetry of Stagecraft." *Voices*, 138 (1949): 4–8.

Brustein, Robert. "American's New Culture Hero: Feelings Without Words." *Commentary*, 25 (February 1958): 123–29.

Buell, John. "The Evil Imagery of Tennessee Williams." *Thought* 38 (Summer 1963): 162–89.

Burks, Deborah G. "'Treatment Is Everything': The Creation and Casting of Blanche and Stanley in Tennessee Williams' 'Streetcar'," *The Library Chronicle of the University of Texas at Austin*, n.s. 41 (1987): 16–39.

Callahan, Edward F. "Tennessee Williams' Two Worlds." *North Dakota Quarterly*, 25 (Summer 1957): 61–67.

"Cardinal Scores 'Baby Doll' Film." *New York Times*, December 17, 1956: 28.

Carlisle, Olga and Rose Styron. "Arthur Miller: An Interview." *Paris Review*, 10 (Summer 1966): 61–98.

Carpenter, Charles A. "Studies of Tennessee Williams' Drama: A Selective International Bibliography: 1966–1978." *Tennessee Williams Newsletter*, 2 (1980): 11–23.

Carr, William H. A. and Malcolm Logan. "Kazan, Tennessee Williams Reply to Spellman Attack on 'Baby Doll'." New York *Post*, December 17, 1956: 5, 42.

Cless, Downing. "Alienation and Contradiction in *Camino Real*: A Convergence of Williams and Brecht," *Theatre Journal*, 35 (1983): 41–50.

Clum, John M. "'Something Cloudy, Something Clear': Homophobic Discourse in Tennessee Williams," *South Atlantic Quarterly*, 88 (1989): 161–79.

Coakley, James. "Time and Tide on the Camino Real." *Tennessee Williams: A Tribute*, ed. Jac Tharpe. Jackson: University Press of Mississippi, 1977: 232–36.

Cohn, Alan M. "More Tennessee Williams in the Seventies: Additions to the Checklist and the Gunn Bibliography." *Tennessee Williams Newsletter*, 3 (1982): 46–50.

Cole, Charles W. and Carol I. Franco. "Critical Reaction to Tennessee Williams in the Mid-1960s." *Players*, 49 (Fall–Winter 1974): 18–23.

Corrigan, Mary Ann. "Realism and Theatricalism in *A Streetcar Named Desire*." *Modern Drama*, 19 (1976): 385–96.

"Memory, Dream, and Myth in the Plays of Tennessee Williams." *Renascence*, 28 (1976): 155–67.

"Beyond Verisimilitude: Echoes of Expressionism in Williams' Plays." *Tennessee Williams: A Tribute*, ed. Jac Tharpe. Jackson: University Press of Mississippi, 1977: 375–412.

Davis, Joseph K. "Landscapes of the Dislocated Mind in Williams' *The Glass*

Menagerie." *Tennessee Williams: A Tribute*, ed. Jac Tharpe. Jackson: University of Mississippi, 1977: 192–206.

Debusscher, Gilbert. "And the Sailor Turned Into a Princess: New Light on the Genesis of *Sweet Bird of Youth.*" *Studies in American Drama, 1945–Present*, 1 (1986): 25–31.

"Trois images de la modernité chez Tennessee Williams: Un Micro-analyse d'*Un Tramway Nommé Désir.*" *Journal of Dramatic Theory and Criticism*, 3 (1988): 143–57.

Dickson, Vivienne. "*A Streetcar Named Desire*: Its Development through the Manuscripts." *Tennessee Williams: A Tribute*, ed. Jac Tharpe. Jackson: University Press of Mississippi, 1977: 154–71.

Dowling, Ellen. "The Derailment of *A Streetcar Named Desire.*" *Literature/Film Quarterly*, 9 (1981): 233–40.

Dowling, Ellen and Nancy Pride. "Three Approaches to Directing *A Streetcar Named Desire.*" *Tennessee Williams Newsletter*, 2 (1980): 16–20.

Downer, Alan S. "Mr. Williams and Mr. Miller." *Furioso*, 4 (summer 1949): 66–70.

"The Two Worlds of Contemporary American Drama: Arthur Miller and Tennessee Williams." *Princeton Alumni Weekly*, 62 (October 20, 1961): 8–11, 17, 20.

Downing, Robert. "Streetcar Conductor: *Some Notes from Backstage.*" *Theatre Annual*, 8 (1950): 25–33.

Dukore, Bernard F. "The Cat Has Nine Lives." *Tulane Drama Review*, 8 (Fall 1963): 95–100.

"American Abelard: A Footnote to *Sweet Bird of Youth.*" *College English*, 26 (1965): 630–34.

Dusenberry, Winifred. "*Baby Doll* and *The Ponder Heart.*" *Modern Drama*, 3 (1961): 393–95.

Ehrlich, Alan. "A Streetcar Named Desire Under the Elms: A Study of the Dramatic Space in *A Streetcar Named Desire* and *Desire Under the Elms.*" *Tennessee Williams: A Tribute*, ed. Jac Tharpe. Jackson: University Press of Mississippi, 1977: 126–36.

Flaxman, Seymour L. "The Debt of Williams and Miller to Ibsen and Strindberg." *Comparative Literature Studies*, Special Advance Issue (1963): 51–60.

Fulton, A. R. "It's Exactly Like the Play." *Theatre Arts*, 37 (1953): 78–83.

Ganz, Arthur. "The Desperate Morality of the Plays of Tennessee Williams." *American Scholar*, 31 (Spring 1962): 278–94.

Gassner, John. "Tennesse Williams: Dramatist of Frustration." *College English*, 10 (1948): 1–7.

Gelb, Arthur. "Williams and Kazan and the Big Walk-Out." *New York Times*, May 1, 1960: section 2, 1, 3.

Genaeur, Emily. "Mielziner." *Theatre Arts*, 35 (September 1951): 34.

Graff, Edward. "Point of View in Modern Drama." *Modern Drama*, 2 (December 1959): 268–82.

Gray, Paul. "The Theatre of the Marvelous: From the Director's Prompt Books." *Tulane Drama Review*, 7 (1963): 143–45.

Gunn, Drewey Wayne. "The Various Texts of Tennessee Williams' Plays." *Educational Theatre Journal*, 30 (1978): 368–75.

"The Troubled Flight of Tennessee Williams's *Sweet Bird of Youth*: From Manuscript through Published Texts." *Modern Drama*, 24 (1981): 26–35.

Hafley, James. "Abstraction and Order in the Language of Tennessee Williams." *Tennessee Williams: A Tribute*, ed. Jac Tharpe. Jackson: University Press of Mississippi, 1977: 753–62.

Hatch, Robert. "Old Hit, New Venture." *New Republic*, 125 (October 8, 1951): 21.

Hawkins, William. "*Camino Real* Reaches the Printed Page." *Theatre Arts*, 37 (1953): 26–27, 96.

Hays, Peter L. "Tennessee Williams' Use of Myth in *Sweet Bird of Youth*." *Educational Theatre Journal*, 18 (1966): 255–58.

"Arthur Miller and Tennessee Williams." *Essays in Literature*, 4 (1977): 239–49.

Hewes, Henry. "The Boundaries of Tennessee." *Saturday Review*, 39 (December 29, 1956): 23–24.

Hilfer, Anthony C. and R. Vance Ramsey. "*Baby Doll*: A Study in Comedy and Critical Awareness." *The Ohio University Review*, 11 (1969): 75–88.

Hirsch, Foster. "Tennessee Williams." *Cinema*, 8 (Spring 1973): 2–7.

Howell, Elmo. "The Function of Gentleman Callers: A Note on Tennessee Williams' *The Glass Menagerie*." *Notes on Mississippi Writers*, 2 (1970): 83–90.

Hughes, Elinor. "Two New Plays of Unusual Conception and Fine Execution." Boston *Sunday Herald* (November 9, 1947).

Hyams, Joe. "Tennessee Williams Turns Critic." New York *Herald Tribune*, December 23, 1959: 13.

Isaac, Dan. "Big Daddy's Dramatic Word Strings." *American Speech*, 40 (1965): 272–78.

Ishizuka, Koji. "Two Memory Plays: Williams and Miller." *American Literature in the 1940s*. Tokyo: American Literary Society of Japan, 1975: 208–12.

Jackson, Esther Merle. "The Problem of Form in the Drama of Tennessee Williams." *CLA Journal*, 4 (September 1960): 8–21.

"Music and Dance as Elements of Form in the Drama of Tennessee Williams." *Revue d'Histoire du Théâtre*, 15 (1963): 294–301.

"Tennessee Williams: Poetic Consciousness in Crisis." *Tennessee Williams: A Tribute*, ed. Jac Tharpe. Jackson: University Press of Mississippi, 1977: 53–72.

Johnson, Kenneth E. "Memory Plays in American Drama." *Within the Dramatic Spectrum*, ed. Karelisa V. Hartigan. Lanham: University Presses of America, 1986: 115–23.

Kahn, Sy. "Through a Glass Menagerie Darkly: The World of Tennessee Williams," *Modern American Drama*, ed. William E. Taylor. Deland, FL: Everett/Edwards, 1968: 71–89.

Kalson, Albert E. "Tennessee Williams at the Delta Brilliant." *Tennessee Williams: A Tribute*, ed. Jac Tharpe. Jackson: University Press of Mississippi, 1977: 774–94.

"A Source for *Cat on a Hot Tin Roof*." *Tennessee Williams Newsletter*, 2 (1980): 21–22.

King, Thomas L. "Irony and distance in *The Glass Menagerie*." *Educational Theatre Journal*, 25 (1973): 207–14.

Knight, Arthur. "The Williams–Kazan Axis." *Saturday Review*, 39 (December 29, 1956): 22–23.

"Lighting Up for *Summer and Smoke*." *New York Times*, December 5, 1948: section 2, 7.

Lolli, Giorgio, "Alcoholism and Homosexuality in Tennessee Williams's *Cat on a Hot Tin Roof*." *Quarterly Journal of Studies in Alcohol*, 17 (1956): 543–53.

McCarthy, Mary. "'Realism' in the American Theatre." *Harper's* 223 (July 1961): 45–52.

MacMullen, Hugh. "Translating 'The Glass Menagerie' to Film." *Hollywood Quarterly*, 5 (Fall 1950): 14–32.

Miller, Arthur. "Morality and Modern Drama." *Educational Theatre Journal*, 10 (1958): 190–202.

Miller, Jordan Y. "*Camino Real*." *The Fifties: Fiction, Poetry, Drama*, ed. Warren French. Deland, FL: Everett/Edwards, 1970: 241–48.

Mitchell, John D. "Applied Psychoanalysis in the Drama." *American Imago*, 14 (1953): 263–80.

Mood, John J. "The Structure of *A Streetcar Named Desire*." *Ball State University Forum*, 14 (Summer 1973): 9–10.

Napieralski, Edmund A. "Tennessee Williams' *The Glass Menagerie*: The Dramatic Metaphor." *The Southern Quarterly*, 16 (1977): 1–12.

Nolan, Paul T. "Two Memory Plays: *The Glass Menagerie* and *After the Fall*." *McNeese Review*, 17 (1966): 27–38.

Parker, Brian. "The Composition of *The Glass Menagerie*: An Argument for Complexity." *Modern Drama*, 25 (1982): 409–22.

Pawley, Thomas D. "Experimental Theatre Seminar; Or, the Basic Training of Tennessee Williams," *The Iowa Review*, 19, 1 (Winter 1989): 65–73.

Pease, Donald. "Reflections on Moon Lake: The Presences of the Playwright." *Tennessee Williams: A Tribute*, ed. Jac Tharpe. Jackson: University Press of Mississippi, 1977: 829–47.

Peterson, William. "Williams, Kazan and the Two *Cats*." *New Theatre Magazine*, 7 (1967): 14–20.

Reck, Tom S. "The First *Cat on a Hot Tin Roof*." *University Review*, 34 (1968): 187–92.

Rice, Vernon. "The Talking Tennessee Williams." New York *Post*, March 18, 1953: 66.

Riddel, Joseph N. "*A Streetcar Named Desire*: Nietzsche Descending." *Modern Drama*, 5 (1963): repr. in *Tennessee Williams*, ed. Harold Bloom. New York: Chelsea House, 1987: 13–22.

Ross, Don. "Williams in Art and Morals: An Anxious Foe of Untruth." New York *Herald Tribune*, March 3, 1957: section 4, 1–2.

Roth, Robert. "Tennessee Williams in Search of a Form." *Chicago Review*, 9 (Summer 1955): 86–94.

Roulet, William M. "*Sweet Bird of Youth*: Williams' Redemptive Ethic." *Cithara*, 3 (1964): 31–36.

Rowland, James L. "Tennessee's Two Amandas." *Research Studies*, 35 (1967): 331–40.

Sacksteder, William. "The Three *Cats*: A Study in Dramatic Structure." *Drama Survey*, 5 (Winter 1966–67): 252–66.

Saroyan, William, "Keep Your Eye On Your Overcoat." *Theatre Arts*, 32 (October 1948): 21.

Schlueter, June. "Imitating an Icon: John Erman's Remake of Tennessee Williams's *A Streetcar Named Desire*." *Modern Drama*, 28 (1985): 139–47.

Schumach, Murray. "Author Changes 'Sweet Bird' Play." *New York Times*, October 27, 1961: 27.

Schvey, Henry I. "Madonna at the Poker Night: Pictorial Elements in Tennessee Williams's *A Streetcar Named Desire*." *From Cooper to Philip Roth: Essays on American Literature*, ed. J. Bakker and D. R. M. Wilkinson. Amsterdam: Rodopi, 1980: 71–77.

Sharp, William. "An Unfashionable View of Tennessee Williams." *Tulane Drama Review*, 6 (March 1962): 160–71.

Sheye, Thomas E. "*The Glass Menagerie*: It's No Tragedy, Freckles." *Tennessee Williams: A Tribute*, ed. Jac Tharpe. Jackson: University Press of Mississippi, 1977: 207–13.

Spector, Susan. "Alternative Visions of Blanche DuBois: Uta Hagen and Jessica Tandy in *A Streetcar Named Desire*." *Modern Drama*, 32 (1989): 545–61.

Stein, Roger B. "*The Glass Menagerie* Revisited: Catastrophe Without Violence." *Western Humanities Review*, 18 (1964): 141–53.

Thompson, Judith. "Symbol, Myth, and Ritual in *The Glass Menagerie, The Rose Tattoo*, and *Orpheus Descending*." *Tennessee Williams: A Tribute*, ed. Jac Tharpe. Jackson: University of Mississippi, 1977: 679–711.

Tynan, Kenneth. "American Blues: The Plays of Arthur Miller and Tennessee Williams." *Encounter*, 2 (May 1954): 13–19.

Vlasopolos, Anca. "Authorizing History: Victimization in *A Streetcar Named Desire*." *Theatre Journal*, 38 (1986): 322–38.

Waters, Arthur B. "Tennessee Williams: Ten Years Later." *Theatre Arts*, 39 (July 1955): 72–73, 96.

Watson, Charles S. "The Revision of *The Glass Menagerie*: The Passing of Good Manners." *Southern Literary Journal*, 8 (1976): 74–78.

Willett, Ralph W. "The Ideas of Miller and Williams." *Theatre Annual*, 22 (1965–66): 31–40.

Williams, Tennessee. "Playwright's 'Letter to the World'." New York *Herald Tribune*, March 15, 1953: section 4, 1, 2.

"Williams Talks on Violence." Philadelphia *Inquirer*, February 1, 1959: amusement section 1, 4.

Wolf, Morris Philip. "Casanova's Portmanteau: *Camino Real* and Recurring Communication Patterns of Tennessee Williams." *Tennessee Williams: A Tribute*, ed. Jac Tharpe. Jackson: University Press of Mississippi, 1977: 252–76.

Young, Vernon. "Social Drama and Big Daddy." *Southwest Review*, 41 (1956): 194–97.

Zlobin, G. "On the Stage and Behind the Scenes." *Inostranaja Literature*, 7 (July 1960): 199–210.

SELECTED REVIEWS AND NEWSPAPER STORIES

"CAMINO REAL"

Atkinson, Brooks. *New York Times*, March 20, 1953: 26; March 29, 1953, section 2, 1.
Bentley, Eric. *New Republic*, 128 (March 30, 1953): 30–31.
Brown, John Mason. *Saturday Review*, 36 (April 18, 1953): 28–30.
Clurman, Harold. *The Nation*, 176 (April 4, 1953): 51–52.
Gibbs, Wolcott. *The New Yorker*, 29 (March 28, 1953): 69–70.
Goghan, Jerry. Philadelphia *Daily News*, March 5, 1953: F, 11.
Hayes, Richard. *Commonweal*, 58 (April 17, 1953): 51–52.
Nathan, George Jean. *Theatre Arts*, 37 (June 1953): 14, 88.
New York Theatre Critics' Reviews, 14 (1953), 330–32:
    Robert Coleman, *Daily Mirror*, March 20, 1953; John Chapman, *Daily News*, March 20, 1953; Walter F. Kerr, *Herald Tribune*, March 20, 1953; John McClain, *Journal-American*, March 20, 1953; Richard Watts, *Post*, March 20, 1953; Williams Hawkins, *World-Telegram*, March 20, 1953.
Sitwell, Edith. Letter to the New York *Herald Tribune*, April 3, 1953.

"CAT ON A HOT TIN ROOF"

Atkinson, Brooks. *New York Times*, March 25, 1955: 18; April 3, 1955: section 2, 1.
Beaufort, John. *Christian Science Monitor*, April 2, 1955.
Becker, William. *The Hudson Review*, 8 (Summer 1955): 268–72.
Bentley, Eric. *New Republic*, 132 (April 11, 1955): 28; 132 (April 18, 1955): 22–23.
Downing, Robert. *Cedar Rapids Gazette*. April 10, 1955.
Gibbs, Wolcott. *The New Yorker*, 31 (April 2, 1955): 68.
Hatch, Robert. *The Nation*, 180 (April 9, 1955): 314–15.
Hawkins, William. "Cat Yowls on 'Hot Tin Roof'." New York *World, Telegram, and Sun*, (March 25, 1955).
Hewes, Henry. *Saturday Review*, 38 (April 9, 1955): 32–33.
[Morrison], Hobe. "*Cat on a Hot Tin Roof*." *Variety*, March 30, 1955.
"'Cat' Censored, But by Whom?" *Variety*, April 13, 1955: 73.
Murdock, Henry T. Philadelphia *Inquirer*, March 8, 1955.
New York Theatre Critics' Reviews, 16 (155): 342–44:
    Robert Coleman, *Daily Mirror*, March 25, 1955; John Chapman, *Daily News*, March 25, 1955; Walter F. Kerr, *Herald Tribune*, March 25, 1955; Richard Watts, *Post*, March 25, 1955; William Hawkins, *World-Telegram*, March 25, 1955.
O'Hara, John. *Collier's*, 137 (March 2, 1956): 6.
Time, 65 (April 4, 1955): 98.
Zolotow, Maurice. *Theatre Arts*, 39 (June 1955): 22–23, 93.

"THE GLASS MENAGERIE"

Brown, John Mason. *Saturday Review*, 28 (April 14, 1945), 34–36.

Cassidy, Claudia. Chicago *Daily Tribune*, December 27, 1944: 11.
Gibbs, Wolcott. *The New Yorker*, 21 (April 7, 1945): 40.
Gilder, Rosamund. *Theatre Arts*, 29 (June 1945): 325–28.
Krutch, Joseph Wood. *The Nation*, 160 (April 14, 1945): 424.
"Mike." *Variety*, January 3, 1945.
Nathan, George Jean. *Theatre Book of the Year, 1944–1945*. New York: Knopf, 1946: 324–27.
New York Theatre Critics' Reviews, 6 (1945): 234–37:
John Chapman, *Daily News*, April 2, 1945; Otis L. Guernsey, *Herald Tribune*, April 2, 1945; Robert Garland, *Journal-American*, April 2, 1945; Louis Kronenberger, *PM*, April 2, 1945; Wilella Waldorf, *Post* April 2, 1945; Burton Rascoe, *World-Telegram*, April 2, 1945.
Nichols, Lewis. *New York Times*, April 2, 1945: 15; April 8, 1945: section 2, 1.
Phelan, Kappo. *Commonweal*, 42 (April 20, 1945): 16–17.
Time, 45 (April 9, 1945): 86.
Young, Stark. *New Republic*, 112 (April 16, 1945): 505.

"A STREETCAR NAMED DESIRE"

Atkinson, Brooks. *New York Times*, December 4, 1947: 42; December 14, 1947: section 2, 3; June 12, 1949, section 2, 1; May, 24, 1950: 36.
Bentley, Eric. *Theatre Arts*, 33 (November 1949): 14.
"Bone." *Variety*, November 5, 1947.
Brown, John Mason. *Saturday Review*, 30 (December 27, 1947): 22–24.
"Firstnighters at Wilbur Enjoy New Play." Boston *Evening American*, November 4, 1947.
F. R. J. New Haven *Journal Courier*, October 31, 1947.
Gaffney, Leo. "'Streetcar' Rumbles a Gloomy Nocturne." Boston *Daily Record*, November 5, 1947.
Gassner, John. *Forum*, 109 (February 1948): 86–88.
Gibbs, Wolcott. *The New Yorker*, 23 (December 13, 1947): 50–54.
Hughes, Elinor. Boston *Herald*, November 4, 1947.
"Ibee." "Plays on Broadway." *Variety*, December 10, 1947.
"Inside Stuff – Legit," *Variety*, December 1947.
Krutch, Joseph Wood. *The Nation*, 165 (December 20, 1947): 686–87,
McCarthy, Mary. *Partisan Review*, 25 (March 1948): 357–60.
Nathan, George Jean. *Theatre Book of the Year, 1947–1948*. New York: Knopf, 1948.
New York Theatre Critics' Reviews, 8 (1947): 249–52:
Robert Coleman, *Daily Mirror*, December 4, 1947; John Chapman, *Daily News*, December 4, 1947; Howard Barnes, *Herald Tribune*, December 4, 1947; Robert Garland, *Journal-American*, December 4, 1947; Louis Kronenberger, *PM*, December 5, 1947; Richard Watts, *Post*, December 4, 1947; Ward Morehouse, *Sun*, December 4, 1947; William Hawkins, *World-Telegram*, December 4, 1947.
Ormsbee, Helen. "That Girl on the New Orleans Streetcar," New York *Herald Tribune*, December 7, 1947.
Sensenderfer, R. E. P. Philadelphia *Evening Bulletin*, November 18, 1947.

Shaw, Irwin. *New Republic*, 117 (December 22, 1947): 34–35.
"'Streetcar Named Desire'." *Christian Scientist Monitor*, November 4, 1947.
"Streetcar Rumbles a Gloomy Nocturne," Boston *Daily Record*, November 5, 1947.
"'A Streetcar' Runs on Electricity," New York *World-Telegram*, October 16, 1947.
"Theater," New Haven *Register*, October 31, 1947.

"SWEET BIRD OF YOUTH"

Atkinson, Brooks. *New York Times*, March 11, 1959: 39; March 22, 1959: section 2, 1.
Brustein, Robert. *Encounter*, 12 (June 1959): 59–60.
Hudson Review, 12 (Summer 1959): 255–60.
Cassidy, Claudia. Chicago *Tribune*, April 26, 1959.
Clurman, Harold. *The Nation*, 188 (March 28, 1959): 281–83.
Driver, Tom F. *Christian Century*, 76 (April 15, 1959): 455; June 17, 1959: 726.
New Republic, 140 (April 20, 1959): 21–22.
Gassner, John. *Educational Theatre Journal*, 11 (May 1959): 122–24.
Hewes, Henry. *Saturday Review*, 42 (March 28, 1959): 26.
Hipp, Edward Sothern. "Williams at Work," Newark *Sunday News*, March 15, 1959.
New York Theatre Critics' Review, 20 (1959): 347–50:
Robert Coleman, *Daily Mirror*, March 11, 1959; John Chapman, *Daily News*, March 11, 1959; Walter Kerr, *Herald Tribune*, March 11, 1959; John McClain, *Journal-American*, March 11, 1959; Richard Watts, *Post*, March 11, 1959; Frank Aston, *World-Telegram & Sun*, March 11, 1959.
"Old But New," Philadelphia *Inquirer*, March 22, 1959.
Tynan, Kenneth. *The New Yorker*, 35 (March 21, 1959): 98–100.
"Williams Off Target," Boston *Sunday Advertiser*, March 15, 1959.

Index